Queering Kansas City Jazz

Expanding Frontiers: Interdisciplinary Approaches
to Studies of Women, Gender, and Sexuality

SERIES EDITORS: Karen J. Leong
                    Andrea Smith

Queering
Kansas City Jazz

Gender, Performance, and the History of a Scene

Amber R. Clifford-Napoleone

University of Nebraska Press | Lincoln and London

Portions of chapter 5 previously appeared in "Prostitution and Reform in Kansas City, 1880–1930," in *The Other Missouri History: Populists, Prostitutes, and Regular Folk*, ed. Thomas Spencer (University of Missouri Press, 2005), 214–36.

Library of Congress Cataloging-in-Publication Data
Names: Clifford-Napoleone, Amber R., 1974– author.
Title: Queering Kansas City jazz: gender, performance, and the history of a scene / Amber R. Clifford-Napoleone.
Description: Lincoln: University of Nebraska Press, 2018. | Series: Expanding frontiers: interdisciplinary approaches to studies of women, gender, and sexuality | Includes bibliographical references and index.
Identifiers: LCCN 2017056171
ISBN 9780803262911 (cloth: alk. paper)
ISBN 9781496210326 (epub)
ISBN 9781496210333 (mobi)
ISBN 9781496210340 (pdf)
Subjects: LCSH: Jazz—Missouri—Kansas City—History and criticism. | Jazz—Social aspects—Missouri—Kansas City—History.
Classification: LCC ML3508.8.K37 C55 2018 | DDC 781.6509778/411—dc23
LC record available at https://lccn.loc.gov/2017056171

Set in Janson Text by Mikala R. Kolander.
Designed by L. Auten.

Contents

Illustrations

Acknowledgments

As with any academic project, there are many people to thank for their support, encouragement, and time. This book has been over a decade in the making, with challenges looming on every corner. It would never have been finished without the support, encouragement, and assistance of many. Without the patient stewardship of this project by Alicia Christensen at University of Nebraska Press, the book would not have been possible. Thank you to Sara Springsteen and Matt Goodwin as well, for their thoughtful and thorough editing. My work benefitted from the thoughtful critiques of several anonymous reviewers as well, and I appreciate their assistance. Deepest thanks to Sherrie Tucker, Cheryl Lester, Ann Schofield, and Bill Tuttle in the American Studies Department at the University of Kansas. My special thanks to Bill for his enthusiasm about my archival work, Ann for her suggestions about haunting, and Sherrie for my introduction to jazz studies and her exemplar writing process and its production. Thanks to the Graduate School of the University of Kansas for their financial support of my research in New York through the William T. Belt Scholarship. I also wish to thank several jazz scholars and archives professionals, whose kindness with their time and skill was so helpful. My thanks to the staff of the Special Collections Department at the Kansas City (MO) Public Library, the staff of the Western Historical

Manuscripts Collection at the University of Missouri–Kansas City, the staff of the Spencer Research Library at the University of Kansas, the County Records specialists at the Missouri State Archives, and the staff of the Lesbian Herstory Archives in Brooklyn, New York. Special recognition goes to Annie Kuebler and Tad Hershorn at the Institute of Jazz Studies at Rutgers University for their hard work, suggestions, encouragement, and to Tad for a talk about Texas a long way from home. Thanks also to Chuck Haddix for help with sources and last-minute questions about Kansas City's musicians. I especially appreciate the generosity of Nathan Pearson Jr., who not only allowed me to interview him but supplied me with copies of his original transcripts and continued to be in contact with me about Kansas City's jazz scene.

I am lucky enough to have many academic "families." My appreciation to my friends and colleagues at the University of Central Missouri, my home in more ways than one, for their ability to keep me working. Special thanks to John W. Sheets II, my friend and long-time mentor, the always supportive Joy Stevenson, my close colleague Jeffrey Yelton, and fellow southerner Vivian Richardson for their friendship, their advice, their support, and their understanding. Thanks as well to Drs. Julie Willett and Randy McBee at Texas Tech University, who introduced me to the history that gave birth to this project. As with all my writing about Kansas City, deepest gratitude to Dr. Arthur F. McClure II, who introduced me to Kansas City's jazz scene. Though we never met, my deepest respect to Edna Mae Jacobs, who left behind the scrapbooks that helped me find these corners of jazz history and, in an unexpected turn of events, helped me find myself as well.

Last, but certainly not least, to my family and friends. My best friend Krisana West, her husband John, and son J.G. saw me through a lifetime of obstacles and joys and never flinched. Thank you, West family. To my parents James and Myrna and my brother Austin: though you did not live to see this work on the shelves, know that there would be no book without you. To my sister-in-law Rachel and nephew Nate, thank you for making my life joyous. Finally, to my wife Tara, who agreed to be my wife with this and many other swords hanging over our heads. Without you this work would be incomplete, unfinished, and lifeless.

1

Rethinking Kansas City's Jazz Story

This is not a book about jazz music. There are many brilliant works on the sounds and performers of Kansas City jazz, including recent works by Chuck Haddix and Stanley Crouch. In fact Kansas City jazz appears in almost every history of jazz, portrayed as a fertile ground for the development of big bands, virtuosic performance, and legendary musicians. At the same time this is not a book about gender. In recent years many writers have undertaken studies of gender in the so-called Jazz Age, focusing tightly on the debates about gender, sex, and society in that fertile 1920s period. Instead this study is about the overlap of jazz places and spaces, gender experimentation, and their erasure from the written history of Kansas City's jazz scene. Erasure of those who disrupted the accepted narrative of Kansas City jazz says as much about that story itself as it does about the players expunged. The jazz scene in Kansas City, Missouri, was fertile ground for the training of famous jazz performers such as Count Basie and Charlie Parker, along with the vice and prostitution often associated with the period. Numerous works have explored the intersection of leisure culture, identity politics, and jazz in New York, Chicago, and other jazz scene cities, but neglected to explore the way that non-normative gender performance, combined with working-class women, racial segregation, and space, created Kansas City's jazz scene. The jazz scene in Kansas City may be remembered for the music, but I argue that its role in the lives of everyday Kansas Citians had little to do with music and much more to do with space, identity, and the transgression of gender norms.

I was first drawn to this topic by my own search for space. Christopher Nealon has proposed that academics who identify as queer engage in historical research in order to find themselves, or "get closer to what they love."[1] I developed my own sense of queer identity as an undergraduate student, and as I sought out spaces where I felt my own identity was accepted I began to wonder about the history of such spaces, places, and people like myself. I discovered that many of the spaces in which I felt at home originated in the jazz scene of Kansas City, creating a subcultural and spatial connection between me and the past. For example the El Torreon Ballroom was founded in 1927 as a "blacks only" dance hall during Kansas City's jazz scene. The El Torreon I knew was the home of Kansas City's predominantly white heavy metal and punk scene. What's important, though, is that while there I was one of a crowd of "my people": I was an outsider, but in the El Torreon I had little concern about my safety or my acceptance. It was a sphere that felt not only like my *place*, but also a *space* where "my people" outnumbered "the man" that included our employers, those who derided "our music," and the mainstream world at large. Compelled by the realization of how space played a role in identity and self-presentation in the present, I wondered about the use of those places in the past: did individuals in the past identify the space, and themselves, as I did? I did rediscover pieces of a forgotten and vital part of Kansas City's jazz scene—silenced lives in the city's past were the foundations of the present—a world where identity was both accepted and bounded by the walls of the space.

KANSAS CITY'S JAZZ SCENE

This reexamination of Kansas City is possible through an analysis of the city's geography of desire, a theoretical approach used to understand the complexity of life in Kansas City's jazz scene in spatial terms. By concentrating on the spatialization of identity it is possible to revisit how those people marked as outsiders commingled spatially, politically, and discursively. Geography of desires combines the critical cultural geography of José Esteban Muñoz and Foucauldian theory to prioritize space in the study of identity, representation, and performance. This approach creates a map of spaces considered marginal in Kansas City's jazz scene history—cabarets, drag clubs, and brothels—and examines how citizens who considered themselves marginalized engaged in worldmaking at these sites of identity formation.[2] A geography of desires depends on using the critical map of spaces as a template to locate the possible identities and workings of power through a Foucauldian analysis and to explore the ways in which space served as a vehicle for worldmaking.

The spatial implications of Foucauldian concepts of resistance, agency, and discursive formation are key to framing Kansas City's jazz scene as a worldmaking scene. Worldmaking is a term I borrow from José Esteban Muñoz, who did not place this reconfiguration in defined space as I do, but rather within the performances and internal narratives of the subjects themselves. These theoretical moves, combining the work of Foucault and Muñoz along with many other scholars in cultural studies, are employed to disrupt and interrupt dominant history of the storied jazz scene. Focused on the jazz scene itself, *Queering Kansas City Jazz* is not about sounds and musicians but instead uses the geography of desires to focus on sites of contested identity—clubs, cabarets, and brothels—that served as worldmaking spaces for the othered folk whose performance of identity transgressed hegemonic notions of gender, sexuality, race, and class.

Jazz flourished in Kansas City from the 1890s until the end of World War II, when city boss Tom Pendergast's patronage of jazz clubs ended with his incarceration for tax evasion in 1941. The city was home to a wide array of clubs, cabarets, and performers from every corner of America. As a railroad terminus Kansas City was the last stop on performance circuits such as the Theatre Owners Booking Association (TOBA), resulting in Kansas City becoming the temporary home for hundreds of African American performers at the end of their TOBA contracts. The grand narratives of jazz history reinforce and replicate the myths of the jazz scene so often portrayed in American popular culture, including films such as *Chicago* and *The Cotton Club*. Images of flappers, speakeasies, and jazz music that permeate the prevailing history of the Jazz Age created a concept of the 1920s as an age of cultural shift and social freedom. Those renderings of the 1920s are just specific icons of a period filled with contention and social clash. The Jazz Age was, in fact, a period in American history as contentious and complex as any other. The lived experiences of Kansas City's jazz scene, as well as the layers of experience buried under dominant written history, illustrate the ideological nature of that popular image. While famous people and events remain in popular memory, the history is complex and many other important aspects have been silenced. The lives of brothel madams, drag performers, table dancers, and other marginalized citizens do not often appear in the written history of Kansas City jazz, but here I excavate the experiences of those citizens and frame the jazz scene in terms of identity and space. The purpose is not to argue that Kansas City was exceptional, but that it represents the complexity of the jazz scene in America rather than a monolithic singularity.

There are several challenges to rewriting the Kansas City jazz story. First, exploring the historical experience and performance of gender identity and avoiding the oversimplified representation of those individuals subjectified by their discursive formation are difficult tasks. Scholars must rely on the representation of gender performance in the historical record, a record where subjects often did not have the opportunity, ability, or even the social and cultural desire to express a gender identity. The difficulties posed by studying historical subjects are further troubled when the subjects were professional performers in an economy in which performed gender variance was both popular and a factor in their livelihood. How do you analyze the "experience" of gender when the represented gender is only biological, or only theatrical, or both? When is the performance of gender purely a performance, and when is it the discursively formed performance of gender? Can the two ever be separated?

This book centers on gender identity as a field of disruption, and looks to the work of postmodern theater studies in order to understand the role that gender identity played in Kansas City. Rather than seeking to understand or define the gender identity of the performers I focus instead on the disruptive space between the performers and the audience/historian. In this scheme performers were not simply the vehicles for the representation of gender. They were, in fact, agents who used their bodies in performance as a way to trouble gender for the audience. In what Daphne Brooks referred to as "opaque performances," performers used their work to challenge the acceptable categories of gender, even if they appeared to reify them.[3] In addition the focus on the space between the performer and the audience/historian provides fertile ground for the critique of a master narrative of history that places gender in socially constructed categories and explores the ways in which individuals were subjectified to the regulatory and disruptive definitions of gender, and the methods those individuals used to disrupt and interrupt those definitions. The gender identity of a historical figure cannot be known or completely understood and I will not try to do so. The gender identity of the performers themselves will remain as they must: in the historical archives of anonymity. This is not, however, a reason *not* to write about identity. What can be understood is the desires of the scholar who seeks to subjectify their subjects. As a historian and a queer scholar I equate subjectivity and disruption. I will attempt to read the experiences of my subjects as an audience member whose desires are played out on the bodies of the performer. I will not be able to assign a single "gender identity" to my subjects, but I do seek to explore and explain the desires that I, and I hope others in the audience, discursively assigned to the subjects.

5

Another problematic feature of this study is the discontinuity of the margins. Studies that focus on insider/outsider or mainstream/margin dichotomies are tasked with defining where those boundaries lie. While many scholars utilize the concept of the margins versus the mainstream, the question is really about the line itself. Here the margin is not a continuous, clearly defined border but a discontinuous, constantly contested boundary. Through this lens the margins are dynamic, changing, and just as problematic as identity to define and categorize, as the "margins" and the "mainstream" move and overlap, depending on the standpoint of the subject. To further disrupt the question of the margins, this work also draws heavily on cultural studies' critiques of dominant written histories. Not only was the margin a moving boundary inside a sociocultural scene, it continues to be a contested boundary among historians.

Given the problematic nature of defining a margin/mainstream boundary, it appears practically impossible to identify. The key is to emphasize the ways in which this margin/mainstream boundary was continuously contested in Kansas City's jazz scene. Rather than discuss groups identified by historians as marginalized, I focus on groups who lived and performed in the jazz scene. As much as possible the emphasis is on groups marginalized *within* the jazz scene as well as by the mainstream who saw the jazz scene as dangerous and damaging.

A third challenge in the revision of Kansas City's jazz story is defining a jazz scene. Despite the image of the American Jazz Age as a unified age of cultural shift, the scenes were interrelated but independent, a temporary culturally and socially specific phenomenon. Kansas City was the site of gender, racial, and class conflict in the first half of the twentieth century, although its written history does not consistently reflect such contested territory. The history of jazz scene Kansas City is instead filled with stories of cowboys, big business, and the excesses of crime, vice, and jazz music more in line with Broadway musicals than lived experience. These stories provide the foundation for the official and scholarly knowledge of Kansas City as a place of civilized roughness.

For all its concentration on progress and urban prosperity, Kansas City was (and still is) a city where inhabitants were unwilling to shed the city's "rough and ready" Western reputation. As one historian wrote: "Machismo was marketable, and bawdiness was big business. The city that limped out of the Civil War had become a cocksure, burgeoning town literally drunk with success."[4] Ross Russell, a historian of Kansas City's jazz scene, depicted the city as a center of heterosexual male pleasure: "For the people of the Plains and the American Southwest 'Kaycee' came to be known as a heavenly place. To its attraction as a prime market was added the allure of high good time as they were then envisioned by the American male—a great plenty of everything, good food, good beer and liquor, dancing, exciting women, and dice rolling on green felt tables—all these pleasurable commodities served well-ladled with the sauce of lively music."[5]

Such heteronormative examples reveal the grand narrative of heterosexual male consumers and willing female commodities. The city's masculine aura, however, depended on the strict control of gender, class, and racial difference, a force since forgotten. The "pleasurable commodities" that Russell suggests included the performances of varieties of gender variance and sexuality. Were these commodities not also part of the desires of the "American male"? The "heavenly place" for people who came to Kansas City during its jazz scene came with a variety of desires, but "machismo was marketable." In fact the very legend of Kansas City's "wide-open" jazz scene continues defend the dominant hierarchy. There was a co-constitutive zoning of non-normative gender performance, race, class, and jazz in the city, but the existence of varied gazes and desires in the city's jazz spaces were subsumed in the city's written history. Bringing these non-normative others and the marginalized spaces to light forces a critical reorientation of Kansas City history as well as an equally important reorientation of jazz history.

The positioning of jazz as both American and transgressive is inextricably linked to the racialization of jazz as a black art form that assim-

7

ilated its African American performers into a European system.[6] While many scholars of jazz history have examined the role of identity and difference in the development of jazz, the dominant history of jazz often focuses on the great performers of "American music." For example as a matter of course musician Charlie Parker appears in jazz histories as the father of bebop whose untimely death signaled a shift in the production of jazz. The story of Parker as an African American jazz musician, a pioneer of sound, is immortalized in everything from the *Grove Encyclopedia of Jazz* to the biographical film *Bird*. Interestingly, however, drugs, sexuality, and inclusion in the jazz "underground" are also part of this Parker history—they serve as a backdrop to describe his downfall, the story of a man who could not deny his desires in favor of his genius. It is one example among many of the ways the Kansas City's written jazz history reflects a society that polices what it produces. At the same time, this backdrop in Parker's story illustrates the importance of this study—ascension into the heights of jazz fame became the "real story" of Parker, glossing over the intersections of gender, sexuality, race, and class that surrounded him.

This is but one example of how gender variance and sexuality, mainstays in the jazz scene, are found most commonly in the background of written history, a kind of theater stage set for the "real story" taking place on stage. The "backstage" was always present, however, part of the culture of the temporary jazz scene, *especially among the players*. Foucault's thought that societies work to speak of the things they cannot say can be seen in the backstage in written jazz history. When it comes to the representation of gender variance and sexuality in dominant jazz scene history, the backstage of non-normative gender performance and sexuality is as obvious as the stage set, but as spectators we are not supposed to see them. For example Nathan Pearson Jr. and Howard Litwak completed an oral history project on Kansas City's jazz scene in the 1980s, and according to the final report of their "Goin' to Kansas City" project, the nationally funded oral history project was a success.

Citing their work with interviewees and the production of a traveling exhibition, Pearson and Litwak reported that their project captured "something of the lives and experiences implicit within the rubric of 'jazz scene.'"[7] One of the project's goals was to study "homosexuality" in Kansas City's jazz scene. Pearson later pointed to an interview with female performer Edna Mintirn as primary evidence of homosexuality in Kansas City's Jazz District. According to Pearson the Mintirn interview was fully transcribed, but only excerpts from the interview were included in the book—those excerpts that seemed to suggest gender variance, which Pearson and Litwak defined as homosexuality. The full interview was never donated to any of the archival repositories where the Pearson and Litwak tapes were archived, and the exact cause of the Mintirn interview tape's "disappearance" from the collections of the University of Missouri–Kansas City, the Institute of Jazz Studies at Rutgers, and the Folklore Archives of the Smithsonian Institution will likely never be known. It is, however, interesting to note that the interviews with famous Kansas City performers from the dominant canon of jazz history, such as Count Basie and Jay McShann, were fully transcribed in 1987 and are available to researchers. Given the fact the Pearson and Litwak suggest the Mintirn interview as the primary evidence of "homosexuality," why is it not valued in the same way as the other interviews? When, and how, did Edna Mintirn's observations and memories become part of "the secret"? Though this example is one of many, it clearly demonstrated the role of written, dominant jazz history in the continued policing of "the secret" in Kansas City's jazz scene, both lived and historically represented.

The temporality of the jazz scene allows for reorientation and focus on performance, representation, and space. This includes not only the lived experience in jazz scene clubs and cabarets, but the spatialization of Kansas City itself. In the typical conception of the Jazz Age the action is concentrated in America's urban eastern cities, though it is understood that the changes of the "Jazz Age" spread across the country. The cultural and social shifts of the jazz scene did not, however, simply radiate from New York City. The changing roles for women, for instance, were seen and felt by Americans in every corner of the country through mass amusements such as jazz clubs and cabarets. Few studies of the American jazz scene have focused on the cities of rural America, which represented the front line in cultural clashes of the period. One such city was Kansas City, considered an urban center by the inhabitants of the trans-Mississippi West.

While the people of Kansas City experienced many of the same social changes as other city dwellers during the American jazz scene, there are aspects of the temporary Kansas City experience that make an excellent case for the geographies of desire. Unlike New York or Boston, Kansas City was a railroad hub on the edge of rural America—the only urban center between Chicago to the east and burgeoning Houston to the south. The city was home to the nation's largest livestock market, which meant an annual influx of thousands of ranchers, farmers, and cowboys along with a consistent population of immigrant workers for slaughterhouses and packing plants. There was also a contentious relationship between the idea of material progress and the city's reputation as "wild and woolly." City fathers embraced the idea of material "eastern" progress, and championed the construction of public buildings, parks, and boulevards. The need to satisfy the expectations of tourists and businessmen seeking entertainment in the Kansas City "frontier," however, also led to odd allegiances within the city. While progressive changes were encouraged in middle- and upper-class sections of the city, the working-class districts near railroad tracks were purposely separated from city planning. City fathers sought to identify these districts as immoral, a place for pleasure-seeking visitors to see the "wild and woolly" west of Kansas City. As Clare Sears explained in her recent book on cross-dressing in nineteenth-century San Francisco, the result was a "purposeful exclusion" that segregated differently gendered people along with racial and ethnic minorities.[8] The sex tourism and non-normative gender performance found in working-class districts were not only part of the city's legend; they were clearly part of the appeal of Kansas City to its many visitors. As Edward Murrow wrote in the *Omaha World-Herald*: "If you want to see sin, forget about Paris and go to Kansas City."[9] To what sins Murrow was alluding is unknown. It was this reputation, however, created by capitalist investment and encouraged by dominant knowledge, that created the myth of Kansas City's jazz scene.

The final challenge of the revision presented in *Queering Kansas City Jazz* is centering space at the center of Kansas City's jazz story instead of music. Rather than position space as secondary or background to performance and representation, geography of desires defines space as an area where identity and representation is contested, tested, and practiced. According to historian Sherry Schirmer, spatialization gave the Kansas City, Missouri, fathers the ability to keep unacceptable racial and gendered behavior geographically separate.[10] This is the application of "moral geography," a term coined by Perry Duis, wherein members of dominant urban societies identify "deviant" districts and neighborhoods. This meant not only the observation of neighborhoods but the observation and discipline of people residing in those "deviant" spaces. The question of space, however, is not simply one of contested territories and concrete maps, but one of *use*. It is important to consider how those who used the spaces of Kansas City's jazz scene, whether patrons, performers, workers or neighbors, saw those spaces as sites of identity formation, representation, and performance and to think about how researchers use space to explain patrons who frequented "deviant" spaces as well as those who considered such spaces their *place*.

In order to highlight the experience of space rather than place, the geography of desires approach depends on critical cultural geography that signifies the workings of power in lived experience on the ground. Space is a concept and term of material reality, and its use in cultural studies has too frequently been relegated to the use of metaphor alone.[11]

Critical cultural geographers, however, position space as a site of experience, not a metaphor. Through the lens of human experience, critical cultural geographers work to examine the various contexts where social differences are "produced, understood, and negotiated" and to understand the connections between space, identity, and representation.[12]

An example of the ways in which space is the site of performance and power is Kansas City Ordinance No. 291, enacted in the 1880s. While the ordinance dealt specifically with sexualized behaviors, the ordinance was written in specifically spatial terms.

> No person shall be or appear in or upon any street, avenue, alley, park, public place or place open to public view, in a state of nudity, or any dress not belonging to his or her sex, or in any indecent or lewd dress, or shall make any indecent exposure of his or her person, or be guilty of an unseemly obscene or filthy act, or any lewd, indecent, immoral or insulting conduct, language or behavior; or shall exhibit, circulate, contribute, sell, offer or expose for sale, or give or deliver to another, or cause the same to be done, any lewd, indecent or obscene book, picture, pamphlet, card, print, paper writing, mold, cast, figure or any other thing, or shall exhibit or perform, or cause or allow to be exhibited or performed, in or upon any house, building, lot or premises owned or occupied by him, or under his management or control, any lewd, indecent, or immoral play or other representation.[13]

Given the ordinance, one would suspect that the spaces where such performances, behaviors, and exhibits appeared were tightly controlled in Kansas City. The jazz scene, however, allowed for flourishing work in sex shows and performances, drag clubs, and in the daily business of prostitution and burlesque dancing. In fact male drag performances were recorded in Kansas City as early as 1880, when one *Kansas City Star* reporter wrote: "As a female impersonator he draws a large salary and is a most remarkable success, but as a man he is a gigantic failure and not worth the powder that would blow his effeminate soul to heaven."[14] The question that remains unaddressed in studies that rely on the metaphorical use of spaces is this: how did the gender impersonator with the "effeminate soul" see "his" identity? What evidence exists that would illuminate this? How did the clubs and cabarets where gender impersonation was welcomed and celebrated serve as sites of identity formation and representation for performers and patrons? At the peak of the jazz scene, drag performers such as the one discussed in 1880 might have performed at the very popular Dante's Inferno, a Pendergast-controlled club in the city's Jazz District. As the home to Kansas City's drag performers, Dante's probably offered a certain level of safety and acceptance to performers and patrons who packed the club every night. How did a club like Dante's serve as a space where the identities of drag performers and their patrons, whatever those identities were, were appreciated and recognized? Did Dante's in fact serve as the site of the production of normative subjects, who could enter and leave this zone of possibilities?

In order both to explore the accepted Kansas City jazz story and to uncover the stories of transgression and difference, this text is arranged so that the erased past comes slowly into focus. It begins with an examination of the accepted narrative of Kansas City's jazz scene and then focuses specifically on the ways in which a very specific group of jazz stakeholders developed that narrative. From there I excavate the history of non-normative gender and sexuality in the city, as aspects of the jazz scene erased from the Kansas City story. Finally I discuss in the last two chapters specific aspects of Kansas City's jazz scene: prostitution and sex tourism, and the lives of cabaret singers often hidden by the stories of jazz greats. Through this organization I intend the book to act as a telescope, focusing more and more closely on the people in Kansas City's jazz scene background.

This book is organized in five sections. Chapter 2 outlines the facets of geography of desires through the story of the Pendergast political machine, which was primarily responsible for the control of spaces in the city's Jazz District as well as the working-class and racially differentiated neighborhoods. Jim Pendergast arrived in Kansas City in the 1870s and with the winnings from a racetrack wager opened saloons in the city's working-class Sixth District. When Jim died and his brother Tom took over the machine in 1911 the Pendergasts controlled and produced prostitution, gambling, jazz clubs, local police, and city government. The power of the Pendergast family and their strict control of daytime activity in the districts was predicated on their own performance and desire for acceptance among Kansas City's wealthy upper class. A working-class immigrant, Tom Pendergast married a former saloon dancing girl and was constantly portrayed in the press as a criminal with a "loose" wife. At the same time government officials and local judges unabashedly sought Pendergast approval and investment, knowing that control of the city depended on the support of Pendergast's working-class constituents and their public amusements. The Pendergast machine itself is a primary example of the ways in which power, space, and performance overlapped in the city. Due largely to Pendergast's segregation rules, the alignment of vice, interracial neighborhoods, and non-normative gender behavior followed codes of dominant morality in Kansas City. White city "movers and shakers," who found the thought of vice in their neighborhoods threatening, deemed it acceptable when segregated to unacceptable neighborhoods already defined as "deviant."[15]

Chapter 3 addresses the research problems by analyzing the official memories of the jazz scene as preserved in written history. The lack of gender variance in Kansas City's historical record is a direct result not only of the city's history, but of the reterritorializing spatialization of the city. That the concept of Kansas City's "cocksure" past silences "othered" subjects in the written record is an issue in jazz scene history, as well as the history of gender, sexuality, and race in the city. Through a discussion of jazz historiography I show how the memories of difference in the Kansas City jazz scene continue to be spatially represented and subsumed in a dominant narrative, while exploring the development of recent jazz historiography. The third chapter addresses the spatial and personal identity of research subjects and the researchers who studied them, and the ways in which those paired identities continue to be territorialized by history, memory, space, and representation in the traditional jazz canon.

Chapter 4 explores non-normative gender performance in the city. Focused on the early twentieth century's changing concepts of masculinity and femininity as well as a burgeoning "homosexual" identity, this chapter discusses the contested representations of "men" and "women." I will also excavate some of the history of gender impersonation in the Kansas City jazz scene, which was far from unknown in Kansas City's jazz scene. Self-identified homosexual performers, gender impersonators, and sex shows were understood as standard components of the jazz scene in Kansas City. Since such clubs and performances were represented and marked as an open secret by historians, however, their space in the jazz scene was silenced and deemed unimportant. Such performers, however, were part of the professional world of performance at the time, and it is important to study the way such performers represented themselves. Did audiences see in the performance something beyond what performers represented on, with, or through their bodies? How did space play a role in the representation of gender impersonators as something "other?" Why does Kansas City's jazz scene history, not to mention much of jazz historiography, not reflect the role of these performers and their performances? Whose desires did they perform? This chapter will excavate the story of changing gender representation in the city, beginning with Oscar Wilde's arrival in 1882. Using the work of theater historians and their conceptualization of spectacle in Foucauldian theory, I investigate how certain performers and performances were eventually represented as "marginal" and "abnormal."

Chapter 5 is focused on the deterritorialization and reterritorialization of space and the ways in which desires were linked to representation through a discussion of brothel madam Annie Chambers. Chambers came to Kansas City in the 1870s and opened the city's largest and most famous brothel, which remained open from 1880 until 1913 thanks to the Pendergast machine and patronage to city officials. Chambers was arrested in 1913 under Missouri's White Slavery Act after a daytime raid on the brothel. Though Chambers sued the City of Kansas City in the Supreme Court of Missouri for violation of her Fourteenth Amendment rights and won, she was forced to close the brothel. Chambers made it clear, in public appearances and in court records, that she considered the brothel a formative space in the creation of her identity as a working-class sex worker. At the same time she saw the brothel space as an important site of the representation of other sex workers, most of whom she portrayed as childlike. The brothel was carefully dismantled by Kansas City leaders and investors, and the house became the City Union Mission—still the largest homeless shelter in the city. Architectural features such as the brothel's famous stained-glass windows found a new home in the most expensive restaurant in Kansas City Plaza shopping district—America's first shopping "mall." The fact that the city's most famous brothel became a Christian mission and its windows became a symbol of the victory of "progress" over "vice" in what is still Kansas City's most elite shopping district illustrates the territorialization of Kansas City's jazz scene.

Edna Mae Jacobs is the topic of the sixth chapter. While thousands of people lived and worked in Kansas City during the 1920s and 1930s, very little information exists about the everyday lives of working-class people in archival records or written histories, making it difficult to write about those whose representation is limited by lack of evidence. One exception is Edna Mae (Whithouse) Jacobs, who arrived in Kansas City as a child in 1905. She lived in the West Bottoms District, the center of Pendergast power and the largest working-class district in the city. As a jazz cabaret performer, table waitress, and later club owner, Jacobs had first-hand experience with the Pendergast machine, jazz clubs, working-class neighborhoods, and the life of women working in the jazz scene. All of these aspects position her as a case study of daily life in the jazz scene. What makes Jacobs so important, however, is the rare availability of primary sources about Jacobs and her life in the city. Jacobs left behind a series of scrapbooks now housed at the University of Kansas, as well as a 1980 interview with Pearson and Litwak for the "Goin' to Kansas City" project. The Jacobs material, therefore, provides a rare opportunity to understand the interplay of space, representation, identity, and power in the actual lived experience and memory of a single individual. How did Jacobs see herself, her identity, and her work at Dante's Inferno? What aspects of the jazz scene, forgotten in the grand narrative, are memorialized in her scrapbooks? How did Pearson and Litwak find Jacobs, why did they interview her, and what did they use her words to represent? Jacobs was never famous, and her papers were donated to the University of Kansas only after other repositories turned them down because she "was not a jazz performer" and deemed "not important enough."[16] Jacobs's story is representative of the problematic work of researching jazz scene lives in Kansas City's history and illustrates the importance of examining identity and performance as a discursive production of space as well as of knowledge. Jacobs's scrapbooks and interview provide "narratives of the self" and insight into the ways she came to inhabit the subject position in the discourse produced by the Kansas City jazz scene.

2

Kansas City's Jazz Scene

In one of the opening scenes of the musical *Oklahoma!*, cowboy Will Parker steps off the train in Claremore and greets his friends at the station. After extolling Kansas City's modernity Will piques the interest of the men and embarrasses the women with tales of his trip to a burlesque show: "One of the gals was fat and pink and pretty," Will informs his small-town friends. "She went about as fur as she could go!"[1]

Oklahoma! was set in 1906, in the early days of Kansas City's rise to fame as a "wide-open town." The music of the "wide-open town" was jazz. Played in the "burleeque" of *Oklahoma!*, in cabarets memorialized in musicals and films such as Robert Altman's *Kansas City*, jazz as a sound was central to the jazz scene in the city. While Kansas City was the site of gender, racial, and class clash during its jazz scene, its written history focuses on this memorialization and does not consistently reflect the contested territories of identity and power in the city. The history of jazz scene Kansas City is instead filled with stories of cowboys in the big city, with the excesses of crime and jazz more easily associated with characters like Will Parker than with lived experience. These stories provide the foundation for the official and scholarly knowledge of Kansas City as a history of civilized roughness.

Such heteronormative examples reveal the grand narrative of Kansas City jazz scene history as the story of heterosexual male consumers and willing female commodities. The city's masculine aura depended on the strict control of gender, class, and racial difference, a control since forgotten and silenced in the grand narrative. In fact the very legend of Kansas City's "wide-open" jazz scene continues to ignore the knowledge of the jazz scene by constantly defining and defending the dominant hierarchy. Anyone interested in the history of Kansas City's jazz scene can read the stories of Charlie Parker peering in cabaret windows or hear about the all-night battles between the city's rival bands. While these famous events of the jazz scene remain in popular memory and written history, many important aspects of the complex jazz scene were forgotten and silenced. What about the lives of the "fat and pink and pretty" girls of the cabarets, burlesque shows, and brothels? What about the girls who were not "pink," or the girls who were not "girls"? How were these areas of "pleasurable commodities" defined and zoned? How did spaces of the jazz scene retain their popularity despite their challenges to the dominant constructions of gender, race, and class? Finally, how did all of those critical challenges to identity, space, and power go forgotten in the city's grand narrative?

Normalcy, explained historian David Goldberg, was the goal of the "Jazz Age."[2] Challenges to the social order were appropriated as a temporary flowering of youth and culture, and threats were transformed by the grand narrative as bumps on the road to modernity. In the grand narrative of the "Jazz Age" Kansas City was positioned as one of the road bumps. The city's railroad terminus meant that performers and musicians from the "big city" found themselves in Kansas City at the end of the line, with no choice but to export their opposition to the status quo.[3] Meanwhile in each of those schemes Kansas City appears as a country bumpkin coming of age, a brief exception in an age of exceptions, the city whose adolescence was felt in the jazz scene.

The problem with that grand narrative is that it does little to explain life inside the jazz scene. Kansas City did not represent a flowering of experimentation or a circumstantial dead end. The city was, in fact, the frontier of the cultural wars fought during the jazz scene: cutting edge, not country bumpkin. As historian Kevin Mumford has explained, a study of jazz scenes must be "premised on the proposition that the shift from rural to urban America, from southern agricultural economies to modern commercial infrastructures, from communal to modern anonymous social relations represented a historic watershed."[4] Kansas City represents that historic watershed that was its *jazz scene*. Unfortunately those disruptions were forgotten, silenced, and lost in a fictional "Jazz Age" that emphasized the road to modernity in the 1920s.

A study of the Kansas City jazz scene reveals an important aspect of life in the city: the threats to the social order were all linked. The sounds of jazz music cannot be divorced from clashes over gender, growing debates about race and ethnicity, the crisis represented by class divides, and the evolving influence of a criminal underworld in the United States. In Kansas City these interrelated subcultures were linked through the Pendergast machine: the Pendergast machine was the fuel for the jazz scene in Kansas City. In fact the jazz scene in Kansas City is part of the Pendergast machine, and vice versa. The Pendergast machine, however, is reduced in the grand narrative of jazz in Kansas City to a backdrop, a criminal element that created the environment of the city's jazz scene, but did not directly influence its events. The subsumed and reductive history of Kansas City's jazz scene is inextricably linked to Pendergast's representations of class, race, and gender in the city. The story of Kansas City's jazz scene is one of spatialization, discursive formation, and the way the reductive representation of the Pendergast machine reflects the desires of historians.

KANSAS CITY'S JAZZ SCENE ROOTS

In his book *Paths of Resistance* historian David Thelen writes of early twentieth-century Missourians:

Traditional Missourians expected to build their communities of resistance, whether of confrontation or escape, from the richly layered associations of their daily lives. Through lines of allegiance and communication among kinship, friendship, and craft groups they built deep and warm participatory worlds of support around their churches, fraternal lodges, saloons, workplaces, and political parties. Shared traditions predisposed them to analyze changes in similar ways and to participate with others in actions to defend or recover those traditions. Their communities turned questions of power into the basic issue of whom to trust and whom not to trust, and they expected political relief to take the more distant form of pressure groups or governmental programs.[5]

The Pendergast world was a world based on Thelen's "lines of allegiance." This was not simply a political machine or a criminal backdrop for the sound of Kansas City swing. The Pendergast world was a system of spaces and loyalties where the dominant "truths" about class, race, and gender were in question. In fact belief in the Pendergast world and the powers it contained were direct challenges to the dictatorial and prevailing ideologies about morality, acceptability, and oppression.

The key to understanding the Pendergast world is framing Kansas City as a *jazz scene*, not part of a fictional "Jazz Age." Jazz scene spaces began to appear in the city in the 1880s, and the jazz scene declined with the end World War II in 1945, dates that coincide with the rise of the Pendergast family. Beginning in the 1880s the immigrant Pendergast family slowly gained control over Kansas City by organizing working-class, immigrant, and African American Kansas Citians. In order to gather their followers the Pendergasts began a system of family-style patronage through working-class saloons and clubs. At its height the Pendergast machine controlled practically every club, cabaret, brothel, and infrastructural business in the city through its network of marginalized subcultures in the city. With Pendergast's approval Kansas City could be shut down. The Pendergast machine itself was seen as a threat to the social order of Kansas City, even while the Pendergast family exerted their influence over the very institutions they threatened. As Kathy Ogren wrote in her book *The Jazz Revolution*, it was the Pendergast machine that kept the jazz scene alive long after the closing of Storyville and through the Great Depression.[6] The jazz scene in Kansas City was literally a Pendergast scene, and all its intricate contestations over space and identity reflected the machinations of the Pendergast family.

Despite the importance of the Pendergast machine in the jazz scene of Kansas City, jazz history's grand narrative continues to reduce the Pendergast machine to a few clichéd terms. These terms tend to illuminate the titillating, voyeuristic aspects of Pendergast-controlled spaces and reify the myth of Kansas City as a "wide-open" stop on the jazz road to New York. One example of this reduction appears in the writing of Dave Dexter, a music critic for jazz publications such as *Down Beat* and a source of information for Driggs and Haddix's book *Kansas City Jazz*. As Dexter wrote: "No other city in the world was quite like Kansas City. Musicians and singers came into the Jackson County town of 400,000 like cattle—in droves. For under the wide-open yet iron rule of Democratic political czar Thomas J. Pendergast there were no closing hours for saloons and nightclubs. Prostitution flourished day and night in the open. There were jobs available for entertainers of every type."[7]

Dexter represents Kansas City as a place where "every type" of entertainer might flourish in the background, suggesting an atmosphere of sexual permissiveness. Another example originated in an essay by Martin Williams, a stakeholder of jazz history and author of the Smithsonian's guides to American jazz. In his essay on Kansas City Williams wrote one paragraph about the Pendergast machine, which positioned it firmly as the backdrop for the development of a musical style. "Kansas City was an 'open' city under the control of the notorious political machine of

Tom Prendergast [*sic*]. There were large ballrooms, and there were less pretentious dance halls, there were cabarets and clubs; there was gambling; there was prostitution. There also was a constant call for music, and like New Orleans before it, Kansas City offered welcoming gestures to the remarkable Afro-American improvisational music called jazz."[8]

Historian of the American West David Stowe, using the books by Pearson and Russell as his only sources, explained Kansas City's jazz scene in much the same way as Williams. "The notoriously freewheeling environment fostered by the administration of Major Tom Pendergast during the 1920s and 1930s," wrote Stowe, "was conducive to the creation of jazz."[9] Musicologist Howard Becker recently continued the same reduction of the Kansas City jazz scene in his autoethnographical account of jazz scene spaces. "Thus, one of the greatest centers of jazz development—Kansas City in the 1920s and 1930s—drew its vitality from the political corruption which made nightlife possible," wrote Becker.[10] Even new jazz studies scholar Krin Gabbard, well-known for his writing against the jazz canon, reduced Kansas City to these diminished representations in a 1997 review of the Robert Altman film *Kansas City*. "Paradoxically, the corruption and violence of the city," wrote Gabbard, "gave us the extraordinary music, the era's one great monument."[11] Such reductive representations entered the jazz canon as a way to prove the authenticity of Kansas City's jazz music. What such reductions silence, however, is the contestations over race, class, gender, sexuality, ethnicity, and power that were at work in Kansas City. These contestations are vital to understanding the development of Kansas City's jazz scene, the role of Kansas City as an urbanized frontier town, and the influence of the Pendergast machine on the lives of Kansas City's population.

A "WIDE-OPEN" TOWN

According to literature scholar Krista Comer, the term "open" to describe a town was coined in the American West to describe white and male spaces.[12] Given the common sobriquet of "wide-open" in descriptions of Kansas City's jazz scene, it would seem that the city was expected to appeal to white, heterosexual male visitors, patrons, and jazz scholars. Much of this representation, no doubt, stems from the Pendergast family and their control of Kansas City in the first half of the twentieth century. Before the arrival of the Pendergasts Kansas City was still a largely rural and typical Western town. An 1882 observer noted it remained a "city in stagnant water much of the year."[13] Founded on river bluffs, the city was still small by urban standards at the end of the Civil War. Most residents lived near the Missouri River and took a dangerous trolley train along the bluffs from the river bottoms to the factories and shops on Main Street.[14] Kansas City was relatively compact, bordered by the Missouri River on the north, the Kansas River bottoms on the west, Thirty-Second Street on the south, and Cleveland Street on the east.[15] There were only wooden sidewalks with no paved streets until 1879.[16] In his recollections of 1882 Lloyd Lewis described Kansas City's rough-hewn character: "Missouri hogs, not yet having fear of packing houses, patrolled the streets. At night, when the hogs were off duty, a billion frogs in the green ponds at the bottom of the choicest unoccupied city lots told their troubles to the stars, and saluted the morning sun with croaks of despair. In wet weather the town site was a sea of mud and in dry weather a desert of dust."[17]

But change was in the air. Between 1869 and 1900 a major population increase, accompanied by booming urban growth, transformed the city. The Hannibal Railroad Bridge across the Missouri River opened in 1869, and Jay Gould made Kansas City his western base of railroad operations in 1880.[18] The city's establishment as a railroad terminus and the rise of meatpacking factories brought thousands of workers and immigrants to Kansas City. A population of only 4,000 in 1865 grew to one of 55,785 recorded in 1880.[19]

The growing modernization of Kansas City created an instant clash between the city's eastern modernization plans and its western typicality.

This clash between "wide-open" western sensibilities and urbanization can be seen as the city's coming of age. Such a coming of age in the West, according to Krista Comer, was inevitably linked to race, class, gender, and sexuality. "Western spaces 'come of age' in the twentieth century," wrote Comer, "via an erotic emplotment that was simultaneously masculinist, heterocentric, nationalist and white supremacist."[20] This coming of age period in Kansas City began in the 1880s, when the city was gaining importance without losing its "wild west" character. The result was a clash between modernization and the rural West. The city had a reputation for "wide-open" permissive behavior and was frequented by cattlemen and farmers who visited it on weekends in search of entertainment.[21] The city directory of 1878 listed eighty saloons—four times the number of city schools, libraries, and hospitals combined.[22] In this sudden clash of rural and urban, Kansas City neighborhoods were clearly stratified. Wealthy city dwellers lived primarily on Quality Hill, a cliffside area on the east side of the city away from livestock barns and the railroad. Quality Hill overlooked the city's working-class neighborhoods, known as the West Bottoms and the North End. The West Bottoms, located between Quality Hill and the Kansas state line along the southern edge of the Missouri River, became the center of industry in Kansas City.[23] Home to meatpacking houses, railroad yards, and factories, the West Bottoms was also home to most working-class Kansas Citians, who lived in overcrowded tenements.[24] Disease and muddy streets in the flood-prone area compounded the poor living conditions.[25] Because the West Bottoms was the city's industrial center its tenements primarily housed newly arrived European immigrant packinghouse workers along with most of the city's African American population. The alleys in some parts of the West Bottoms were so narrow that residents had to walk single file.[26] The city's other principal working-class neighborhood, known as the North End, was located just north and east of the West Bottoms. Called the "dingy North End," the neighborhood was the center of Kansas City's red-light district.[27] What the North End lacked in industry it made up for in gambling halls and brothels. Most red-light activity took place in the North End's Knob Hill section, where one-third of Kansas City's police force was concentrated from 1870 to 1875.[28]

While Kansas City grew as an industrial center and railroad terminus, its lack of infrastructure reflected its frontier origins. On the surface Kansas City appeared to be a progressive city. Kansas City's police system was established in 1874 with the celebrated artist George Caleb Bingham as the first chair of the Board of Police Commissioners. The state of Missouri, however, retained control over the commissioners and the youthful chief Tom Speers until 1889.[29] Though Kansas City's population depended on industry and the railroads, their operations were strictly concentrated in the West Bottoms away from the residential and financial districts. Downtown and Quality Hill Districts boasted a library, cable cars, and a telephone system by 1887.[30] The Kansas City passenger railroad depot, a 384-foot-long terminus in the Kansas River Bottoms, opened in 1878 to annual ticket sales of $1.5 million.[31] These institutions, however, were largely facades that disguised the city's rural foundations.

While outwardly Kansas City appeared to be a major metropolis, it was a city in crisis. The city's rapid growth and expansion outpaced the ability of its officials to address the problems of a burgeoning urban area. For instance in 1880 the city had only a primitive sewer system in Quality Hill and no provisions for garbage collection. Most city dwellers dumped their garbage into the Missouri River. Dead animals floated in the river or littered the streets.[32] Only five hundred yards of Kansas City's eighty-nine miles of street were covered with sandstone paving blocks. Sixteen miles were covered in crushed limestone that caused clouds of dust and dissolved into mud during inclement weather. The few pine-plank sidewalks remained constantly filthy.[33] Conditions were so bad that members of the Kansas City Equal Suffrage Society voted in 1893 to raise their hemlines three inches. While the suffragists intended the decision to bring attention to their cause, they also used the occasion to reprimand Superintendent of Streets John May about city conditions.[34] Their concern was not just the streets but their own respectability and representation as progressive thinkers. As one suffragist told the *Kansas City Evening Star*: "Besides saving dresses and keeping mud out of the house the fulfillment of the new plan will be a badge of honor and will serve as an advertisement of the society. Any member walking the streets will irresistibly attract attention and be a monument of higher progression."[35]

The Kansas City fathers' preoccupation with railroad development caused them to ignore the city's infrastructure. Railroads were the cornerstone of the city's economic system. As a railroad terminus Kansas City had national importance. The city's livestock and meatpacking industries attracted businessmen and investors as well as a large transient workforce.[36] Railroads brought seventy thousand people to Kansas City in 1869, the first year the Hannibal Bridge was open. In the 1880s only San Francisco and Chicago exceeded Kansas City in miles of street railway track. City promoter Kersey Coates owned eleven rail lines in the West Bottoms and died a millionaire.[37] The number of livestock brokered yearly in Kansas City rose from approximately one hundred thousand in 1870 to almost one million by 1880.[38] Cattle brokers and meat packers, who depended on the railroads, soon controlled Kansas City government and business. The Kansas City Livestock Exchange was founded in 1871 and governed by a group of local railroad tycoons.[39] When the Plankinton and Armour meatpacking plants made Kansas City their base of operations in the late 1880s, the West Bottoms became the nation's leading packing district.[40] Despite all this prosperity, however, the city's working class and immigrant inhabitants saw little material improvement in their lives. Poverty and homelessness were rampant and likely exacerbated by the transient nature of the city's population. Squatters on railroad tracks and abandoned families were common in the city. Forty homeless boys working as bootblacks were discovered clustered around a heater in the Board of Trade building in 1885. According to newspaper reports the city was home to seven thousand prostitutes in 1887.[41]

THE RISE OF THE PENDERGAST FAMILY

In this confusing clash of rural and urban, wealth and poverty, the Pendergast family began to build power in the 1870s and 1880s. Jim Pendergast came to Kansas City in the 1870s as a transient railroad worker from a Polish-Irish family. He moved into the West Bottoms and frequented the working-class saloons and gambling halls there. In 1881 a lucky racetrack wager brought Pendergast an unexpected windfall that he used to buy a West Bottoms saloon on St. Louis Avenue that he renamed Climax. Pendergast opened a second saloon in 1891 in the North End and quickly gained popularity in the city's working-class districts.[42] He put up bonds for arrested neighbors and cashed paychecks for railroad and packinghouse workers from the saloon safes.[43] In 1884 Pendergast was chosen to represent the "Bloody Sixth" Ward in the West Bottoms on the city council.[44] At that time city fathers began to express concern about the number of inhabitants in the city's poorest districts—the West Bottoms and the North End. When ward lines were redrawn in 1886, putting the West Bottoms and the North End in a single district, Pendergast was chosen to represent the new First Ward.[45] From the First Ward Jim Pendergast built his political machine and gained a reputation as a fighter for the working class.[46] Pendergast used his machine to protect his investments in gambling and prostitution while building a coalition with the Kansas City police.[47] He also gained a reputation as a defender of the city's working class and immigrant populations in the First Ward.

One of the keys to the early construction of the Pendergast machine was the saloon. Until the 1880s the most important leisure space in American society was the saloon. Saloons offered working-class men shelter, a place to discuss politics and labor concerns, and a haven from the world of work.[48] However, in an attempt to reorganize leisure space after 1880, saloon owners sought to limit the more objectionable aspects of saloon culture, such as smoking and the use of profanity. The owners of these establishments attempted to encourage heterosocial behavior by limiting the homosocial side of male culture. Saloon owners hoped to attract more business by opening the doors to women, and they believed that the only way to attract "respectable" women was to limit the homosocial saloons hallmarks of gambling and prostitution. The key to this reorganization of culture was the reorganization of space.[49] For instance traditional saloons were spaces for men to congregate, and women were only allowed through back entrances.[50] When women were allowed as patrons, saloon owners moved prostitutes upstairs and allowed women to enter the saloon from the street. To make leisure space more enticing to women, owners had to alter the space and the men inhabiting that space. Jim Pendergast's early political machine was based in saloon business. While he continued to gain income from gambling, drinking, and prostitution in the saloons, he also offered loans, meals, and assistance to First Ward women who came to the saloon for his patronage. He also used his headquarters in the saloon as his place of business—anyone dealing in the North End, whether political or social, had to start at Climax, his West Bottoms saloon.

Jim Pendergast continued to gain power and prestige in the North End through the 1880s, coinciding with the growth and urbanization of Kansas City. For instance the city fathers believed that the adoption of an 1889 Kansas City charter would laud the beginning of a new wave of city development in the 1890s. Business leaders led by William Rockhill Nelson initiated plans to create a city charter intended to limit corruption—a direct threat to the growing Pendergast machine. Pendergast and his supporters, including the city's saloon owners and railroad operators, repeatedly defeated charter propositions. When a city charter was finally approved in 1889, it was only after backers made concessions to Pendergast and his supporters. One of those conces-

KANSAS CITY'S JAZZ SCENE

sions was that the city police would remain under local control, which meant that Pendergast could retain his system of patronage for the local police. It seems, however, that with the rise of Pendergast in the First Ward came an increased move by upper-class Kansas Citians away from the West Bottoms. The finished charter led to a new movement of well-to-do Kansas Citians outside the city center. Charter propositions included the formation of a Parks and Boulevards Commission, as well as a Board of Public Works, both designed to formalize the map of the city. This new map included a clear partitioning of the First Ward District. As the working-class First Ward grew in both population and political power, upper-class Kansas Citians moved out of Quality Hill across Grand Avenue and away from First Ward tenements.[51] The city's primary retail district remained within seven blocks of the Missouri River, while tenements from the First Ward began to expand. An area known as the Bowery, one of the city's primary African American neighborhoods, began to grow south along Troost and Woodland Avenues.[52] Despite the work of Jim Pendergast and his supporters, the power of the Pendergast machine remained within the borders of the First Ward.

In the politically charged and increasingly contentious atmosphere of the 1890s, Tom Pendergast joined his brother Jim in Kansas City. Originally Tom arrived in Kansas City to help his older brother consolidate power in the First Ward, but he quickly rose through the ranks. Through Jim's patronage Tom Pendergast served as Jackson County deputy marshal in 1896 and superintendent of streets in 1900. Meanwhile Jim Pendergast was grooming Tom to take over as boss of the First Ward. It was Tom who would build the Pendergast machine into a city-wide institution and bring the family and its supporters to the height of their power. Though the Pendergast family lost some of their control over city politics with the creation of the 1889 charter, the First Ward was still a Pendergast stronghold. With his political offices and his brother's patronage Tom Pendergast continued to provide his constituents with work, food, and other necessities through

31

Pendergast-owned saloons and businesses.[53] From those beginnings Tom began to increase the machine's control of the city's leisure spaces. The Pendergast machine drew its sustenance from the types of business the city fathers hoped to control: liquor, prostitution, gambling, and entertainment in clubs and cabarets. Tom Pendergast owned at least two hotels where prostitution was an open secret—he took a cut of the income from prostitution to pay the local police.[54] Tom then founded the Pendergast Wholesale Liquor Company, which supplied liquor to hotels, clubs, and the businesses in the Pendergast machine. For instance Pendergast protected cabarets such as the El Torreon Ballroom and the Chesterfield Club in exchange for their continued purchase of Pendergast liquor.[55] With the support of the working-class patrons and employees, as well as the city police (many of whom were working-class as well), Pendergast control of the First Ward went unchecked. Kansas City, known by the 1920s for its available entertainment and liquor, had zero felony convictions under prostitution laws for the entire period of Prohibition.[56] When Jim Pendergast died in November 1911 he left Tom in full control of the family businesses. Tom subsequently expanded the machine's geographic and political influence so that it went from a First Ward protection system to a massive political machine that controlled Kansas City's streets until the end of World War II.

Traditionally historians of the "Jazz Age" have positioned the underworld in one of two ways: as a criminal backdrop for the permissiveness of the fictional "Jazz Age," or as a criminal, mob-dominated periphery to the sound of jazz music.[57] One such depiction of the underworld in Kansas City's "Jazz Age" was written by oral historian Nathan Pearson: "The relationship between gangs and mobsters and musicians in those days was mostly complementary. Musicians minded their business; the gangsters minded theirs. . . . The cancerous vice that infected the city rarely harmed the musician, and often helped him."[58]

Such historical hindsight depends on the practice of depicting the underworld as a backdrop of criminals and degenerates, stage dressing for the performance of music. In the written history of Kansas City this grand narrative portrayal of the underworld is especially clear. For instance, one of the most frequently quoted statements about Kansas City in the Pendergast era comes from Edward Murrow: "If you want to see sin, forget about Paris and go to Kansas City."[59] Using this quote is an example of how the grand narrative focuses on vice and "wide-open" aspects of the city. Murrow's recollections, like those of many others who recalled the jazz scene in Kansas City, associated his representation of vice and crime with jazz, and jazz meant Pendergast. That the Pendergast machine was an underworld of crime and vice may be a fact, but it was not the simplified, homogeneous system so easily portrayed in Jazz Age creation. In fact the Pendergast jazz scene combined many of the contentious aspects of life that other historians have silenced. The Pendergast machine relied on three important yet contentious aspects: race and ethnicity, the intersection between gender and class, and jazz. Through the machine Tom and his constituents made a world of their own, one that was lost in the written history of jazz and the history of the Pendergast machine.

RACE, ETHNICITY, AND THE PENDERGAST WORLD

According to historian Lawrence Larsen, the Pendergast machine was based on a block system, and each city precinct had several block captains who reported to a ward boss. Captains handled interpersonal conflicts in their precincts and then reported larger problems directly to the ward boss. There were sixteen ward bosses in Kansas City, each of whom regularly reported to Tom Pendergast himself. The captains and ward bosses were not, unlike their historical and popular portrayal, all white. In fact Pendergast employed African Americans as both captains and ward bosses in African American neighborhoods.[60] An important supporter of the machine was Casimir Welch, an African American and head of the Second Ward that included the Bowery and the Twelfth and Vine area that became known as the Jazz District. The Second Ward was the city's poorest district, but under the 1890s control of Welch it became known as "Little Tammany." Pendergast supported Welch's debts at the Riverside race track and used those debts to gain Welch's support.[61] Eventually Pendergast financed an "American" paper for African Americans in Kansas City, much to the opposition of Chester Franklin, editor of the African American newspaper *Kansas City Call*.[62]

While some historians have claimed the Pendergast machine was "color blind," the idea ignores the contestations over race and segregation in the city.[63] In fact it continues a denial of race in Kansas City's jazz scene, a city enmeshed in a struggle over the expansion of blacks into predominantly white neighborhoods.[64] Editor Chester Franklin, who rallied against Pendergast's black newspaper, regularly featured blacks engaged in "block busting" in white neighborhoods in the *Kansas City Call*.[65] At the same time black neighborhoods were increasingly zoned by whites through moral geography. The most notorious cabarets in Kansas City, those that featured female impersonators and live sex shows, were in the predominantly black districts such as the famous Eighteenth and Vine Jazz District.[66] Kansas City's white mainstream saw this as a clear defense of moral geography—blacks were represented as deviant. For blacks this representation led to the zoning of their neighborhoods as deviant and to the harassment of black citizens. The alignment of the Pendergast machine with vice meant that the machine had a great influence in black neighborhoods. According to the *Kansas City Times* blacks voted for Pendergast as a way to defend vice, since it was the spaces of vice that brought income into the homes of "deviant" citizens.[67] The result of an alignment with Pendergast was a double-edged sword for blacks in the city's jazz scene districts. Pendergast's patronage brought those citizens income, protection from reformers, and work on public projects throughout the city. In fact blacks in Kansas City may have voted for Pendergast candidates because the "redneck" officers employed by the Pendergast machine were not as feared by black citizens as the police put in power by vice reformers.[68] At the same time it only supported the representation of blacks as "purveyors of deviance."[69] While the Pendergast machine may have *appeared* color blind, Tom Pendergast used the moral geography of racism in the city both to extend his sphere of power and to encourage patronage in the jazz scene spaces that he controlled. The zoning of race in the city, inextricably tied to the Pendergast machine, was about the commodification of race, gender, and sexuality in the deviant zones of the city.

Another part of this construction of race in the Pendergast world is the fact that Pendergast himself was part of the wave of immigrant labor in Kansas City. Though Pendergast himself is often represented as a white man with an ironclad hold over Kansas City politics, the positioning of race in the city was not that clear-cut. The Jewish, Italian, Irish, and Polish immigrants that made up the massive waves of immigration to the United States were considered racially inferior.[70] In the actual construction of neighborhoods in America, racially inferior European immigrants were inevitably neighbors with African Americans who left the south during the Great Migration period.[71] Therefore the Great Migration was perhaps not only African Americans moving north and west, but also Europeans moving across the Atlantic. As one Italian immigrant to Kansas City remembered of the 1920s: "When I was growing up in the Lower East Side, there were four kinds of people. Italians, colored people, Jews and Americans. Anybody who wasn't one of us or colored or Jewish we always talked about as an American."[72] The result of racial and ethnic marginalization for these groups of migrants was social exclusion. Racially and ethnically identified groups in Kansas City banded together through the Pendergast machine as a way of protecting their own livelihoods. As Kansas City police commissioner Herman Davis remembered: "We probably ought to understand what we mean by organized crime. . . . Many people believe that this confederation is the Mafia or the Cosa Nostra or something of that kind. It is not. It involves other ethnic groups, Jews, the blacks. They're all involved, so it's wrong to call it a mafia."[73]

Given the early rise to power of the Pendergasts, these disparate groups had to follow the lead of Tom Pendergast. By the time the Pendergast machine peaked in the 1920s, Italian and Jewish mobsters escaping investigation in Chicago and New York had come to Kansas City as well. Pendergast's machine was so well organized and diverse that even those new migrants had to succumb to Pendergast's leadership.[74] Kansas City's position as a railroad terminus, with all of its transient and immigrant laborers, were something that Pendergast turned to his favor.

Finally, in the Pendergast world race was not simply a factor of segregating African Americans. Master narratives of Kansas City's jazz scene seem to suggest that African Americans were relegated to one neighborhood at Eighteenth and Vine, a "self-contained community." For African Americans in the American West, however, such a clear segregation was not tenable. African Americans who migrated north and west in the Great Migration inevitably mixed with other immigrant populations as well as native white populations. Consequently the "modern" conception of racial segregation as a way to prevent miscegenation was difficult to maintain.[75] In Kansas City the mixture of African American migrants from the south, European immigrants, and rural whites gave rise economically to the city's vice districts. For instance Casimir Welch was in charge of the Second Ward, which included the Eighteenth and Vine Jazz District. This was Kansas City's poorest ward, its most racially and ethnically diverse, and the ward with the largest number of brothels and boarding houses.[76] In an effort to enclose that space Kansas City's reformers codified the segregation of the Second Ward in the belief that such enclosure would render the district invisible. As historian Alecia Long wrote of the jazz scene in New Orleans, reformers believed that an enclosed space would be easier to control and limit.[77] The result was that the Second Ward, the city's center of race, ethnicity, and sexuality, was territorialized and represented as a zone of deviance. Pendergast used this territorialization to his advantage by locating his most prurient entertainment spaces in the Second Ward, and then representing the Second Ward as a space for arousal, eroticism, and the race mixing that mainstream society marked as immoral. Using the enclosure of the Jazz District as a tool, Pendergast kept the African American community in Kansas City subordinate to his representation of African Americans as exoticized commodities and purveyors of deviance.[78] Pendergast kept African American culture subsumed, a move that jazz historians continued in the master narrative of jazz history.

GENDER AND CLASS IN THE PENDERGAST WORLD

Another major aspect of the Pendergast world was the intersection between gender and class in the lives of Kansas Citians. Kansas City was the front line of clashes between urban and rural society, as well as between Victorian society and working-class culture. The spaces of femininity that existed before 1880 were rapidly disappearing in the early twentieth century.[79] Such spaces were increasingly challenged by working-class women who tested boundaries, challenged acceptability, and shifted the representation of the female in society. Working women felt burdened by a social system that defined a world of work as a masculine space because such definitions made it impossible for working-class women to support themselves and their families.[80] For working-class women in Kansas City, the support of the neighborhood and the machine was far more important than concerns about the morality of women, whatever their work. As one Kansas Citian born at the end of the Pendergast era explained: "Nobody cared what you did, as long as you took care of each other. Some ladies in my neighborhood did questionable things, but you just didn't care as long as they didn't."[81]

Working-class African American women in Kansas City were likely not as invested in Victorian standards as their white counterparts. In fact it would appear that African American working-class women in the city were frequently part of the Pendergast world out of sheer necessity. According to historian Lawrence de Graaf African American women were more concentrated in urban towns in the American West than white working-class women. De Graaf wrote that 50 percent of African American women in the urban West worked outside the home from 1890 to 1920, compared to only 12–25 percent of white women.[82] Most of these working-class women were migrants to western towns such as Kansas City, where they worked as domestic workers or laundresses. For these women, however, the contact with sex work and sexual identifications was more immediate than it was for white working-class women. African American migrant women exchanged the sexual terrorism of the South for identification with eroticism in the North and West.[83] The myth of black hypersexuality was placed on African American working-class women in the West, who were then perceived as erotic and sexually available. When coupled with the fact that American cities and towns often had vice districts enclosed in racially segregated neighborhoods, the resulting identification is obvious. The proximity of prostitution in black neighborhoods made such work easy to find, and as a result prostitution became associated with African American working-class women.[84] African American women became one more commodity that Pendergast used to fuel the jazz scene.

In the Pendergast machine the intersection of gender and class also meant a reliance on women as a commodity for the cabarets and brothels. It also meant, however, that Pendergast's own family was a subject of local debate. Carolyn Elizabeth Pendergast, Boss Tom's wife, was a West Bottoms native who had worked her way from the streets to a job in one of the Pendergast saloons when she married Tom. While there is no clear proof, it was suspected that Carolyn Pendergast was a crib girl or an employee at one of the Pendergast brothels when the two met. The two constantly fought for some level of middle-class (if not upper-class) respectability.[85] Pendergast built the family home in Quality Hill, the premiere upper-class neighborhood of Kansas City. He and his wife attended performances at the respectable theaters and held parties where city leaders and their families were invited. Despite these attempts Pendergast and his wife were always outsiders in upper-class Kansas City circles. As one Kansas City historian wrote, "There was no way a former saloon owner and suspected bawdy-house owner and his West Bottoms woman were ever going to gain complete social acceptance in Kansas City."[86] Ironically, the very people that Pendergast sought for approval were the ones who had to seek his assistance in operating the city.

Pendergast's ironic position as the wealthy leader of a working-class conglomerate was not lost on him. While the Pendergast machine made money from liquor sales, it was famous for its influence in prostitution and men's clubs. The Pendergast "sin palaces" were a system of 250 different brothels and cribs east of downtown Kansas City on Fourteenth Street. In addition to the sin palaces, Pendergast also controlled a series of "men only" cabarets and clubs that catered to the city's middle- and upper-class inhabitants who worked downtown. Only a few blocks from Pendergast's downtown headquarters at the Jefferson Hotel, the sin palaces brought in nearly $12 million each year in prostitution income for the machine.[87] While the brothels were located on Fourteenth Street, men's clubs were located much closer to the city's political center. The most famous of these clubs was the Chesterfield Club, located less than a block from the Jackson County Courthouse. At the Chesterfield patrons could gamble, drink, or meet with Pendergast for an "official" lunch. Each Friday Pendergast had a luncheon for his captains and bosses at the Chesterfield, sometimes with judges and city officials eating in the main room. The featured attractions at the Chesterfield were the waitresses. Brought in each morning by the madams at Pendergast's brothels, the women who worked at the Chesterfield were always an even ratio of white to African American. The waitresses wore only high-heeled shoes and a change belt. Four feature waitresses were specially identified: the two African American waitresses had their pubic hair shaved in the shape of a spade or club, while that of the two white waitresses represented hearts or diamonds.[88] First, this

39

particular form of racial mixing flaunted Pendergast's refusal to follow miscegenation laws. At the same time, however, the feature waitresses clearly displayed the position of working-class women in the Pendergast world: both white and black women were on hypersexual, erotic display. Second, their display as playing cards points to their representation as a commodity, a game, and a site of amusement. By identifying the women with playing cards, perhaps specifically "poker," the feature waitresses were represented as nothing more than another exciting entertainment to lay on the felt tables of the Chesterfield. Finally, the waitresses at the Chesterfield clearly represented the territorialization of women in the Pendergast world as zones of sexual pleasure and erotic arousal. The Chesterfield was a clear message to the city's officials and elected leaders: whatever they desired in life—drinks, food, sex, working-class support, loans, or political help—could only come from the very man they shunned in society. In the Pendergast world the intersection of gender, race and class that revealed itself in brothels and clubs was a more than just the titillation of a red-light district. Pendergast brought the representations of gender, sexuality, and class from the jazz scene directly into the "respectable" neighborhoods of Kansas City's leadership, thereby flaunting his ability to defy the city's official zoning by creating interzones.

THE PENDERGAST WORLD AND MUSICAL SPACES

The final, and perhaps most important, aspect of the Pendergast underworld was jazz spaces, and the role that jazz played in changing the map of Kansas City. It was the underworld, with its economic and spatial influence, that established jazz. "It [the success of jazz] had everything to do with the fact that a high value had been placed on the music they played by certain infamous admirers willing to pay handsomely for its performance," wrote historian Ronald Morris, "and *who economically determined its sphere of influence* [emphasis added]."[89] Eddie Durham, a pioneer guitarist and musician for such bands as the Bennie Moten and

Count Basie Orchestras, remembered the link between musicians and the underworld this way: "Those guys paid you double for anything you ever done in Kansas City. They never owed a musician a nickel. The gangster always protected. . . . Those gangsters would always treat everybody right."[90]

The nineteenth-century saloons were slowly taken over by the underworld in the early twentieth century. With their representation as colorblind and their reliance on working-class neighborhoods, underworld organizations could not afford to ignore the growing popularity of jazz.[91] The underworld provided the protection, support, and spaces where jazz could be performed, and pulled jazz musicians out of the saloons and honky-tonks where such risqué music was marginalized. While musicians played an important role in creating jazz, their patrons in the underworld were the vital link between jazz musicians and social acceptance. The underworld made jazz a national phenomenon, and took the sound of jazz with them into the spaces of America's jazz scenes. Ronald Morris explained: "Musical historians have tended to treat themselves to the easy way out, concentrating on the musician in his own milieu, uncritically suggesting that a limited network of associations—mainly other musicians—influences his development. Needless to say, the links with underworld characters, for better or worse, are invariably omitted."[92]

The inextricable link between the underworld and jazz is especially clear in the history of Kansas City. Pendergast's influence included the First and Second Wards—the two areas of Kansas City that served as home to the centers of jazz performance. Pendergast himself owned four cabarets in the First and Second Wards: the Blue Goose, the Bowery, the Oriental, and Jubilesta.[93] In addition the Pendergast machine exerted its influence over the clubs and cabarets in the city's Jazz District. The more deviant the performance according to mainstream white Kansas Citians, the deeper in Pendergast territory it lay. While "black-and-tan" clubs were open to white patrons in the Jazz District along Eighteenth and Vine, black-only clubs were farther inside the Second Ward between Charlotte and Cleveland Streets.[94] Meanwhile live sex shows, some featuring both humans and animals, took place deep in the West Bottoms at Smokers and the Antlers Club.[95] Drag acts and female impersonators were featured along Independence Avenue, south of wealthy Cliff Drive, sandwiched between the Jazz District and the West Bottoms. Buildings where buffet flat parties were held were concentrated on what is now called Truman Road, linking Independence Avenue to the West Bottoms District. The Pendergast family controlled some of the most famous clubs, cabarets, and performance halls in Kansas City: the Cherry Blossom club where Count Basie made his Kansas City premiere and the Subway Club where a young Charlie Parker peered through the windows. Together the Pendergast-controlled clubs were known popularly as the "devils of the night."[96] Interestingly it is the clubs that featured the visible performers, the men who eventually became a focus of dominant jazz histories, that remain featured in Kansas City history. The Cherry Blossom and Subway clubs were in the Eighteenth and Vine District, where white slumming among the "purveyors of deviance" was an everyday occurrence. Spaces of performance that contested the very concept of deviance were written out of history, despite the fact that they flourished and attracted the desires of Kansas City patrons throughout the jazz scene.

An examination of some of the "devils of the night" reveals much about the absolute dependency of jazz performance and the underworld in Kansas City. Due to the lack of written records, however, much of the evidence of the "devils of the night" are of clubs in the Eighteenth and Vine District. For example one of the most important club owners in Kansas City was Felix Payne. Payne was a saloon-keeper in the early days of the Pendergast machine who became a Tom Pendergast precinct captain in the First Ward. Payne owned the famous Twin Cities Club, a large jazz club that straddled the Missouri-Kansas state line. After Prohibition ended, Payne helped Pendergast purchase clubs throughout the First and Second Wards. Two of these clubs were the Sunset Club at Twelfth and Vine and the Subway Club at Eighteenth and Vine. The Sunset was managed by Piney Brown, a well-known African American drummer and fixture in Kansas City's African American community. Pendergast purchased Kansas City's first public address system for the Sunset, and Brown used to amplify performances out into the street.[97] The Subway Club was a basement club well-known by musicians as a welcome place to hold jam sessions after hours. The Subway became the most popular club with musicians and lasted well into the Great Depression.[98] Pendergast also had the support of Ellis Burton, a leader of the African American criminal establishment and owner of the Yellow Front club in the Jazz District. Burton had a criminal record in his own right, and was rumored to have robbed trains with the Mafia.[99] Another club in the Pendergast sphere was the Reno Club. The Reno was owned by Papa Sol Epstein, a white immigrant and Pendergast supporter. Located on Twelfth Street between Cherry and Locust, the Reno featured a low wall that segregated white patrons from black patrons. The Reno also featured four floor shows each night, featuring performers who traveled on the TOBA circuit and arrived in Kansas City on the railroad. Money from the Reno did not, however, come just from jazz patrons. Behind the Reno was a meeting place for Pendergast and his cronies, as well as a space for dealing in drugs and prostitution. Two-dollar tricks with crib girls were sold behind the Reno, and after the deal was finalized there was a private stairway leading to the Reno's second floor cribs.[100] In addition to Pendergast-owned clubs, there were many other clubs in Kansas City that catered to jazz performance and patrons. Even these clubs, however, had to deal with Pendergast to secure such things as liquor, day laborers, or protection. White dance halls such as the Pla-Mor Ballroom and the Century Room burlesque were dependent on Pendergast for protection from police raids, especially during Prohibition.[101]

In the grand narrative of Kansas City's "Jazz Age," many clubs are known more for their association with individual musicians than for their connection to the Pendergast world. For instance the Reno is always associated with a particular story about the legend of Charlie Parker. Parker often loitered behind the Reno to fraternize with musicians taking breaks between sets. Parker was underage and could not go into the Reno, and lunchwagon owner John Agnos took pity on Parker and offered him leftover chicken each night—chicken that was referred to by local musicians as "yardbird." In the jazz canon annals of Kansas City's written history, the Reno was the place where Parker earned his nickname "Bird."[102] This kind of spatial representation, however, further reduces the influence of the Pendergast world on Kansas City's jazz scene. What role did the Pendergast world play in the performance of jazz, and therefore the creation of the jazz scene, inside clubs like the Reno?

The subsumation of the Pendergast world into an argument about Kansas City's jazz authenticity silences the important role that the underworld played in the production of jazz music and its spaces. One example of the grand narrative's ignorance of the underworld lies in the story of Bennie Moten. Moten was one of the most influential and important jazz musicians in Kansas City. Moten got his start as an occasional player at clubs and parks before forming his Bennie Moten Orchestra in the 1920s. Eventually the Moten Orchestra became the most popular and famous band in the city, and featured such musicians as Eddie Barefield and the early appearance of Count Basie.[103] In fact, in terms of the history of jazz music the Moten Orchestra was a constellation of stars: Walter Page, Buster Smith, Oran "Lips" Page, Eddie Durham, Lester Young, Ben Webster, Dan Minor, Eddie Barefield, Jimmy Rushing, and Count Basie.[104] Moten was also the earliest of Kansas City bands to gain popularity outside the Kansas City area through his many recordings with RCA in the 1920s and early 1930s.[105] Moten is best known as the originator of the "Kansas City sound," also known as "Kansas City swing."[106] When Moten died as the result of a botched tonsillectomy in 1935, a resulting split in the orchestra left Count Basie in charge of the group eventually known as the Count Basie Orchestra.[107] Basie then took Moten's "Kansas City swing" to New York and immortality. According to Kansas City's grand narrative of the "Jazz Age," it was Moten's musical success, and his ability to gather such talents, that made him a success. With the inclusion of the Pendergast machine in that story, however, the history of the Moten Orchestra is upset. Moten had clear ties to the Pendergast machine and was well known as a good friend to Kansas City's underworld, including Felix Payne and Sol Epstein. "Through contacts of this kind," wrote Ronald Morris of Bennie Moten, "he was able to control all the good jobs and choice locations in and around Kansas City."[108]

Another illustration of the difference between the grand narrative of Kansas City's "Jazz Age" and life in the city's jazz scene lies within the biography of Mary Lou Williams. Williams was a pianist and singer who was discovered in Pittsburgh and joined the TOBA circuit in 1925 at fifteen years old.[109] Two years later she married saxophonist John Williams and began a second career as an arranger and pianist for the TOBA circuit. Williams came to Kansas City in 1929 and was so enamored with the Kansas City scene that she quit the TOBA circuit and joined Twelve Clouds of Joy, an orchestra led by musician Andy Kirk.[110] Williams immersed herself in the sounds of Kansas City swing, as well as the protections and connections that night life offered in the Pendergast world. "If you were without funds, people would make you a loan without you asking for it," Williams told biographer Linda Dahl. "[They] would look at you and tell if you were hungry and put things right."[111] In her private notebooks Williams recalled Kansas City as "a place to be enjoyed even if starving."[112] Williams also wrote of the interactions she had with the Pendergast world. For instance when one member of the Twelve Clouds of Joy was arrested for molestation and would not make a performance at Fairyland Park, one of Pendergast's cronies intervened. Known to Mary Lou Williams only as "Stumpy," this Pendergast agent freed the bandmember and paid the jail wardens.[113] Williams continued to play regularly in Kansas City, both with the Kirk orchestra and as an individual pianist at the Sunset and Subway clubs. After Count Basie took over for Bennie Moten Williams began to play piano for Basie at the Cherry Blossom Club in Kansas City—another Pendergast club.[114] Despite the Depression and the problems of poverty, Williams was never unemployed in Kansas City. The Depression did not affect Kansas City during the Pendergast era as it did other cities. Performers such as Mary Lou Williams continued to come to Kansas City throughout the 1930s and early 1940s.

REFORMING THE PENDERGAST WORLD

It was the Pendergast world, this unique combination of racial and ethnic power, gender, and class issues, and the performance of jazz that made Kansas City the jazz scene that it was. But how did Kansas City's Pendergast world, a city machine so clearly important, get so reduced in the history of the "Jazz Age?" Ironically, the very thing that made Kansas City pivotal was what caused the grand narrative of the "Jazz Age" to treat the Pendergast machine in such a reductive manner. The Pendergast world of prostitution, jazz music, and interdependent neighborhoods of blacks, immigrants, and working-class natives did not fit within the jazz canon image of Kansas City as a spontaneous source of jazz evolution. While other cities saw their jazz scenes decline in the 1930s, Kansas City's jazz scene remained strong and popular until the end of World War II. The city's reputation as a "wide-open" town, predicated on the very underworld that the canon reduced to a backdrop, is likely what saved Kansas City from the worst effects of the Great Depression. In the traditional history of Kansas City and of jazz, however, the jazz scene is portrayed as a backdrop for the evolution of jazz music, a temporary flowering before reformers brought law and order back to the city.

Kansas City reformers actually began their work with the city charter of 1889, the same charter that allowed Jim Pendergast to begin building his power base. In the 1889 charter was the creation of the Parks and Boulevards Commission and the Board of Pardons and Paroles. While originally intended to plan the city's twentieth century road and park system, the Parks and Boulevards Commission eventually turned its attention to the "healthy" use of parks and other leisure spaces. At the same time, Pardons and Paroles officials became increasingly interested in how their clients lived once out of city institutions. Reformers began to think of urban areas as sites for environmental reforms that went far beyond the building of parks: the focus was on policing leisure places around the city and on a more careful observation of the behavior of Kansas City's citizens. The result was the creation of the Board of Public Welfare, an outgrowth of the Board of Pardons and Paroles and the Parks and Boulevards Commission. Kansas City was the first American city to create a welfare department, which opened in 1910.[115] The first act of the Board of Public Welfare was to form a Recreation Department, whose officials were social workers or parole officers charged with controlling problems such as crime and poverty in Kansas City's leisure spaces: everything from clubs and cabarets to dance halls and movie houses.[116]

Kansas City's Recreation Department commissioned a recreation census and survey in 1912. Officials hoped to use the survey as a method of gathering data and suggesting solutions for the social and moral problems inherent in city leisure spaces. The Recreation Department hired Rowland Haynes, a New England schoolteacher and representative of the newly formed Playground Association of America, to consult on the survey. Along with Recreation Department superintendent Fred F. McClure, Haynes visited and recorded every known leisure space in Kansas City, from roller rinks to cabarets.[117] The results of the 1912 recreation survey effected almost all the reform attempts aimed at working-class leisure spaces in Kansas City. McClure's recommendations concerning amusement parks resulted in the regulation of dance halls. Haynes's observations about Kansas City movie houses and nickelodeons led to further film censorship at the movie houses. The recreation survey of 1912 did exactly what its authors intended—it identified for eradication the problem of working-class amusements and all offenses that violated middle-class morality and gender. Haynes and McClure sought to put health and morality back into urban amusements, and they did so by attempting to destroy or appropriate what they deemed to be unacceptable gender and sexual behavior throughout the city. The reformers discursively engaged, constantly, the unacceptable aspects of the city.

The clubs, cabarets, and brothels of the Pendergast world were inherently part of a working-class existence in the city. These aspects of working-class life, however, were not easily appropriated into the dominant concept of morality. While dance hall owners and movie house managers managed to strike deals with the Board of Public Welfare, the operations of the Pendergast world did not. For example owners of white dance halls such as the Pla-Mor Ballroom made compromises with the Board of Public Welfare that allowed board agents to periodically visit dances, as well as mandating minimum age requirements for entrance to dance halls. In Kansas City, as well as other cities such as Chicago, those compromises did not extend to nightclubs and cabarets.[118] Reformers in Kansas City, led by the Board of Public Welfare, continued to investigate every aspect of working-class leisure in the city. Using a 1927 federal law mandating that all clubs or cabarets allowing patrons to fill their own glasses were in violation of the Volstead Act, the board began to investigate and close Pendergast clubs. Through the 1930s the board closed movie houses and nickelodeons, cabarets, and clubs, and worked to enforce Missouri's 1913 White Slavery Act. At the same time, Tom Pendergast's activities were under investigation by the federal government in the blanket investigation of mob-related activities undertaken in the 1930s. Though Pendergast kept both vice and jazz running in Kansas City through the Depression, the Pendergast world was under increasing pressure to reterritorialize itself to fit dominant culture. The Reno Club was closed due to Board of Public Welfare violations in 1938, followed by other cabarets and clubs along Twelfth Street. In 1939 Pendergast was finally found guilty of tax evasion for not reporting a bribe he received for a gambling debt. Pendergast spent fifteen months in federal prison at Leavenworth before his release in 1941. He died in his home on Ward Parkway in 1945.

According to the accepted version of Kansas City history, the incarceration of Pendergast was a victory against vice and the end of Kansas City's jazz scene. Nathan Pearson refers to the "downfall" and "aftermath" of Pendergast in musical terms: musicians who came to Kansas City after the demise of the Pendergast era were "musically sophisticated, and used the swing-style as their jumping off point" in New York or Chicago.[119] Still other jazz historians refer to Kansas City as a stopping point on the Southwest circuit and the home to Basie and Parker, and not much else. None of this reflects the interplay of jazz spaces and the Pendergast machine in Kansas City's jazz scene. Instead this grand narrative of Kansas City's jazz scene history positions the Pendergast world as one of crime and vice, a background to the spontaneous rise of Kansas City jazz, a world eliminated by the work of reformers and moral citizens.

3

The Myth of the Wide-Open Town

Jazz studies has, as a discipline, increasingly questioned the grand narrative of the history of jazz music. Writing what jazz historian Andrew Clark called "internalist musicology," the traditional jazz historians were record producers and critics such as Nat Hentoff, or musicologists such as Smithsonian scholar Martin Williams who were focused specifically on the sounds of jazz as America's classical music.[1] Rather than continue to focus on the sound of jazz emphasized by traditional jazz historians, scholars in new jazz studies have focused on the cultural moments and jazz artifacts that existed with the sound of jazz as their backdrop. "The time has come for an approach [to jazz history] that is less invested in the ideology of jazz as an aesthetic object and more responsive to issues of historical particularity," wrote Scott DeVeaux, "Only in this way can the study of jazz break free from its self-imposed isolation, and participate with other disciplines in the exploration of meaning in American culture."[2] This focus on the "other history" disrupts the traditional history of jazz music and relies on critical theory to understand the creation of jazz scenes.[3] The grand narrative history of jazz music is clearly evident in the written history of Kansas City's jazz scene. This chapter will demonstrate the role of Kansas City's written jazz history in marginalizing the non-normative cultural moments of the city's jazz scene for an accepted canon focused on great musicians.

Jazz stakeholders built, and continue to build, an official history that silences gender difference in the Kansas City jazz scene. Indeed, a very select group of stakeholders and their work is the site of Kansas City's jazz story production, a production that is as performed as the music it is based upon.

The official history of jazz has several unique components. Each of these constructed components creates an official knowledge of jazz by silencing aspects of the social milieu of jazz scene cities in America. The first of these is a focus on music as performed and recorded. Histories of jazz created a canon of great performers. This focus stems from an internal debate about jazz between patrons and performers of different periods. Debates over the meaning and importance of jazz music began in the 1920s, when white vendors of jazz began to align the sound to European roots.[4] At the same time, largely African American performers of jazz celebrated jazz music as a patently cultural sound. As different styles of jazz developed, the debate further splintered purveyors and performers of jazz. Through this debate jazz became identified with an essence that carried it through evolutionary periods. By giving jazz an inherent identity historians effectively removed jazz from sociocultural roots. As DeVeaux wrote: "This envisioning jazz as an organic entity that periodically revitalizes itself through the upheaval of stylistic change while retaining its essential identity resolved one of the fundamental problems in the writing of its history: the stigma of inferiority or incompleteness that the notion of progress inevitably attached to earlier styles."[5]

In this continuing debate over the past (and future) of jazz, the key is the sound and skill of jazz performance. In an interesting reiteration of European musical history, jazz historians developed an evolutionary scale of musicians and sounds. Historians focused on jazz music as a seamless progression rather than exploring the cultural disruptions that led to its development. The result is an official history of jazz that is solely focused on styles and performers. Peppered with a few women such as Billie Holiday and Lena Horne, and linked with key recordings and performances, this official history presents jazz as a clear, natural development from slave quarters to Harlem. The problem, however, is that the official narrative of jazz sound does nothing to explain the culture that created that sound. Jazz is a culture, not just a sound.[6]

The second feature of the official history of jazz is an oversimplified view of race. In terms of race traditional jazz historians have tended to draw a binary black/white divide that positioned jazz as an established African American folk music that was absorbed as American art form.[7] This leads to important questions about the position of race in the jazz canon. Exploring race in jazz history means uncovering a complex system of relationships and constructions, and that complex system puts whiteness in a precarious position. Renewing the "problem of whiteness" takes away the part of the jazz canon that posits white musicians as "outsiders."[8] The canon depends on a clear binary, and without such a binary the canon does not work. Substitutions to the race binary in the jazz canon intentionally prevent exploration of any specific cultural moment. As David Ake wrote: "The alternative [to disrupting the jazz canon] only reduces individuals and historical communities to impermeable if internally mutating constructs and hampers opportunities for increased understanding across and even within cultural boundaries."[9]

Oversimplified and hegemonic representations of sex and gender are another integral part of the grand narrative of jazz history. Traditional jazz history relies on the "great man theory."[10] According to the great man theory jazz history is the history of individual male performers, their skill as musicians, and their contributions to the development of jazz music. While a few women are included in traditional jazz history, these women are often represented as either skilled exceptions to the norm or stereotypical women admired more for their bodies than their musical abilities. Vocalists such as Bessie Smith were remembered for their lyrics, but the social and cultural realities that caused those lyrics were ignored.[11] In addition race and gender cannot be separated in the history of jazz. For instance, as jazz scholar Sherrie Tucker wrote of the role of women in the history of swing: "There is no room in dominant swing discourse for women who participated in the complicated processes of crossing race and gender boundaries in the performance and production of the marginalized jazz product known as all-girl bands."[12]

While women are central to the oversimplification of sex and gender in jazz history, the problem is not limited to women. Integral to the jazz scene were female impersonators, men whose performance of sex and gender did not fit the period's construction of the hypersexual "jazz man," performers who identified as gay and lesbian, and an untold number of patrons and city dwellers whose lives defied mainstream conceptions of gender. For instance historian Kevin Mumford studied the role of sex districts in the construction of jazz scene racial and gendered identities. This significant aspect of jazz history was also a significant aspect of its commodification, as it was a factor in the spatialization of jazz scene spaces as simultaneously "uplifting" and "slumming."

Together these factors of jazz's grand narrative created a story that denied and ignored the cultural moments that served as the foreground of jazz music. The role of this grand narrative was not, however, simply a creation for the sake of art. It is, at its core, a debate about the cultural capital of jazz. By defining authentic jazz as an art form traditional jazz history effectively disconnected jazz from its popular culture environment. High culture, with its concentration on the authenticity of its forms, has economic and cultural power supported by cultural institutions.[13] It therefore has cultural capital and can defend itself by canon-building. By denying the social and cultural scene of jazz traditional scholars claimed their concept of jazz authenticity as truth.

HISTORIOGRAPHY OF KANSAS CITY JAZZ

In the jazz canon Kansas City appears as little more than a geographical birthplace for certain styles and sounds of jazz music in the canon of jazz history in America. The "jazz myth" represents Kansas City as a marginal stop between New Orleans and New York, a temporary flowering of vice and corruption that, through its jazz spaces, produced Charlie Parker and professionalized Count Basie. The growth of jazz studies has had little impact on that representation. For instance, in his award-winning book on Charlie Parker titled *Kansas City Lightning* Stanley Crouch described Kansas City this way: "People came to guzzle the blues away, to chase the night long, to take the risk of leaving in a barrel as they laid bet after bet, and, as ever, there were those who came to involve themselves in the mercantile eroticism of the high to low courtesans."[14] Any discussion of the cultural and social milieu of Kansas City jazz is erased in the grand narrative of jazz music. Instead the city is exoticized, and its gendered outlaws, its sexual tourism, and the city's minority and female populations are reduced to backdrop.

This historiography of Kansas City's jazz scene is a linear progression of four works. These works are the essay "Kansas City and the Southwest" (1959) by Franklin Driggs and the books *Jazz Style in Kansas City and the Southwest* (1971) by Ross Russell, *Goin' to Kansas City* (1987) by Nathan Pearson, and *Kansas City Jazz: From Ragtime to Bebop—A History* (2006) by Franklin Driggs and Chuck Haddix. Taken together these four works successfully defended Kansas City's place in the jazz canon and continue to serve as the main points of evidence about Kansas City's jazz scene. Each of these works, however, also follows the four main points of jazz history's grand narrative: a focus on music, an oversimplification of race, a reduction of gender and sexuality, and a concentration on proving the authenticity of Kansas City jazz as part of the art of jazz music. While these works build on each other, and each work makes different claims to disrupt the jazz canon, all four in fact reify the grand narrative of jazz in Kansas City.

As with other jazz historiography, an interesting facet of Kansas City's jazz scene historiography is its reliance on oral histories of jazz performers. Frank Driggs did a series of interviews for nearly forty years that included Kansas City jazz musicians, and Nathan Pearson (with his colleague Howard Litwak) did over one hundred interviews of Kansas City performers and city dwellers for the Pearson book. In each case interviewers sought to elicit "facts" from their subjects, with the belief that the resulting interview and/or transcript would serve as a text of jazz history. As jazz scholar Burton Peretti has discussed, however, jazz history interviews are not a precise historical account of fact. Interviews do not fit within the traditional concept of a historiographical account because the interviews themselves spring from the specific memories and recollections of the informant. The result is that jazz historians may have believed they were constructing a history of specific "facts" when they actually were creating a text that could only *interpret the context* of the interview subjects.[15]

Jazz history is based much in jazz folklore, Peretti wrote, and therefore confirming the memories of informants is practically impossible.[16] Kathy Ogren, in her essay "Jazz Isn't Just Me," explained that the lack of truth-claim evidence in jazz autobiography created a performance of "self-aggrandizement on the part of the narrator, or the possibility of distortions created by editors."[17] The concept of an interview as performance is especially interesting in the case of jazz history interviews. In these interviews trained and experienced performers were "performing" the text, which requires a great deal of contextualization and corroboration on the part of jazz scholars.[18] According to jazz scholar Christopher Harlos, this is precisely why jazz oral histories are used only as support of the master narrative of jazz history. Interviewers ask questions about "fact" and interpret those facts as part of the grand narrative because the underlying context of the interview is so difficult to understand.[19] It is not difficult to comprehend the use of oral history in the grand narrative of jazz, given the reality that the grand narrative avoids anything problematic due to its threat to the power of the narrative itself.[20] This is the role that jazz history interviews have played in Kansas City's jazz scene historiography—to support the grand narrative and strengthen that narrative's positioning of Kansas City.

"KANSAS CITY AND THE SOUTHWEST"

While Kansas City was frequently mentioned in the works of the jazz canon as the birthplace of Parker and the Basie Orchestra, the first traditional jazz scholar to focus on Kansas City as an independent location for jazz was Franklin S. Driggs. Driggs began his career as a jazz scholar upon graduation from Princeton in 1952. At that time Driggs started collecting oral histories and ephemera from jazz performers living in New York City. Driggs traveled to Kansas City several times in the 1950s, collecting oral histories with funding from the Institute of Jazz Studies at the Smithsonian Institution.[21] Driggs caught the attention of John Hammond, the record producer who led the movement of jazz music into the American mainstream. With Hammond's cooperation Driggs began to produce reissued recordings of jazz albums. He continued to work as a record producer through the 1980s, winning several awards including a 1991 Grammy. As a jazz historian Driggs was best known through the hundreds of liner notes he wrote for albums. Driggs also wrote "Kansas City and the Southwest," a chapter in Nat Hentoff's *Jazz: New Perspectives on the History of Jazz by Twelve of the World's Foremost Jazz Critics and Scholars.* This chapter was the first major addition of Kansas City to the traditional jazz canon. "It may surprise a number of readers," wrote editors Hentoff and McCarthy in their introduction to Driggs's essay, "to find many names here who have never before been included in a jazz book."[22] When the Driggs essay was published in Hentoff's *Jazz* in 1959 it literally became the benchmark explanation of Kansas City's jazz scene.

As a record producer and reviewer Driggs had a clear interest in maintaining the evolutionary framework of jazz history. He served as a producer for Columbia and Decca records, for many years the home recording studio for Charlie Parker. This experience was reflected in "Kansas City and the Southwest." In this essay Driggs made several important statements about Kansas City that seemingly sealed its position in the jazz canon. Some of these statements were a result of the first focus of the jazz canon: a focus on the performance and production of music. Driggs asserted that Kansas City's major role in jazz history was as a center for territory and circuit performers, giving rise to a period of experimentation that led to the creation of such jazz greats as Parker. In his discussion of such Kansas City musicians and bandleaders as George Lee, Bennie Moten, and Andy Kirk, Driggs positioned Kansas City's jazz sound as one that led to the development of greater musicians. In addition Driggs's essay concentrates on an established trajectory for each musician discussed: each musician comes to Kansas City from the South or Southwest, develops skills in Kansas City, and then moves to New York, where each either succeeds or fails. One example is Driggs's summary of the career of Jay McShann. McShann was a pianist and bandleader who came to Kansas City from Oklahoma in 1935. McShann employed Charlie Parker sporadically until 1940, when Parker joined his orchestra.[23] According to Driggs McShann took the orchestra to New York, where promoters noticed Parker. "Bird soon accepted Budd Johnson's tenor chair in Earl Hines' bop-oriented band of 1943," wrote Driggs. "McShann came out of service in 1944 and reorganized his band."[24] There is no further mention in the essay of McShann, who continued to play and record until his death in 2006. For Driggs, however, McShann's story was over once the production of America's classical music moved on to New York.

Driggs's essay also replicates the oversimplification of race found in the grand narrative of jazz history. Throughout the essay Driggs includes little discussion of race. His references to race are related to the concept of Kansas City as a temporary flowering and to the practice of delineating jazz as black music. Driggs's first mention of race appears in a short discussion of the Pendergast machine: "Although no one I interviewed would admit it publicly, both whites and Negroes hankered for the return of what Pendergast stood for. Pendergast was the musician's friend, and in some quarters he is sorely missed."[25] Driggs then made no effort to explain what was "hankered for," or how Pendergast was a friend to jazz musicians regardless of race. The second reference to race is in Driggs's conclusion, where he admits that he has not discussed any white musicians: "Thus far the white musician's story has been ignored, although many fine white jazzmen were working in the Southwest before moving on, in some cases to greater fame. Theirs, apparently, is a separate story, which should be written."[26] In a clear reification of the jazz canon Driggs positions race as something separate and simply divided into black and white. In addition this quotation is further evidence of Driggs's dependence on the canon and its positioning of Kansas City as a temporary training ground for musicians on their way to more important places.

The reduction of gender and sexuality found in the grand narrative of jazz history is also found in Driggs's essay. In fact in the entire essay on Kansas City and its jazz scene only one woman is mentioned by Driggs: Mary Lou Williams. Williams and male musician Marion Jackson were pianists for the Clouds of Joy, an orchestra led by Andy Kirk. In this excerpt, the only discussion of women in the essay, Driggs explained how Williams replaced Jackson:

> On the afternoon of the Clouds' first session, pianist Marion Jackson failed to show up, so Andy made a call to Mary Lou Williams, piano-playing wife of his altoist John Williams, who was then in Kansas City but not playing music. Mary Lou came over and made the date, knocking out the musicians and recording people alike. Andy rewarded her for her fine work by giving her the privilege of making the balance of the Kansas City session, so she sat up with Andy and worked out some arrangements, which they used on the sessions. Some time later, when the band was scheduled for another session in Chicago, Marion Jackson was back at his piano chair. When Kapp [Jack Kapp, a record executive] heard them rehearsing, he didn't like what he heard, and told Andy it didn't sound like the

THE MYTH OF THE WIDE-OPEN TOWN

same band, and that he had to have Mary Lou. She came up from Kansas City and continued to make all the recordings at Kapp's insistence, and not with Andy's reluctance. She finally joined the band in 1931, after they had come back from their first trip East.[27]

In this lone discussion of female performers in Kansas City, Driggs's work as a historian of the jazz canon is clear. First, Williams is not referred to as a musician or pianist, but as a "piano-playing wife." Then, according to Driggs, Williams was "rewarded" with the "privilege" of playing with the band, though she clearly was not "privileged" enough to join the Clouds of Joy in Kansas City. Driggs positions female performers here as accidental exceptions to the rule who are lucky to have male bandleaders and executives willing to include them. Through omission Driggs made a specific canon-building point about gender and sex: the history of jazz is a history of great men.

Traditional jazz history also focuses on the authenticity of jazz as an American art form, and Driggs's essay followed that focus as well. The key to authenticating Kansas City jazz, however, is to explain its temporality while positioning Kansas City neatly in the "jazz myth." Traditional jazz historians were enamored with one question about Kansas City: why did such a strong jazz scene develop in Kansas City? In order to explain how Kansas City became so exceptional, Driggs positioned Kansas City as a site of temporary jazz production that revolved around the political machine of Tom Pendergast. It was Driggs who wrote about Kansas City as a "wide-open town," a city where a momentary period of criminality allowed jazz to flourish. By positioning the Kansas City scene in such limiting terms, Driggs was able to retain Kansas City's position in the jazz myth as a stopover between New Orleans and New York. According to Driggs the performance and influence of jazz in Kansas City was practically nonexistent before Pendergast came to power. "At that time [after the closing of Storyville in 1917] there was neither a great demand for nor much knowledge of jazz in Kansas City," wrote Driggs.[28] Driggs explained, however, how quickly that changed after Pendergast came into power:

Tom Pendergast was boss of the Democratic party in Kansas City from 1927 to 1938, and the men he chose for office held all the key positions of power in Kansas City during those years. Pendergast himself held political office as early as 1902, and ran a wide-open hotel, the Jefferson, from 1907 until 1920, with police protection. He encouraged gambling and night life; clubs as such appeared during his years of power in vast proliferation, and all had music of one sort or another. Many could house full bands, and many of the owners had political connections. It is significant that nearly all the developments in Kansas City's music took place during Pendergast's reign. Since his conviction in 1938 for income-tax evasion, relatively little of importance has occurred, and only the 1942 Jay McShann band, with Charlie Parker and Walter Brown, has made any further impact on the jazz world at large.[29]

With that paragraph Driggs created a major component of the jazz canon of Kansas City's jazz scene history that presents a reductive representation of the Pendergast machine as a producer of spaces where jazz took hold. Once Pendergast was gone, according to this representation, so was jazz. Representing Kansas City as a temporary site of jazz performance, and using the Pendergast machine to give that temporality both an explanation and a date, became the most well-known aspect of the jazz canon in Kansas City. Beginning with Driggs jazz historians gave little thought to Pendergast-era Kansas City beyond simple references to gambling, vice, and being "wide-open." In fact Driggs is still considered by many jazz historians to be the authority on Kansas City's jazz scene history, specifically because of his positioning of Kansas City as a temporary, Pendergast-controlled stop en route to New York. "Thus, one of the great centers of jazz development—Kansas City in the 1920s and 1930s," wrote jazz scholar Howard Becker in 2004, "drew its vitality from the political corruption which made nightlife possible."[30] As the citation for the quotation above, Becker used Driggs's 1959 essay.

JAZZ STYLE IN KANSAS CITY AND THE SOUTHWEST

Another traditional jazz history stakeholder has written more extensively on the role of Kansas City in jazz music's "organic" development. Ross Russell was the owner of Dial Records, a New York City music label that specialized in bebop recordings, especially those of Charlie Parker. Early in his career Russell worked for two years as Charlie Parker's personal manager.[31] Russell also wrote for the magazine "The Record Changer," a specialized publication for collectors of rare jazz recordings.[32] Russell, according to jazz scholar Scott DeVeaux, was one of the first traditional jazz historians to suggest that jazz had an inherent and organic developmental path from New Orleans through Kansas City to the art form known as bebop.[33] Russell's study of Kansas City, titled *Jazz Style in Kansas City and the Southwest* and published in 1971, was based largely on the uncredited collections of interviews completed by Frank Driggs.

Russell's book depends entirely on the work of Driggs, both in terms of sources and organization. First and foremost Russell is interested in discussing Kansas City as a site of jazz performance, where a handful of jazz "greats" gained skill and moved on to fame. In his book Russell positioned Kansas City as an oasis in the Southwest circuit. Pointing to the factors already identified by Driggs—Pendergast, the territory, and the Kansas City jazz sound—Russell discussed the jazz scene in Kansas City as a series of clubs and performers. Each of the performers identified by Russell played some part in the development of the "Kaycee" sound, leading eventually to Charlie Parker and the rise of bebop.[34] Russell went on to use the same sources and conclusions in his later book *Bird Lives!*, a biography of Charlie Parker. Through his study Russell continued the focus on great performers and the sound of jazz as a way of retaining ownership of jazz history for its stakeholders.

As one reviewer explained, Russell wrote a "work consisting chiefly of sketches of the individual musicians and bands which set the style."[35]

Russell's position as a jazz history stakeholder, and his reliance on Driggs's material, is further evident in his discussions of race. In fact, in a nod to both Driggs and the jazz canon that emphasized the African American roots of jazz, the only mention of race or ethnicity in the Russell book are references to whiteness or simply drawn black/white binaries. Russell does not identify the race or ethnicity of jazz performers in Kansas City unless they were white, and even then they are mentioned sparingly and as a group. For example Russell engaged in a discussion of selected club owners and managers, among them Papa Sol Epstein. Epstein was a white Pendergast crony who owned a black-and-tan club along with other saloons in Kansas City's First Ward. In his discussion of other club managers such as Piney Brown and Joe Turner, Russell made no mention of race.[36] Russell's silencing of race as a facet of the jazz canon is further evident in his discussion of clubs in Kansas City. He took great care to identify white performance spaces such as the Muehlebach Hotel and the Pla-Mor Ballroom and to reiterate their position as "whites only" spaces every time they were mentioned. What Russell termed "black dance halls" were only identified as such when in the same paragraph as a "white dance hall."[37]

Russell's dependence on Driggs, and therefore on the grand narrative of jazz history, is further evident in his lack of discussion about gender, sex, and sexuality. Unlike Driggs Russell did include some mention of spaces in Kansas City that could easily be considered spaces where the definitions of gender and sexuality were contested. While Driggs wrote nothing about sexualized and gendered spaces in the City's jazz scene, Russell does include mention of prostitution and burlesque. For instance Russell specifically mentioned prostitution at the Reno, where "tricks" were taken up the back stairs behind the club for two dollars each.[38] Russell also referred to burlesque performances at the Century Theater.[39] Each of these references, however, is exoticized as further evidence of the corruption of the Pendergast era and the "wide-open" atmosphere. For example Russell's discussion of prostitution at the Reno is only a backdrop for his lengthy discussion of Charlie Parker, who according to Russell got his nickname thanks to John Agnos, a lunchwagon owner who parked behind the Reno.[40] Russell's reference to burlesque is intended as a glimpse of the "wide-open" nightlife in Kansas City, portrayed by Russell in the pages before as "Pendergast prosperity."[41] Though Russell seems on the surface to develop a deeper understanding of the jazz scene in Kansas City, it is essentially Driggs's argument with the exciting backdrop of sexual license and marginal performance. In this manner Russell further pushed female jazz performers into the backdrop and advanced the canon-based concept that jazz was the production of great men. For Russell what were important were not the prostitutes behind the Reno, or the female musicians who may have been performing inside, but the young male musicians watching them from the lunchwagon.

Finally Russell depended on Driggs's positioning of Kansas City as a temporary, Pendergast-driven jazz scene in order to complete his work. According to Russell Kansas City was a southwestern city that was "off the beaten track," positioned as an isolated city that lent itself to a temporary cultural explosion.[42] Another example from Russell's book is his discussion of "Kaycee," previously discussed in this work. While more exciting-sounding than Driggs's explanation, Russell's positioning of Kansas City as a "wide-open town" is nonetheless clear. For Russell the "Pendergast prosperity" lasted from 1927 until 1934, when jazz died in Kansas City.[43]

Kansas City, as Russell explains, was the site of a style creation, the birthplace of Parker, and a fleeting moment of jazz production thanks to the excess of Pendergast. Though Russell expanded on Driggs's exploration of musicians and their careers, as well as the social and cultural scene in Kansas City, Russell's work did not deviate from the jazz canon. Ross Russell's *Jazz Style in Kansas City and the Southwest* was for many years considered the definitive book on jazz history in Kansas

City. One reviewer wrote that the Russell book "reveals new insight for historians to ponder and consult for reference."[44] "It will more than adequately serve as the standard reference work," wrote reviewer Frank Gillis, "for jazz researchers and scholars for many years."[45]

GOIN' TO KANSAS CITY

Out of the work by Driggs and Russell grew the most formative study of Kansas City jazz, which appeared in book form in 1987. The book, titled *Goin' to Kansas City*, was written by scholar Nathan Pearson based on the interviews he conducted with Howard Litwak from 1977 to 1980. Pearson and Litwak were folklorists who had studied jazz history in New York City as college students: Pearson, in fact, was a jazz patron.[46] The two relied heavily on previous work by Driggs and Russell, and carried the assumptions made by those stakeholders into their own work. Though not well known to jazz historians outside Kansas City, the work of Pearson and Litwak became the template for jazz history in Kansas City. In addition the traditional scheme of jazz history presented by Pearson and Litwak continues to be a factor in all other studies of Kansas City's jazz scene.

In terms of oral history collections, *Goin' to Kansas City* was part of a national project. The "Goin' to Kansas City" (GTKC) project was a subsection of the larger Jazz Oral History Project. Originally founded in 1968, the Jazz Oral History Project (JOHP) was designed to collect oral history interviews of jazz performers. National Endowment for the Arts funding was used to pay jazz "elders" for their interviews: as much as $2,000 for a five-hour interview.[47] The GTKC project had its impetus in the JOHP. While not officially part of the JOHP at its beginning, the GTKC project was completed in conjunction and with the assistance of JOHP officials at the Smithsonian and Rutgers.[48] Upon its completion Pearson and Litwak had "interviewed forty-seven musicians, dancers, politicians, civic leaders, band managers, and night club owners significant to the Kansas City jazz scene."[49]

Since the project's completion the GTKC interviews have become major sources of information about the jazz scene in Kansas City. Like the other interviews completed under the auspices of the JOHP, the interviews did much to preserve the memories of early jazz performers and their patrons. Many researchers have, however, identified problems with the JOHP interviews. The first of these problems is the transcription of the interviews. In many cases the transcriptions of interviews in the JOHP remain unfinished.[50] In addition transcripts that were completed were done by volunteers, so the quality and detail of transcripts varies in terms of cancellations, mishearings, and what jazz scholar Burton Peretti called the "bowdlerization by typists."[51]

The GTKC project also suffered from the transcription problems at the JOHP. Of the forty-seven interviews completed, only twenty-five were transcribed.[52] JOHP administrators Martin Williams and J. R. Taylor originally agreed to transcribe the GTKC interviews, but after completing only ten transcripts the men backed out of their agreement with Pearson and Litwak.[53] Pearson and Litwak completed an additional fifteen transcripts in the grant period and then deposited the full collection of twenty-five interviews at the Smithsonian for the JOHP and at the University of Missouri–Kansas City. Between 1977 and 1983 Pearson and Litwak completed the remaining transcripts for their own use—full transcripts were never placed at any archival repository.[54] As Pearson and Litwak wrote in their Final Report to the NEA in 1977: "Our only serious difficulty was that the Smithsonian did not completely live up to its promise to transcribe interviews with musicians. . . . We have compensated by continuing to transcribe interviews ourselves without remuneration."[55]

While some of the concerns about interview quality in the JOHP are evident in the GTKC project, others are not. For instance Pearson and Litwak were not jazz journalists. Unlike Driggs and Russell they were trained academic scholars and musicologists, who conducted interviews that tried to focus as much on the social milieu of Kansas City as the music. From the beginning Pearson and Litwak planned to explore aspects of race, gender, sexuality, and the sociocultural scene in Kansas City at greater depth than Driggs or Russell. At the same time, and despite their plans, the Pearson and Litwak interviews have frequent references to aspects of Kansas City that were part of the jazz canon. For instance nearly all the transcribed interviews contain questions by the interviewers about meeting Count Basie or Charlie Parker. Additionally the outline used by Pearson and Litwak to guide their interviews belies an interest in cultural moments, but focuses instead on jazz music and its development in Kansas City. For the project a GTKC interview outline was broken into five categories: family background, early music, professional music, adult experiences, and Kansas City. According to Pearson and Litwak adult life inquiries centered on marriages and children, as well as illegal activities (drug use, alcoholism) and the musician's "retrospective attitudes toward music as a profession."[56] Finally Pearson and Litwak sought information about life in Kansas City during the jazz scene. According to Pearson and Litwak those queries were: "The Pendergast machine; voting experience; ward politics; segregation; streetcars; well-known figures such as Piney Brown, Felix Payne, and Ellis Burton; retrospective attitudes about black life in Kansas City, etc."[57]

While it is clear from the transcripts that Pearson and Litwak tried to pursue interview subjects' memories with further questions, the interviewers also appeared to go on what Burton Peretti characterized as a "fishing expedition" for information that followed their outlines.[58] A good example of this interview concern occurs in the Pearson and Litwak interview with Ernest Williams. Williams (1904–86) was a vocalist and drummer, best known as the director and lead vocalist for the Blue Devils and the Rockets. Pearson and Litwak interviewed Williams on May 18, 1977, in Kansas City. Throughout the interview Williams discussed his experiences as a director and vocalist, and his knowledge of other musicians in the Kansas City scene. During the interview, however, Pearson and Litwak seem to ignore Williams's statements in an effort to follow their own outline.

LITWAK: Peeny Johnson, where'd he get that nickname?

WILLIAMS: Made it up. I don't know where that name was from, Peeny, played trumpet.

LITWAK: Where did he come from?

WILLIAMS: Kansas City.

LITWAK: You found him right here in town?

WILLIAMS: Yeah, and he worked with the Dean's of Swing then.

LITWAK: The Dean's of Swing, oh sure, Charlie Parker's little band?

WILLIAMS: Yep, well it wasn't Charlie Parker's. . . .

PEARSON: Do you recall this session?

WILLIAMS: Yeah.

PEARSON: This recording session?

WILLIAMS: I was the one that directed the session.

PEARSON: Yeah, right. Do you think the sound of this does justice to the way the Rockets sounded? Is this a pretty fair representation?

WILLIAMS: Yeah, it's fair.[59]

As this short excerpt demonstrates, Pearson and Litwak were primarily interested in aspects of the master narrative of jazz—namely in this instance, Charlie Parker. Williams seems to refute the conclusion of the interviewers, that Parker led the Deans of Swing. Those pauses and dropped thoughts were ignored by the interviewers. Rather than follow the lead of the subject both Litwak and Pearson turned the interview to their own purposes.

Pearson and Litwak's interpretation of the interviews was organized into a single text, the Pearson book *Goin' to Kansas City*. For the interpretation of the GTKC interviews Pearson relied on two sources: transcripts of the interviews and their memories of the oral history encounter. The transcripts were different depending on their source. Interviews transcribed by the Smithsonian were available for the researchers, but additional transcription was done by Pearson and Litwak themselves. In preparation for a book Pearson and Litwak chose to focus only on those interviews that they felt yielded the most information about Kansas City jazz. As a result only 41 of the 123 interviews completed were described in the finished book. In addition interviews used in the book were carefully edited and rearranged with no discussion of the interview itself. Subjects were introduced to the book with a short biographical statement followed by fragmented quotes from their interviews. The arrangement of chapters was based on the researchers' outline of interview topics. As Pearson wrote in the introduction to the 1987 book: "The oral histories that tell the Kansas City jazz story are taken, with very few and noted exceptions, from Howard's [Litwak] and my research. They are arranged by theme and content rather than by speaker. Supplementary words, phrases, and explanations are occasionally added by me for clarity and are marked by brackets."[60] The book then listed the interview subjects in two appendices: one that restated the short biographical statement and one that listed their major recordings and the recordings of the jazz musicians mentioned in the book.

The role that performance played in the interviews is absent in the book. In fact the only discussions of interview subjects in the book, aside from their edited recollections of Kansas City jazz, are in footnotes by Pearson. These footnotes contain clarifications, but more importantly they frequently discuss the performers at the interview or correct their memories. This editing is an important facet of the traditional jazz canon, as it focused on positioning the informants in terms of their careers and performance history, followed by their role in the temporary flowering of Kansas City jazz. For instance Pearson interviewed Jesse Stone, a well-known bandleader, arranger, and composer of American jazz in the 1930s and 1940s. Pearson and Litwak asked Stone about Count Basie, and how Basie became a member of Bennie Moten's orchestra. While Stone explained that Basie joined the band because he was following them around "like a valet,"[61] Pearson wrote this correction about Stone's memories:

Jesse Stone is probably incorrect in stating that Basie was just hanging around the Moten band before he was taken in. Most other accounts agree with Stone that Basie was well known to the other band members before he joined (due in part to his prior experience in Kansas City), but also assert that he was vigorously recruited by Moten. Stone is correct in implying that Moten recognized his own limitations as a pianist, and wished to devote more time to leading the orchestra. Basie was the perfect and much sought-after choice to take his place at the piano bench.[62]

Clearly, in this example, Pearson uses his (and other historians') "knowledge" of jazz history as a way of editing Stone's memories. It is unclear, however, how Stone's memories are somehow "incorrect." Instead it appears that Pearson is working to protect Basie, and his position in the grand narrative of jazz history, from Stone's recollections. In addition Pearson used this correction to reiterate the focus of the master narrative on skills, great men, and the sound of jazz. The end of the statement by Pearson has nothing to do with Stone's statement—it is instead a replication of the master narrative, and its insistence on the skills of "perfect" performers and their intended "place at the piano bench."

While some notes by Pearson corrected memories of interview subjects, still other notes presented a romanticized view of aging performers. These statements did not rely on the interviews themselves, but on the concept of loss of skill to age and morbidity. In one particular example Pearson discussed an encounter with Joe Turner, a well-known blues singer from Kansas City. Though Pearson did not include any interview selections with Turner in the finished book, he did discuss an interview encounter with Turner in a footnote attached to another informant's memories of Turner. Pearson wrote:

Joe was not only a brilliant blues singer, sensitive, swinging, and inventive; he was also the loudest singer I ever heard. My first personal encounter with Big Joe was in 1976 at Barney Joseph-son's Cookery in New York City. Joe was sixty-five years old and no longer the big, well-built lady-killer of his youth. He must have weighed at least three hundred pounds and could barely walk (later he was forced to use crutches and a wheelchair because of his weight), but he could still sing. He held the microphone down below his waist, and raised his voice to the crowd. People in the first few tables were deafened, but everybody was impressed. In his prime, at the Sunset Club, he must have been truly awesome.[63]

If Kansas City's scene is dead then its performers must be antiques, and both are "no longer the big, well-built lady-killer" of the past. Kansas City jazz, in both scene and performance, was past its prime.

The interpretive decisions that Pearson and Litwak used for the interviews also became a cornerstone of Kansas City's jazz monument: the American Jazz Museum and Hall of Fame. The foundation of the museum was the traveling exhibition "Goin' to Kansas City," admin-istrated by Pearson and Litwak. "Goin' to Kansas City" was composed of thirty-seven exhibit panels featuring images Pearson and Litwak had gathered during their research, along with music clips, a twenty-five minute documentary film on Kansas City jazz, and an interpretive program.[64] The exhibit followed a clear four-part narrative based on the periods of Kansas City jazz music: sources of the Kansas City sound from the 1890s, a section titled "Jazz Emerges" that focused on the 1920s, the 1930s series "The Jumping Town," and the last series "End of an Era."[65] The interpretive program opened with a short narrative history of jazz in Kansas City and an essay by Pearson and Litwak about the importance of the Midwest in jazz history. The rest of the program provided quotes from the GTKC interviews with no captions, biographical information, or explanation. The program was also filled with images taken from the exhibition, images that Pearson and Litwak gathered from their informants during the GTKC project or borrowed from other local collections. Only three musicians are discussed at length in the program: Bennie Moten, Jay McShann, and Charlie Parker.[66] Cosponsored by the Mid-America Arts Alliance, the Kansas City Museum, and the National Endowment for the Humanities, the finished exhibit opened in Kansas City on May 24, 1980. In an article titled "Goin' to Kansas City: In Search of Heroes," Kansas City reporter Terry Teachout interviewed Pearson and Litwak and discussed their GTKC project. After discussing their project and their academic backgrounds, the two researchers discussed the goals of the exhibition, goals that clearly reified the jazz canon in Kansas City. When Teachout asked Litwak about his hopes for the exhibition, Litwak replied: "If I had to pick one thing as a goal for the exhibit, it would be to make the people in this region realize that it's the style here that truly fed into the mainstream of jazz. People around here just don't realize how influential the heritage of jazz in Kansas City is . . . even the influence of Charlie Parker himself—that all came right from Kansas City."[67]

"Goin' to Kansas City" opened at the Kansas City Museum and then toured the Midwest for three years. Upon completion of the tour the Mid-American Arts Alliance placed the exhibit in storage at the Kansas City Museum. At that point backers and historians in Kansas City began to create an interest in opening a museum about the city's history of jazz. Pearson and Litwak began to work separately in 1983—Pearson on the book *Goin' to Kansas City* and Litwak as an advisor for the committee working to build a jazz museum. Eventually Litwak used the same interpretive scheme used in the GTKC project in the creation of exhibits at the American Jazz Museum and Hall of Fame. According to Nathan Pearson the exhibits at the American Jazz Museum were devised and created under Litwak's direction. While Litwak focused on the creation of a jazz museum, Pearson began to write the long-awaited book *Goin' to Kansas City*. With its publication in 1987 Pearson

THE MYTH OF THE WIDE-OPEN TOWN

and Litwak's GTKC project finally closed. There is no doubt that the GTKC project was the most important project in the historiography of Kansas City jazz, leaving behind images and interpretations that shape the official knowledge of Kansas City jazz to this day. It is important to note, however, that despite its lofty goals the GTKC project did only support the official jazz canon and the knowledge that the canon produced. Harold Brofsky, who reviewed the Pearson book for the journal *Ethnomusicology*, even wrote that the book was at its core "a reliance on Russell—or perhaps they both go back to Frank Driggs, the earliest historian of Kansas City jazz."[68]

KANSAS CITY JAZZ: FROM RAGTIME TO BEBOP—A HISTORY

Though the GTKC project closed in 1987, it was the beginning of a renaissance of traditional jazz history in Kansas City. This reiteration of the jazz canon also brought the written grand narrative of Kansas City back full circle to its founder, Franklin S. Driggs. Driggs, who first wrote about Kansas City in a canon-building 1959 essay based on his own interviews and research, continued to do interviews and study jazz in Kansas City from the 1950s through the 1980s. In 1977 Driggs was awarded a contract by Oxford University Press for a book on Kansas City jazz.[69] At the same time Chuck Haddix was "working in the record business" before becoming jazz and blues producer at radio station KCUR-FM in Kansas City.[70] The two men began to collaborate in 1987, when Haddix took over as director of the Marr Sound Archives at the University of Missouri–Kansas City (and the same year the Pearson book was published).[71] In the 1980s Driggs donated his collection of oral history interviews to the Marr Sound Archives, where it came under the direction of Chuck Haddix.[72] As Haddix wrote of the Driggs work on Kansas City: "The oral histories, conducted from 1956 to 1986, capture the truths of the development of jazz as related by a host of musicians and band leaders who defined the tradition."[73] A longtime jazz patron and collector, Haddix began to add interviews

73

to the Driggs Collection through his work as the director of the Marr Sound Archives. Haddix also began to host "Fish Fry," a public radio program dedicated to classic jazz recordings. Through his relationship with Driggs Haddix began to do research about Kansas City jazz. The result is the most recent addition to the historiography of Kansas City jazz: *Kansas City Jazz: From Ragtime to Bebop—A History*, published by Oxford University Press in 2005 as a completion of Driggs' original 1977 contract.

Kansas City Jazz explores a little known-aspect of Kansas City jazz: the local musicians and musical styles that did not gain national and international fame. The Driggs and Haddix book is a major work in Kansas City jazz history because it focuses so directly on the music and style of Kansas City jazz. It also reinforces the master narrative of the jazz canon. In fact, despite its efforts to deepen the history of Kansas City jazz, it only continues to reify the major aspects of the master narrative: authorship by white stakeholders, an emphasis on music over cultural contestation, and a reduction of the jazz scene in the city to the "Kaycee" of existing historical representation. *Kansas City Jazz* relies on four major sources of information: the Driggs oral history collections, further interviews done by Driggs and Haddix, Kansas City newspaper "coverage of the bands, musicians, and others who created the Kansas City Jazz style," and articles about Kansas City's jazz scene in stakeholder outlets such as *Metronome* and *Down Beat*.[74] The result is a book that does two things. First, it challenges the jazz canon by focusing on local Kansas City musicians, including territory bands, who did not go on to gain fame in New York. In this respect it is a ground-breaking study of the Kansas City sound. Second, it reifies that same canon by representing Kansas City as a fleeting "wide-open" time where contestations over race, gender, sexuality, and jazz scene spaces were far less important than the music itself.

Driggs and Haddix unmistakably focused on the first aspect of the jazz canon in *Kansas City Jazz*: the sound of jazz music as performed and recorded. This is most obvious in one simple move that the authors use: throughout the book the phrase "Kansas City Jazz" always appears with "Jazz" capitalized. Through this subtle piece of typography Driggs and Haddix undoubtedly identified Kansas City as a musical style and a sound, not as a scene of socio-cultural contestation. For example in their discussion of the development of "Kansas City Jazz" Driggs and Haddix wrote: "Rooted in the ragtime, blues, and concert band traditions, nurtured in the 18th and Vine area, Kansas City Jazz grew into a hearty hybrid."[75] That analysis firmly locates Kansas City as the site of a musical production, and not much more. Much like the Driggs essay in 1959, *Kansas City Jazz* also discussed Kansas City bands, musicians and recordings in a chronological arrangement. This chronological discussion attempts to slightly jar the jazz canon by focusing on Kansas City's local musicians. This attempt is not entirely successful, however, because in every instance Driggs and Haddix juxtapose local musicians who remained local with musicians who left Kansas City for fame in New York City. One such passage involves Mary Lou Williams and Marion Jackson, in a continuation of the story about Williams's inclusion in Clouds of Joy that first appeared in the Driggs 1959 essay. "At first, she [Mary Lou Williams] played piano duets with Marion Jackson, similar to Moten and Basie in the Moten band," wrote Driggs and Haddix.[76] This is the last time Jackson is mentioned in the book, and Moten's death appears in the book only thirty pages later. Williams and Basie, however, appear in the epilogue as the major examples of "Kansas City Jazz" stars who found fame outside the city. Such juxtapositions continue throughout the book, most obviously with the continual juxtaposition of Kansas City musicians Jay McShann and Charlie Parker. In fact the focus of chapter 8 of the book is entirely on the roughly parallel careers of these two men, but with two eventually fatal diversions: McShann never left Kansas City and became a local hero, while Parker went to New York and died a young hero of jazz. While such juxtapositions surely insert many Kansas City musicians into the jazz canon, they still defend the canon by creating these juxtapositions between the local musicians of "Kansas City Jazz" and the musicians "who changed the course of American music."[77]

The second aspect of the jazz canon that appears in *Kansas City Jazz* is its oversimplification of race, ethnicity, and racism in Kansas City and in American jazz scenes in general. In a nod to the 1959 essay Driggs and Haddix make little mention of race in Kansas City other than an admission of segregation and an identification of "whites only" versus "blacks only" spaces. One such example is in the discussion of the Moten band's tour of New York, where Driggs and Haddix explained that "the band moved comfortably between white audiences in upstate New York and African American audiences in Harlem."[78] Even more telling about the silencing of race in the Driggs and Haddix book is their exploration of segregation. According to Driggs and Haddix segregation in Kansas City was practically limited to the Jazz District around Eighteenth and Vine, which the authors contend was "a self-contained community."[79] In their short examination of the Jazz District Driggs and Haddix seemingly represent the district as one where segregation was not only appreciated, but perhaps even preferred and enjoyed by Jazz District residents. "Born of necessity and reared by industry," wrote Driggs and Haddix of the Jazz District, "the 18th and Vine area quickly grew from its humble beginnings into an urbane center for African American commerce, culture, and music."[80] In the passages on the Jazz District Driggs and Haddix suggest that race itself was bounded in the city. In addition, by representing race in the city as "self-contained" and "an urbane center," the authors reterritorialized the Jazz District as a location within which racially segregated residents were happy in their enclosed and urbane enclave. This brief examination of Jazz District segregation is the only such discussion until the book's epilogue, where the same unexplained reterritorialization of race continued: "Segregation remained the rule in Kansas City, but the African American community grew steadily by establishing a strong foothold in

THE MYTH OF THE WIDE-OPEN TOWN

the northernmost stretch of Troost Avenue and shouldering south past 27th Street. Eighteenth and Vine survived as an entertainment center, but the business district followed the migration of the community and gradually shifted south along Troost and Prospect Avenues."[81] Through the use of phrases such as "strong footholds" and "shouldering south," Driggs and Haddix represent African Americans in Kansas City as a group retaining a burden of labor, and then continue to marginalize African American neighborhoods and sections of the city as growing in spite of inexplicable segregation.

In their discussion of sex, gender, and sexuality, Driggs and Haddix did not depart from jazz canon practices. Women appear in *Kansas City Jazz* in one of three representations: performers who were exceptions to the grand narrative, band wives supporting their musician husbands, and sex workers in the Pendergast era. Very few women are mentioned specifically in *Kansas City Jazz*, and the ones that are included in this narrative were either mentioned in Driggs's 1959 essay or were famous outside the Kansas City scene. Mary Lou Williams, the most frequent female subject of *Kansas City Jazz*, appears in the book first as a band wife and then as an exception to the "great men of jazz" narrative. For instance Driggs and Haddix wrote that when Williams arrived in Kansas City she was not allowed to join Clouds of Joy. "Instead, she found herself relegated to the role of band wife," wrote Driggs and Haddix, "working odd jobs—at one point driving a hearse while playing music for her own pleasure."[82] Williams's biographer Linda Dahl, however, wrote that Williams was uncomfortable in her role as a "band wife," a position she dealt with by working as a table waitress in the Subway club, a hearse driver, and a piano teacher.[83] While Driggs and Haddix seem to be simply noting how Williams's gender affected her career in Clouds of Joy, it is interesting to note that Driggs and Haddix did not discuss the work in the jazz scene that Williams engaged in that was not directly related to the well-known local band. Later in the Kansas City narrative, after Williams had distinguished herself playing against

Marion Jackson, Driggs and Haddix explain that "Williams joined [Clouds of Joy] as a full-time member after Kirk finally put aside his reservations about having a woman in the band."[84] What reservations did Kirk have about a female band member? In this and other passages Williams is represented as an exception to the rule, a woman who became a skilled musician despite her sex. Williams is often juxtaposed with Julia Lee, a local pianist who did not tour, and instead found fame and a following in Kansas City. Lee, injured in a tragic car accident in 1930, refused to travel and tour like Williams. The result is Lee's representation as one of the "local girls," damaged by an accident and unable to fulfill her potential.[85]

Even more oversimplified is the juxtaposition of band wives and sex workers. Several women are mentioned only once in the book and are referred to as "band wives." Along with Mary Lou Williams, other women called "band wives" include Vivian Winn Basie (wife of Count Basie) and Charlie Parker's third wife Doris. These women are represented as little more than faithful wives who seemingly played no part in the city's jazz scene. One example is the book's only mention of Count Basie's wife by name, in a description of the departure of Moten's band for a New York tour: "Vivian Winn Basie and other band wives joined nearly a hundred well-wishers jamming the sidewalk in front of the Moten-Hayes music shop."[86] Mentioned in even fewer instances are the sex workers, including everyone from prostitutes to cabaret dancers that were such a fixture in the popular imagination of Kansas City's "wide-open" status. In fact sex workers appear only twice in the Driggs and Haddix book, and in those passages the women are couched in terms that both titillate the reader and silence the evidence of sex workers in the jazz scene. There is a short discussion of madam Annie Chambers, taken entirely from a single newspaper report published in 1932 about her arrest.[87] Another brief passage is a mention of the infamous Chesterfield Club, a Pendergast-owned diner and bar in downtown Kansas City. "Downtown, at the Chesterfield Club on

9th Street, waitresses clad only in shoes and see-through cellophane aprons served up a businessman's lunch. For adornment, they shaved their pubic hair in the shape of playing card pips. Briskly circulating among the tables by cigar puffing politicos, businessmen, and shy high school boys on a lark, the waitresses skillfully picked up tips without using their hands."[88]

The open secret of sexuality is again represented as a backdrop for the jazz scene in this passage. The stripped women of the Chesterfield, who "served up a businessman's lunch" with their amusing genitalia for the delight of politicians and aroused boys alike, is portrayed as a site of commodity and amusement. The waitress, doing what we are left to imagine in order to make a day's wage, is far removed from the steadfast band wife waving good-bye to her husband. Is it possible that some of these waitresses were also band wives? For Driggs and Haddix the roles that women, gender, and sexuality played in "Kansas City Jazz" are simple: women were a commodity, a faithful companion, or an exceptional "one of the boys."

The final aspect of the master narrative of the jazz canon is a focus on the authenticity of jazz music. The method commonly used in Kansas City's jazz scene historiography to authenticate Kansas City jazz is the Pendergast era. Through the use of the Pendergast era, Kansas City jazz historians can easily enclose the jazz scene in terms of spaces and dates, both of which fit easily into the "jazz myth" that positions Kansas City as a stop on the way to New York. Since Driggs was one of the innovators of this method for authenticating Kansas City jazz, it would seem obvious that such a reductive representation of the Pendergast era appears in *Kansas City Jazz*. In fact Driggs and Haddix establish in the introduction that their narrative does not stray from the well-worn path of the jazz canon. "Kansas City's government, ruled from 1911 to 1939 by a Democratic political machine driven by Tom Pendergast, a burly Irishman with a twinkle in his eye, fostered the wanton nightlife rife with gambling, prostitution, and bootlegging. Twelfth Street, a tawdry string of taxi dance joints, bars, and gambling dens, stretched a mile east of downtown. The red-light district on 14th Street thrived in the shadow of city hall. Kansas City Jazz, a hardy hybrid, flourished in this immoderate environment. This is the story of Kansas City Jazz."[89]

This portrayal echoes the writing of Pearson and Russell, and originally of Driggs in 1959. Portraying Kansas City as "wide-open" provides an explanation for Kansas City's temporary rise in the written history of jazz. The same explanation is used to explore the eventual decline of Kansas City's jazz scene, an event represented in the jazz canon as an inevitable step to the success of jazz music. For Driggs and Haddix Kansas City seems haunted by its jazz history and by a past it can never hope to rival. Representing Kansas City as "a genteel elderly lady of former ill repute reluctant to discuss her notorious past," Driggs and Haddix suggest that the music is the only point worth mention in Kansas City's past.[90] As Driggs and Haddix wrote:

> Twelfth Street, a one-time neon riot of bars, gambling dens, and taxi dance halls, fell victim to urban renewal and the freeway that choked the life from the city core during the 1960s. The wise guys who lorded over the strip packed up and moved years ago to sunnier venues in Las Vegas. An untidy surface parking lot for the adjacent police department occupies the hallowed site of the Reno Club, where Charlie Parker witnessed Lester Young and Count Basie making jazz history. No plaque marks the spot. . . . The jazz museum, situated on the corner of 18th and Vine, showcases the legacies of Ella Fitzgerald, Louis Armstrong, Duke Ellington, and Charlie Parker.[91]

Of all the musicians in "Kansas City Jazz" only Parker seems to merit remembrance.

Reviews of *Kansas City Jazz* criticized some omissions, but still supported the book as the definitive work on Kansas City's jazz scene. One review, written by historian Robert Rawlins, questioned the continued representation of Kansas City's jazz as a direct result of Pendergast's machine politics. According to Rawlins: "There seems to be a historic connection between jazz and licentious behavior. Could it be that the real connection lies between jazz and freedom, and that where there is freedom there is bound to be behavior that many will not condone? The authors do not address such issues, or even comment on Pendergast politics. *Kansas City Jazz* sticks to the facts throughout, with little personal opinion from the authors, musical or otherwise."[92]

Despite this concern about the reductive representation of the Pendergast machine, Rawlins considered *Kansas City Jazz* a definitive work. "A serious history of Kansas City jazz has been lacking for some time," wrote Rawlins, "and this book may become the standard reference for this subject."[93] In fact the Driggs and Haddix book was considered such an important publication when it appeared that it was featured in the premiere issue of *Jazz Perspectives*, an interdisciplinary journal of new jazz studies. After a short review of Kansas City jazz historiography that situates *Kansas City Jazz*, review author Brian Priestley wrote that the role of the Pendergast era in Kansas City's jazz scene was "well-rehearsed," still underestimated. "While this aspect of the story is a constant background factor," wrote Priestley, "what is in the foreground is an enormously detailed picture of the comings and goings of venues and musicians, their activities interlocking with the gradual development of an identifiable regional style."[94] Priestley concludes by agreeing with Rawlins and portraying *Kansas City Jazz* as "the publication we have been waiting for from Driggs, and Haddix's contribution has made it even more valuable than might have been expected."[95] With that, the jazz canon written around Kansas City had come full circle and continued to reify the master narrative of music and authenticity above all.

If the historians of the grand narrative of Kansas City jazz reduced Kansas City's jazz scene, then what was it? The following chapters will attempt to excavate the jazz scene of Kansas City, a scene reduced to a backdrop by traditional historians of Kansas City jazz. Rather than position the Pendergast machine as an "era" that served as a colorful background for the temporary flowering of Kansas City "style," Kansas City was home to a Pendergast *world*: a site of contestations about race, gender, sexuality, and class, and a spatialized social and cultural scene in Kansas City history poorly understood by jazz historians. It was this world that made "Kansas City jazz," and the music was the background for an incredibly contentious American cultural scene.

1. Photograph of a performance couple from Dante's Inferno, signed to Edna "Eddie" Jacobs. Edna Mae Jacobs Collection, Kenneth Spencer Research Library, University of Kansas Libraries.

2. Photograph of Art West, who performed under the name "Mr. Half-and-Half," signed to Edna "Eddie" Jacobs. Edna Mae Jacobs Collection, Kenneth Spencer Research Library, University of Kansas Libraries.

3. Promotional photograph of the Dante's Inferno interior from the scrapbooks of Edna Mae Jacobs. Edna Mae Jacobs Collection, Kenneth Spencer Research Library, University of Kansas Libraries.

4. Portrait of Edna Mae Jacobs, wearing a leopard-print dress that she claimed she made for Ella Fitzgerald. Edna Mae Jacobs Collection, Kenneth Spencer Research Library, University of Kansas Libraries.

5. Exterior view of the Paradise Club, featuring Baby Lovett. Edna Mae Jacobs Collection, Kenneth Spencer Research Library, University of Kansas Libraries.

6. Page from Edna Jacobs's scrapbook, showing clippings about Dante's Inferno and an image of Jacobs in a sailor costume with an unidentified colleague. Edna Mae Jacobs Collection, Kenneth Spencer Research Library, University of Kansas Libraries.

ELI MADLOFF

7. Page from Edna Jacobs's scrapbook, showing photographs of Edna Jacobs during her time as an employee at Dante's Inferno, including a photograph of Jacobs and another performer in their infamous devil costumes. Edna Mae Jacobs Collection, Kenneth Spencer Research Library, University of Kansas Libraries.

4

Sissy Nights at the Spinning Wheel

The term "jazz" is a piece of coded language from African Americans, prostitutes, and homosexuals in the early twentieth century, a slang term for sexual intercourse.[1] The term, however, became associated with music and the sexual attractiveness of male jazz musicians: its original meaning was lost. This is only one small example of the reordering of gender and sexuality in American jazz scenes. The famous "Jazz Age" of written history and popular memory is marked by a redefinition and reduction of gender. While largely subsumed in the grand narrative of jazz history, gender transgression played a major role in the discursive formation of gender in the "Jazz Age" of the first half of the twentieth century. Gender transgression also created spaces of worldmaking for those who did not feel represented by the changing discursive formations of gender in that period. People who identified with, or were represented as, members of a group seemingly outside "modernity" were an important part of the jazz scene. As jazz historian Lawrence Levine wrote: "It was this quality of course [being 'out of phase with the period's concept of culture'] that made jazz one of the houses of refuge in the 1920s for individuals who felt alienated from the central culture."[2]

Much of the gender transgression of the jazz scene was an outgrowth of Victorian gender norms. While the Victorian social and moral codes sought to protect women and empower men, they had an important side effect: the creation of homosocial and homosexual American subcultures. Due to sex segregation Victorian society encouraged the development of homosocial culture for both men and women.[3] While the men's homosocial culture revolved around the concept of camaraderie and saloon culture, women's relationships were supposedly based on romantic companionship. Even passionate relationships between women were permissible so long as the social rules of heterosexual marriage and family were followed.[4] Consequently women had an outlet for self-expression and same-sex attachment that was considered acceptable in mainstream society.[5] This began to radically shift in the 1920s, as gender and sexuality were closely redefined and policed by city fathers, reformers, and the trappings of popular culture.

Kansas Citians adhering to Victorian social mores upheld a national concern about the dangers of women's sexuality. According to one reformer working-class women seeking amusement were a source of social danger. In his investigation of working-class girls the reformer wrote that he feared the cultural effect of "girls who were idling along, seeking some diversion, some amusement, girls who were loitering on the edge of that precipice over which so many fall to destruction."[6] The reordering of leisure space also meant that previously masculine spaces, such as the saloon, were altered. American society was faced with a new "gender question": how to overthrow the Victorian system that segregated the sexes without permanently damaging the masculine underpinning of American culture.[7] The fear of damaging male culture in America quickly overshadowed any belief about the possibilities of the efforts by New Women to reform leisure spaces.

The other consequence of the reordering of the male/female gender binary in the 1880s and 1890s was the creation and development of homosexual as a category of identity. "The growing differentiation of sexual object choice from sexual roles and gender characteristics, and the growing importance of object choice in the classification of sexuality," wrote George Chauncey, "were reflected, albeit inconsistently, in the increasing frequency with which the term 'homosexuality' was used."[8] In effect the development of hypermasculinity and hyperfemininity in the early twentieth century created a homosexual identity, positioning binary hypergendered behavior as "normal," and presupposed homosexual behavior as "deviant." As historian Elizabeth Drorbaugh wrote: "Perversity, the dumping ground at the turn of the century for women who confounded norms of sex, gender, and sexuality, was a restive place from which proprietary norms continued to be disturbed, since labeling degenerates did not seem to make them go away. Degeneracy, relegated to the category of 'wrong,' became a necessary boundary: one could not otherwise fully comprehend 'right.'"[9]

It was in this atmosphere in the 1880s and 1890s that the concept of a "queer" community began to develop.[10] Eventually anyone who transgressed "straight" heteronormativity was seen as "queer" and territorialized into "queer" spaces. The sexual topography of jazz scene cities facilitated the development of those identities.[11] Cabarets, theaters, and red-light districts were marked as "queer" and deviant spaces that required both careful policing and eventual reform by "straight" culture. "Queer clubs and taverns," wrote historian Nan Alamilla Boyd, "existed at the intersection of vice and reform."[12] While often portrayed as a development of the early twentieth century, this "crisis" over gender identity and sexual orientation actually began in the 1880s. In addition, the "crisis" had clear foundations in race. Beginning in the 1890s white and of color gay men and lesbians increasingly frequented African American clubs and cabarets, since queer enclaves and black enclaves frequently overlapped in both geography and social marginalization.[13]

While upper-class theater audiences accepted the representation of different gender roles on stage as an illusion of the theater experience, they were not so accepting of gender difference in daily life. For instance many sensational accounts of working women "passing" as men to gain more economic advantages appeared in the American press.[14] The influence of gender transgression in the theater did, however, create a subculture of homosexuality in the American working class despite hegemonic discourse. While legitimate theaters catered to the Victorian sense of gendered entertainment and working-class reality, working-class theaters featured both vaudeville and burlesque performances that attracted large audiences in Kansas City.[15] According to a 1912 recreation census of Kansas City, thirty-one thousand city dwellers attended a vaudeville performance each week.[16] An increase in theater openings in working-class areas paralleled the boom in legitimate theater building in Kansas City's more prosperous areas. When the Coates Opera House opened in 1871, so did the Free and Easy Theater on Fourth Street. By the 1890s there were several theaters that catered strictly to working-class patrons: vaudeville at the Orpheum, burlesque at the Century and Gayety theaters in the red-light district.[17]

The increased interest in leisure and its growing acceptance as a vehicle for experimentation with gender roles made theaters, in Kansas City and across the country, especially important. Theaters promised to provide realism or escapism in a safe setting. Increasingly theater owners found themselves questioning how to meet female audience demands without turning away their male patron base. The result was the creation of two types of working-class theater experiences, the "hot shows" and the "cold shows."[18] So-called hot shows attracted a predominantly white male audience of mixed-class patrons who attended primarily saloons, vaudeville shows, and burlesque productions. They usually included sexual innuendo, sexually explicit performances, or strip-tease acts that intended to appeal to heteronormative masculinity. While hot shows attracted larger audiences and generated more ticket sales, theater owners that booked them were subject to more police attention and greater social pressures than other owners of working-class theaters. "Clean shows," featuring vaudeville variety shows and cabaret entertainers, attracted a broader audience of both men and women across racial lines.[19] In many ways the clean shows of vaudeville and cabaret bridged the gap between legitimate theater and burlesque, and brought aspects of working-class neighborhoods into the world of legitimate theater. Kansas City's working-class neighborhoods were home to both vaudeville and more sexual "hot show" clubs.

Vaudeville and cabarets had their foundations in the male saloon culture of the post–Civil War era. Saloons were male homosocial spaces whose only female occupants were prostitutes and entertainers. The space was marked as one reserved for men and was a prominent part of the male public sphere.[20] With the creation of a new market for women in the 1880s, saloon keepers began to transform their spaces to accommodate female patrons. Drinking was moved to barrooms in the saloon, while back rooms were redesigned to accommodate vaudeville performances for working-class audiences.[21] Though the vaudeville stages in saloons remained primarily male spaces, vaudeville soon spread to larger theaters and theater circuits. However many vaudevilles and burlesque theaters kept their connection with saloons. In Kansas City a few vaudevilles even retained a connecting door to a neighboring saloon into the early twentieth century.[22]

Vaudeville was one of the most popular working-class amusements in Kansas City. Kansas City's thirty-six-week vaudeville season extended from September to June. The vaudeville theaters were concentrated in the city's central business district near the tenements and cable car lines.[23] The vaudeville theaters with the largest audiences were the Orpheum on Ninth Street and the Globe Theater on Walnut at Thirteenth—only eight blocks from the red-light district.[24] The Orpheum Vaudeville Circuit, a vaudeville company that toured the United States, leased the Orpheum Theater beginning in 1898.[25] Patrons at the Orpheum paid twenty-five cents for a balcony seat and fifty cents for a floor seat at the show. Eventually the Orpheum was relocated to Baltimore Street to cater to visitors staying at the Muehlebach and Baltimore hotels.[26] Performers were quartered at the Centropolis Hotel at Fifth and Walnut inside the red-light district, where there were "special rates for show people and bands."[27] Another vaudeville company was the Theater

Owners Booking Association (TOBA), which booked African American performers. Kansas City was the western base and terminus of operations for TOBA, and many of the jazz scene performers who made their home in Kansas City did so by spending the off-season there.[28] According to Kansas City jazz musician Ernest Williams, vaudeville shows (which included TOBA shows) were variety shows:

> You got the show where them skits, have to do so much in so many acts and then get the, dance, girls dance, actors dance, got a dancing act, like you'd have the jugglers or something out there, you know. You see, he'd juggle that. And then they'd have a scene, or a comedy, have a whole lot a comedy. See, like Strawberry Rush and them used to box that, have a boxcar scene, where the guys like to ride the freight train, got it, got the electricity fixed up so you see, the guy, you get the guy say 'I'm from Oklahoma, I'm getting off the spit,' and it would fire up and do all this kind of stuff. Then after that, the other acts, go on with the show, change the clothes.[29]

Vaudeville theaters in Kansas City also hosted cabarets and minstrel shows. Minstrelsy had its foundations in the Jacksonian period, when four white performers developed a caricature of the freed urban ex-slave.[30] Minstrelsy gained popularity in Kansas City through the early decades of the twentieth century, probably due to the continuing importance of TOBA, which featured minstrel singers for many years. Its popularity in Kansas City was a reflection of the national popularity of minstrelsy in post–Civil War America. By the early twentieth century, however, minstrelsy had taken on a new meaning. With the rise of modern masculinity, black men were increasingly portrayed as libidinous creatures drawn to white women.[31] Minstrelsy featured black men cross-dressing and wearing exaggerated makeup, so the minstrel shows of the early twentieth century distorted gender and racial stereotypes.[32] Minstrel shows included men in blackface as the primary characters and choruses, and their performances were mostly song-and-dance shows.[33]

The result was that minstrelsy stripped away the image of the libidinous black male and put in its place an effeminate and weakened "song-and-dance man." Evidently the most popular minstrel show in Kansas City was U. S. Epperson's Megaphone Mastodon Minstrels, featuring stage costumes and comedians.[34] A special citywide minstrelsy performance by U. S. Epperson's minstrels was held in Kansas City's first Convention Hall on April 3, 1899. This show was produced by William Rockhill Nelson, an upper-class city leader and owner of the *Kansas City Star* newspaper. A benefit for Nelson's planned public bath, the 1899 show attracted fifteen thousand people and ended with a parade of local citizens and minstrels in silk costumes and blackface. The daylong performance raised nearly twelve thousand dollars for Nelson's project.[35]

Cabarets also experimented with gender roles and stereotypes, but with a very different method than contemporary minstrel shows. While minstrel performers were seen as race illusionists, cabaret performers challenged dominant gender constructs in the early twentieth century.[36] Cabarets featured floor shows and singers as well as a public dance floor. The mixed-gender contact in the cabaret positioned the cabaret as a heteronormative space, while challenging that position by placing women in a position of power. Cabaret performers were often women who were portrayed by critics as asexual beings. That portrayal resulted in the identification of cabarets with homosexuality. Cabarets were open to diverse populations, but their environment of sexual expressiveness and experimentation attracted a working-class crowd. Critics of the cabaret quickly derided such establishments as lower-class spaces that were "influencing and infecting good women of better classes."[37] Cabaret was essentially a sensual space for mixed-gender crowds. Unlike vaudeville and minstrel shows children were not allowed in cabarets. Performance in cabarets took place on the same floor level as the audience.[38] These conditions in the cabaret removed barriers between genders and destroyed the illusory barrier between performance and reality that legitimate theater institutionalized. Victorian critics saw the cabaret as a much bigger threat to gender separation than vaudeville or minstrel shows. "The ultimate fear was that once off the pedestal," wrote historian Lewis Erenberg, "respectable married and single women would find lower-class men in the cabaret better able to satisfy their cravings for pleasure."[39] Cabarets were financially and morally marginalized, and tended to occupy small spaces that could quickly empty in cases of a police raid.[40] Vaudeville performers in that period worked sexual language and homosexual references into their acts as well.[41] Kansas City likely had more cabarets than other jazz scene cities. Kansas City's geography and association with western America meant that there were several clubs with few amenities, and that cabarets opened and closed quickly.[42]

Even more transgressive than cabarets were working-class burlesques. Beginning in the 1880s plays and burlesque acts increasingly portrayed sexual behavior.[43] While most vaudeville theaters in Kansas City were built near Market Square area, burlesque theaters were deeper in the working-class districts, usually near the brothels of the railroad district. According to the Board of Welfare statistics twenty-two thousand Kansas Citians attended burlesque performances weekly.[44] The two leading Kansas City burlesques were the Free and Easy Theater at Fourth Street and Main and the Theater Comique located next door to the Jackson County Railroad Stables at Fourth Street and Walnut.[45] The Theater Comique mixed burlesque with bawdy plays such as "Forbidden Pleasures" and "Mountain Meadow Massacre."[46] Another Kansas City burlesque was Standard Theater, which opened in 1900 with the Fulton and Miaco's Jolly Windows Grass troupe. The performance featured blue humor comedians and female "leg art."[47] One Board of Welfare inspector discussed the Standard and Century theaters as morally dangerous: "Every report from the two burlesque theaters was similar in one respect. They tell of the exhibition teaming with salacious lines and situations suggestive of immorality in song and act appealing to the sensual. Scenes carefully worked out by skilled directors convey clearly the lewd story without giving evidence that would stand in court. The entire moral trend of burlesque is downward."[48] While minstrel shows exaggerated gender stereotypes, and cabarets challenged gender roles, the burlesque theaters solidified them.

The leading discourse about gender roles in the burlesque was not only from Victorian morality, but also from working-class masculinity. According to working-class male patrons, upper-class white men fell prey to the feminine wiles of female burlesque performers while working-class men retained power at home. This reification of masculinity positioned upper-class men as effeminate, giving working-class men across racial lines subcultural power that they lacked outside the spaces and homes of the working class. The phrase "gold-digger," which suggested a working-class woman seeking financial gain through liaisons with a wealthy man, was coined in the burlesque theater of the 1890s.[49] Burlesque was increasingly seen by upper-class reformers as something to "clean up," and burlesque performers were portrayed by the bourgeoisie as prostitutes, not performers.[50] Burlesque posters produced by working-class burlesque owners, showing upper-class white men as overweight fools unable to control themselves in the presence of wily burlesque girls, intensified the criticism. As burlesque historian Robert Allen wrote: "It [the burlesque performer's sexual appeal] can be used to obtain the trappings of the high life through an inversion of 'normal' sexual power relations: the woman is clearly in control of the situation; the wealthy admirer is clearly taken advantage of."[51]

According to jazz musician Ernest Williams cabaret and burlesque was not simply a source of entertainment in the jazz scene: it was a source of employment for the wives and sisters of African American male jazz performers. Williams told interviewers that his wife, along with the wife and sister of musician Virgil Hall, performed as dancers in Kansas City burlesques and cabarets such as the Gayety and the Midland.[52] In fact Williams suggested that Kansas City women who worked in burlesque frequently worked as prostitutes as well. "Some of 'em used to do it, I know some of 'em used to do it right here, down here," Williams told interviewers.[53]

GENDER IMPERSONATION IN THE JAZZ SCENE

Found in a variety of cabarets, vaudevilles, taverns, and theaters, gender impersonation was of major importance in the jazz scene. In the dominant discourse of jazz history the sexualized performances in cabarets and burlesques seldom appear, or appear only as an implied colorful backdrop to the dominant narrative. Minstrelsy is portrayed as a precursor to jazz music, but not connected to either performance or to the dominant concepts of masculinity in the jazz scene.[54] In fact the grand narrative of jazz scene history portrays the subculture of working-class sexualized performances, as well as same-sex city dwellers and their spaces, in a totalizing manner. Sexuality is most often totalized into a single image: the buffet flat or the rent party. A space of both sexuality and a challenge of social convention, buffet flats or rent parties were indeed a part of the jazz scene. The analysis of sexuality in the jazz scene, however, is more often than not symbolized by a poorly understood single phenomenon. Buffet flats are positioned as the single space where alternative sexuality was welcome. At the same time, buffet flats are frequently portrayed with titillation and a proverbial "wink," as though they need not be taken seriously as an aspect of the jazz scene. As jazz scholar David Levering Lewis has written: "Social analysis, whenever it ventured beyond the Cotton Club, pretty much contented itself with the fabled Dark Tower and the rent party as sufficient paradigms."[55] A good example is from an article by Ellen McBreen about Harlem artist Richard Bruce Nugent: "Nugent's openness was more like those Harlemites 'in the life,' who were indeed publicly shouting 'I love prick' in the cellar clubs, buffet flats, and rent parties of Harlem's thriving entertainment scene."[56] This totalizing effect is evident in the written history of Kansas City's jazz scene as well. Scholar Nathan Pearson wrote that prostitution, drag acts, and sex shows were not directly related to jazz.[57] Kansas City jazz historian Chuck Haddix told the author that shows that included female impersonators were very common, but not very important to the "Jazz Age."[58]

If female impersonation was common, then how did it become unimportant? What was "in the life"? Does gender impersonation represent the public appearance of a queer subculture in jazz scene cities?[59] Historians of gay and lesbian history have uncovered what they have termed strong "queer" subcultures in many cities during the jazz scene, and much of their evidence has relied on accounts of gender impersonation. According to historian Sharon Ullman gender impersonation likely marked a "private practice" of homosexuality in the early years of the twentieth century.[60] David Hurewitz, in his book *Bohemian New York*, suggested that the female impersonator was "emblematic" of early homosexual subcultures. "That Eltinge was both homosexually active and a female impersonator," wrote Hurewitz, "does not make him a 'fairy,' though."[61] Further is the work of George Chauncey, who clearly located a world of homosexual people "in the life" in New York before World War II in spaces such as Harlem drag balls. What jazz historians have often silenced is the important role that these subcultures played in the jazz scenes of America. Even clearer is the fact that the homosexual subculture of the jazz scene was centered on cabarets, taverns, and neighborhood enclaves. Historian Barbara Kukla explained that entertainment spaces were a means of social survival for African Americans and sexual minorities in jazz scene Newark.[62] In her study of early San Francisco Nan Alamilla Boyd explained that queer communities created their own social world in San Francisco and then fought to secure that space by preventing "outsiders" from entering.[63] According to Boyd the queer community of the jazz scene in San Francisco developed as early as 1905 and was centered on gender impersonation clubs and bars that "offered practical and ideological responses to policing" that members of the queer community dealt with in daily life.[64] Such worldmaking was not limited to San Francisco. Art historian Ellen McBreen has explained that the queer community was central to the jazz scene in Harlem. While African Americans in Harlem used the jazz scene as both a community creation and a vehicle for political agency, homosexuality in Harlem was as tightly policed as any other city. As McBreen wrote:

> Harlem society had, in fact, both embraced and rejected its thriving gay community. The same papers that ran front-page, celebratory stories on drag ball winners also ran articles in support of the Reverend Adam Clayton Powell's much publicized efforts to out and banish homosexual ministers from Harlem pulpits during the early 1930s. Other [Harlem] Renaissance critics campaigned vigorously for the projection of an image of the New Negro that would combat stereotypes of the lascivious and primitive sexual Other. *Collier's* magazine labeled Harlem a "synonym for naughtiness" in 1933, reflecting the idea that Harlem itself was an escapist sexual commodity for downtown whites, many of them gay men, wishing to indulge in a rebel and exotic sexuality without fear of censure by their own social group. Not surprisingly, Harlem's cultural leaders sought to counter this racist and touristic characterization. Homosexuals and gender impersonators were afforded a good deal of tolerance in Harlem, then, so long as their antics were confined to the space of performance. For many prominent critics, however, decadence, perversity, and blatant homosexuality were unacceptable themes in the higher forms of art and literature that they hoped could advance the race.[65]

As that quotation demonstrates, gender impersonation was seen as an indicator of queerness, even though the performers themselves were not necessarily homosexual. In addition much of this identity building seemed to hinge on queer sex tourism in jazz scene spaces. "Slumming" in jazz scene spaces represented both a deterioration of moral and economic hegemony and an adventure in the borderlands of acceptability. Some whites engaged in queer sex tourism may, indeed, have gone slumming in search of sexual encounters with other queer city dwellers. Many others, however, were interested only in the exoticism represented by slumming. By engaging in queer sex tourism in the jazz scene, whites "slumming" in search of the exotic equated queer sex with racial segregation and miscegenation, since queer enclaves were usually in racially mixed vice districts. "Slumming turned on the asymmetry between the slummer and the object," wrote Kevin Mumford, "but remember that some slummers were sympathetic outsiders with a genuine sense of affinity whereas others were more concerned with exploitation than appreciation."[66]

The silencing of homosexual subcultures in the jazz scene was, therefore, directly linked to twentieth-century masculinity, African American rejection of primitivist representation, and the representation of jazz as art. The debate over the history of jazz resulted in its representation as an American art form, and homosexuality and gender impersonation were portrayed and positioned in the jazz scene as anything except art. At the same time, jazz history's attachment to the "great man" theory relied on the masculinity of its heroes. While scholars of post-Stonewall gay and lesbian history have discussed the worldmaking role of bars and clubs, jazz historians have continued to marginalize the role of the possibility of queer community in the jazz scene.[67]

Given the work of other historians, it seems that the key to excavating the history of possibly queer communities in the jazz scene is gender impersonators, most commonly female impersonators. Whether gender impersonators had onstage representations identical to their offstage identities is unknown, but their representation of gender transgression in jazz scene spaces served as a signpost, an indicator on the city's jazz scene map for members of the city's queer individuals to locate and interact. Homosexual city dwellers saw in gender impersonation a representation of their own desires and identified spaces that hosted impersonators as "queer spaces."[68] The result was the policing of gender impersonation and the clubs that hosted such performances, from the jazz scene through its historical representation. Gender impersonators "walked a line between respectability and deviance."[69] They embodied the increased scrutiny of homosexual behavior that accompanied the rise of masculinity, but at the same time female impersonators were imitators of the counterpart to that masculinity: hyperfemininity. Last, but certainly not least, these performers' stage personas were not literal translations of their offstage personas. The audience was left without any real knowledge of the queerness as a possible identity, faced with only an ambiguous representation of what *they* saw. In this way female impersonators represented the development of a possible queer community and changing discourses about gender, even if they did not identify with the gender identity they represented. They secured spaces for displays of queerness such as cabarets and bars by presenting an illusion, one that fed into both the popular conception of heterosexuality and the subjugated knowledge of queers "in the life." This was indeed worldmaking, but in a way that used space as both offense and defense. For female impersonators and their peers in the queer jazz scene the social geography of queers "in the life" was one where being *onstage* was just as political and subcultural as life *offstage*. Since gender impersonation represented queerness in mainstream heteronormative culture, historians took gender impersonation as an indicator of homosexuality. By placing primary importance on the masculine performance of the "art that was jazz," jazz scholars continued to silence the subjugated knowledge of the queerness in the jazz scene by subsuming the history of gender impersonation. In order to excavate the importance of gender impersonation scholars must understand the role of worldmaking *within* the systems of power/knowledge during the jazz scene. As critical geographer Donald Moore wrote: "If critical analysis dispenses with the notion of an authentic insurrectionary space 'outside' of power—nurturing either an originary and insubordinate individual consciousness 'offstage' or sustaining the 'autonomy' of insurgent collectivities—then how does one begin to conceptualize sites of resistance; and from what cultural ground? What, in turn, do such theoretical moves imply for understanding the polyvalent politics of place?"[70]

Along with the role of female impersonation onstage came jazz music. According to historian Marybeth Hamilton female impersonation was incredibly popular in the "Jazz Age."[71] In fact the era 1900–1930 is considered the "golden age of female impersonation" by theater historians.[72] There can be little doubt that gender impersonation involved the music later called "jazz" by historians, as it was played in cabarets and clubs. With the codification of jazz history, however, the popularity of gender impersonation was marked as offensive and marginalized. Since those performances, that *world*, was centered in specific jazz scene spaces, those spaces were ignored and silenced as well. This is the case in Kansas City's jazz scene history. As Haddix admitted, female impersonation was a popular component of the jazz scene in Kansas City, but its position in the city is completely subsumed in the city's jazz canon. At the same time, the possibility of queerness was practically erased from Kansas City's written history. Instead Kansas City "jazz music" has been positioned as a precursor to bebop and therefore high art, while the more "vulgar" performance of gender impersonation is denied.

What made female impersonation so important to worldmaking was the fact that impersonators created more questions than they answered. While impersonators supposedly symbolized the transgression of heteronormativity, they in fact destabilized the very boundaries of "inversion."[73] In this sense gender impersonation was internally contradictory—and had its biggest implications onstage.[74] First, gender impersonators occupied an intermediate identity, somewhere in the spectrum between heterosexual and homosexual. While audiences (and future historians) assumed that impersonators were homosexual, such was not the case. One example is Julian Eltinge, a famous female impersonator at the turn of the twentieth century. Eltinge was an extremely popular impersonator, but offstage he loudly proclaimed his masculinity and heterosexuality. Perry Hammond, a theater critic who wrote about Eltinge's performances, coined a new term to describe his persona: *ambisextrous*.[75] Female impersonators who did not reify masculinity offstage were, however, portrayed not as impersonators but as degenerate "fairies."[76] Historian Robert Toll, a scholar of late Victorian female impersonation, further explained the transgressive zone that impersonators occupied between heterosexual and homosexual. According to Toll the popularity of female impersonation was specifically based on the fact that the actual *performance* was not transgressive at all until the 1930s.[77] While the offstage life of the impersonator was seen as degenerate and dangerous, the onstage persona displayed a hyperfeminine understanding of dominant culture. "Billing themselves as 'female illusionists,' impersonators were lauded as skilled magicians," wrote historian Marybeth Hamilton, "able to conjure themselves across gender boundaries that all observers believed to be fixed and immutable."[78]

Did gender impersonation signal a queer subculture, as other historians have suggested, or did it exist in a more transgressive, marginal zone of commodification than that simple binary suggests? According to theater historian Kristina Straub gender impersonation and its popularity must be understood as a function of what Foucault termed "scopophilia," or the obsessive pleasure of looking that relates directly to the subject position of the spectator.[79] Through this desire to look, to be a voyeur, spectators form a discourse between the performance and themselves. According to Foucault such scopophilia was compelled by "an unacknowledged search for illicit pleasure and a desire which cannot be fulfilled."[80] It was this search for pleasures, this commodification of desires, that spectators of gender impersonation in Kansas City sought. According to Straub, in this field of desires and pleasures discourse about the sexuality of performers became a site of hegemonic struggle about definitions of sexuality and gender.[81] At the same time, however, the marketing of gender impersonation depended upon the concept that such performances were contained in the space of the theater.[82] It was in the jazz scene spaces of gender impersonation, therefore, that sexuality was both contained and displayed, both discussed and silenced. "Theatrical cross-dressing," wrote Straub, "constitutes a site of cultural resistance to this narrowing of masculine and feminine down to certain opposite, prescribed roles, even as it serves as one of the grounds of its construction."[83]

As a site of resistance, spaces where gender impersonation was performed may have developed into what Deleuze and Guattari termed "uncertain desire-zones."[84] These zones contained subordinate groups who sought to defend their territory by representing an alternative to hegemonic social systems.[85] Consequently gender impersonation may have served as a symbol of an alternative queer subcultural zone that was just beginning to develop. As a subculture nurtured and created by the working class, queer communities existed in inner-city enclaves of clubs and homes that heterosexuals knew little about.[86] As such, gender impersonation did not exist outside the mainstream or solely inside a queer enclave. Instead it occupied a space (both literally and figuratively) of desire-zone. Gender impersonators were represented as the public face of queerness, and in doing so corrupted the very gender system their personas represented. Queer spectators sought, in the spaces of gender impersonation performance, the representation of their own desires. "Seeing the other is a social form of self-reproduction," explained Peggy Phelan, "For in looking at/for the other, we seek to re-present ourselves."[87]

As Foucault theorized, once it was identified as a domain to control, "sex became a matter that required the social body as a whole, and virtually all of its individuals to place themselves under surveillance."[88] Gender impersonators were under constant surveillance onstage by the audiences and fellow performers. The theater, however, was a space of illusion. Whether that theater was on a cabaret floor, a tavern table, or a legitimate stage, the illusion of theater meant that surveillance itself could be corrupted. The consequence of corruption in Kansas City was both profit and a call for reform. While gender impersonation remained popular in the jazz scene, it was increasingly policed and attacked by mainstream reformers. Part of this attack on gender impersonation was because Americans began to link impersonation to prostitution. In terms of social geography this was not a difficult connection to make. Cabarets and clubs that featured gender impersonation were often in or along the borders of a city's red-light district, "at the intersection between vice and reform."[89] Queer communities were often located in red-light districts as well, because such districts were predicated on the concept of silence placed there on behalf of sexual tourists. Beginning in the 1930s, however, gender impersonation was increasingly seen as dangerous outside its connections to prostitution. As vice investigations occurred across America in the jazz scene, investigators began to connect impersonation with the subculture it represented. No longer seen as an illusion, gender impersonation became identified as an attack on the masculine underpinnings of American culture. Impersonators were marked as degenerate, and their performance was positioned as a clear indicator of their sexual orientation. As anthropologist Esther Newton explained in her 1970s study of drag performers in New York: "The work [female impersonation] is defined as 'queer' in itself. The assumption upon which both performers and audiences operate is that no one but a 'queer' would want to perform as a woman."[90] Once impersonation was stigmatized as a homosexual practice it lost both its popularity and its position in the jazz scene. The resulting stigma of impersonation as "popular" and "gay" meant its marginalization in the written history of jazz. Gender impersonation was banned by municipal and state authorities as part of a larger crackdown on homosexual culture that occurred nationwide during the Depression.[91] "Impersonators were no longer seen as performers—they were performing homosexuals," wrote Marybeth Hamilton. "In a culture that demonized homosexuality, that was enough to exclude them all from the mainstream, to put them out of business once and for all."[92]

The first appearance of female impersonation in Kansas City is impossible to pinpoint. Gender impersonators were doubtless part of vaudeville, cabaret, and burlesque performances in the city, and they were certainly part of minstrel shows in the city. What makes the case in Kansas City so interesting is that a municipal statute barring cross-dressing and gender impersonation was on the books as early as the 1880s—not the 1920s and 1930s as in other urban jazz scenes. This early policing of gender crossing is inextricably linked to Kansas City's location in the American West. According to Laurence Senelick the American West was a "breeding ground" for gender crossing because the limited female population in western towns created a general acceptance of female impersonation.[93] At the same time the women on the western frontier often engaged in transvestism as a way to gain upward mobility.[94] The municipal statute that policed gender crossing in Kansas City was City Ordinance No. 291, codified in the 1880s and first mentioned in chapter 1.

No person shall be or appear in or upon any street, avenue, alley, park, public place or place open to public view, in a state of nudity, or any dress not belonging to his or her sex, or in any indecent or lewd dress, or shall make any indecent exposure of his or her person, or be guilty of an unseemly obscene or filthy act, or any lewd, indecent, immoral or insulting conduct, language or behavior; or shall exhibit, circulate, contribute, sell, offer or expose for sale, or give or deliver to another, or cause the same to be done, any lewd, indecent or obscene book, picture, pamphlet, card, print, paper writing, mold, cast, figure or any other thing, or shall exhibit or perform, or cause or allow to be exhibited or performed, in or upon any house, building, lot or premises owned or occupied by him, or under his management or control, any lewd, indecent, or immoral play or other representation.[95]

As mentioned earlier, perhaps the first recorded female impersonator performance in Kansas City, however, was reported in the *Kansas City Star* in 1880. "As a female impersonator he draws a large salary and is a most remarkable success," wrote the reporter in his article "Strange Men," "but as a man he is a gigantic failure and not worth the powder that would blow his effeminate soul to heaven."[96] As Kristina Straub demonstrated, the representation of female impersonators as "failed men" was clearly connected to the discursive formation of masculinity. The very concept that these biological males were "failed men" acted as a mirror on masculinity, that both spatially and discursively identified such performers as feminine in appearance and therefore perhaps in desire.[97] Indeed this mirror was also part of the marketability of gender impersonation. According to City Ordinance No. 291 public cross-dressing was illegal, but no attempt was made to halt the performance recorded in 1880. In fact Kansas City's reputation as a "wide-open town" was predicated on the fact that any of the performances listed in Code 291 were perfectly allowed in *certain spaces* and as *nighttime entertainment.*

The representation of female impersonators as failed men, indeed as failed *women*, appears again in a report in the *Kansas City Star* in 1927. In the anonymous report titled "'Sissies' Brought In by Rude Police; Fined $500 Each by Judge," the author represented impersonators as feminine and hypersexual:

"It was just too terrible, my dear!" "The rude police have no sense of propriety," let the "sissies" of the city tell it. When officers of the law raided a cabaret at 1520 East Twelfth street early yesterday morning, terror and consternation spread from manly breast to manly breast underneath the frilly garments of the feminine sex, worn for the evening's pleasure.

When the last screams and squeals had coyly come forth from throats originally designed for some he-occupation like calling hogs, the police had seven men—six were all clad in dainty chiffon things, cute little pumps, silk hose and other frills.

Yesterday morning the sight of six men in flimsy clothing evidently had a bad effect on Judge Carlin P. Smith because he fined each of the frequenters $500 each and also fined Ben Payne, the proprietor of the place, $500. They are the heaviest fines ever assessed against frequenters of a cabaret.[98]

While it is unclear what the "sissies" and cabaret proprietor were fined for, it is clear that the men arrested did not follow the reporter's definition of "men." These men were a spectacle of coy squeals and dainty chiffon, hiding their manly breasts under layers of pleasure.

With the jazz scene in Kansas City came increased visibility of gender impersonators, especially female impersonators. Among the few sources of information about female impersonators was the Pearson and Litwak interview with musician Booker Washington. Washington played with the Bennie Moten Orchestra and the Kansas City Rockets, and frequently played at Kansas City clubs and cabarets. Washington remembered female impersonators in performance at the Spinning Wheel:

WASHINGTON: . . . we'd have different acts but really the place consist more of uh female impersonators.

INTERVIEWER: Uh huh. Really?

WASHINGTON: They didn't publicize that, female impersonators.

INTERVIEWER: That was kind of a featured act?

WASHINGTON: That was featured. Each one of them would do something different. They had a special to do, each one of them, see, but uh you never heard.

INTERVIEWER: Would they do impersonations of people like Mae West or Greta Garbo?

WASHINGTON: Oh no! This is, they dressed like women. They stayed dressed like women. They went around throughout the crowd as women. They were "women." You know and they didn't, wasn't nothing uh, uh, funny or faking with them, they were genuine, see.

INTERVIEWER: Would you only have them as performers or in other words would a lot of female impersonators just come to the Spinning Wheel as their favorite club?

WASHINGTON: No, these were hired. They were hired. This is uh, they had about oh there was between six and eight of them and they worked every night, see. In fact, uh, the most of them, that's where most of our money came from, the impersonators. They'd go out and do their numbers. And they would get tips and what tips they'd get, they'd throw in the "kitty."[99]

Washington's memories underscore the popularity of female impersonators in the Kansas City jazz scene. Not only were such performers "genuine," they were beneficial to the economic success of bands who depended on the money impersonators threw "in the kitty." Another jazz musician who recalled female impersonators was Herman Walder. Walder was one of the most famous saxophonists in Kansas City and was considered by many to be a major influence on the bebop sound. In Walder's interview he recalled an interest in a particular female impersonator.

WALDER: Well, they had female impersonators, mostly.

INTERVIEWER: Really?

WALDER: And a—yeah, they was sharp, too, man. One cat like to got in a fight with one of them man—

INTERVIEWER: Oh—yeah.

WALDER: Yeah.

INTERVIEWER: Who were the female impersonators, do you remember their names?

WALDER: I don't remember none of their names. One of them was named Billy—that's one I'd like to have a fight over.

INTERVIEWER: Uh-huh.

WALDER: And they would come from out of town, not here.

INTERVIEWER: Would they sing songs or would they dance?

WALDER: Songs and dance. All kinds of artist and with these marionettes—

INTERVIEWER: Marionettes?

WALDER: Marionettes, yeah, man they had all kinds, man.

INTERVIEWER: Was that a popular thing here in town, female impersonators?

WALDER: Oh, yes. Still.[100]

According to Walder female impersonator performances were advertised in newspapers. In what Walder referred to as a cabaret show, female impersonators performed two or three nights per week at the Spinning Wheel, with other floor shows the rest of the week.[101] At one point Walder began to discuss Elmer Orrie, the leader of a four-member dance team that appeared weekly at the Spinning Wheel. Walder remembered that Orrie "got in a little bit of trouble at times because his features are kind of effeminate. He's a very delicate looking man."[102] When interviewers asked Walder to elaborate, he explained the rotating schedule at the Spinning Wheel and its connection to queer culture.

WALDER: In other words, on Monday—so and so's night—Tuesday—so and so's—next was Men's night—next is—is sissy night—they come on out then, you know. Yeah. . . . Female impersonators, they come on out, man.

INTERVIEWER: And that's when a lot of homosexuals would come?

WALDER: Yes, um huh—yeah. And everybody else—they'd come to see 'em dance.

INTERVIEWER: They'd come to see the act?

WALDER: See the—what's going on. . . . Well, hell, mean, they was—look here, ah, people—we judge people by what they want to be themselves, you dig what I mean? And those people were good—they're always good to you, dig what I mean, huh? They'd fill up the kitty man—if they make some money man, they'd come and fill up the kitty.[103]

For Walder impersonators were part of the jazz scene and also perhaps a developing subculture. Walder's recollections of "sissy night" and judging "people by what they want to be themselves" serve as interesting glimpses of queerness in the jazz scene.

As each of these interviews reveal, female impersonation was an important and popular part of Kansas City's jazz scene. Perhaps most important, however, is the fact that female impersonation may have represented a possibly burgeoning subculture in the city. The jazz scene in Kansas City is not as simple as male performers and female performers, or the even more simplified jazz babies and virile musicians. Instead the jazz scene was a mixture of gender identity and sexual orientation that written history has ignored. According to scholar Judith Butler drag performance such as those by female impersonators reflected the primary ways in which gender is/was *performance*: beyond the stage itself, gender combined "anatomical sex, gender identity, and gender performance."[104] In Kansas City the female impersonators that were likely seen as a necessity in the pre-1880s frontier were increasingly a homosexual subject in the jazz scene. This subjectification not only defined "the homosexual" in Kansas City's jazz scene, but it defined and marked "the heterosexual" as well. While the development of queerness was part of the jazz scene, the increased backlash against female impersonation in the 1930s and 1940s drove that symbol of queerness further into its own spaces. For the master narrative of jazz, the influence of female impersonation and queerness on the jazz scene was ignored. In his book on Kansas City jazz the only reference made to homosexuality by Ross Russell is a sentence about buffet flats on Truman Road. In Pearson's *Goin' to Kansas City* female impersonation and homosexuality are included in the chapter "Wide-Open Town," a chapter that featured "a remarkable body of exotic, sensual, and lurid tales."[105] Pearson wrote in his introduction to the chapter: "This chapter is split into four sections, covering each of the major vices that were prevalent in K.C. during those years: gangsters; gambling and gamblers; prostitution and other open sexuality; prohibition, bootlegging, and narcotics. Each was common in K.C. then and each had positive (or at least relatively benign) and negative aspects."[106]

By positioning homosexuality and female impersonation as "other open sexuality" and part of a list of jazz scene events that were clearly illegal, jazz historians such as Pearson made a clear statement. Gender transgression, in whatever form it appeared, was ancillary, illegal and immoral, and not an important piece of the jazz scene. Such representations of the historical jazz scene, however, do not reflect the contested spaces of gender and sexuality in the jazz scene. The popularity of gender impersonation, along with the changing discursive formations of gender and sexuality in the jazz scene, demonstrate that this particular "other" needs to be excavated and included in the narrative of jazz history. As jazz historian Krin Gabbard wrote: "Isn't there some value in writing this other history of jazz?"[107]

5

Crib Girls to Criminals

While prostitution was an integral part of American jazz scenes, the role of sex tourism as an economic and social factor in the development of jazz scenes has attracted little attention from traditional jazz historians. More often than not prostitution is relegated to the backdrop of the jazz scene by the authors of the jazz canon, and sex tourism is represented as an exotic factor of jazz scene life that was simply indicative of the vice of "wide-open" towns. While the best-known example of this marginalization of sex tourism is Storyville in New Orleans, such marginalization is also a factor in the master narrative of Kansas City's jazz scene. For example Driggs and Haddix discuss the red-light district of Kansas City's jazz scene sparingly, and describe it as a "brazen display of flesh in the large windows of the 'dreary flats' lining 14th Street."[1] These examples illustrate the subsumation of sex tourism, and its role in the economic and social production of jazz scenes, in the jazz canon. In Kansas City that meant that sex tourism was enclosed in the First and Second Wards, the center of the Pendergast world and the city's jazz scene. As seen in previous chapters, the contested territories of gender, sexuality, race, and class were the spaces of the Pendergast world. Sex tourism was not the backdrop to this world; it was an integral part of it. At the same time, while sex tourism was centered in the jazz scene, the efforts to criminalize prostitution in the twentieth century eventually led to the removal of sex tourism from the Kansas City story. The crib girls of the jazz world quickly became the criminals of a mythical underworld and were removed from the jazz story itself.

In the case of sex tourism and jazz scene sex districts, it is important to note that jazz scene cities often developed, encouraged, and exploited their sex districts as a way to draw in sex tourists. As Alecia Long demonstrated in her study of Storyville, New Orleans's reputation as a decadent city in the nineteenth century was exploited by city leaders for its economic advantages.[2] New Orleans became a site of "pleasure pilgrimage" where sex tourists traveled to trade in the commodities of sex districts: prostitution, racial mixing, and desire. In a move that signaled "modernity" prostitution became the backbone of commercial sexuality.[3] Enclosure was central to the success of sex tourism in jazz scene cities such as New Orleans. As the railroad's western terminus and the temporary home to hundreds of migrant, immigrant, and native workers of all classes, there is little doubt that Kansas City attracted plenty of tourists. Sex tourism, however, was a major draw. As part of the Pendergast world sex tourism was a constant source of income, business, and patronage for Pendergast, his machine, and the city of Kansas City. Enclosure and the creation of boundaries around sex work were a key factor in sex tourism in the jazz scene. This was not enclosure simply as a way of keeping "fallen women" policed: it was a method of enclosing sex tourism and therefore enacting a space for a socially sanctioned sex trade.

Sex tourism and sex workers played an important role in the development of Kansas City's jazz scene. The best-known prostitute in the Kansas City jazz scene was Annie Chambers, a brothel madam and famous city dweller. Chambers was linked with the Pendergast machine and worked for decades as the "mother" to hundreds of young rural and immigrant women who found themselves at Kansas City's Union Station. Despite her position in the jazz scene traditional jazz historians even represent Chambers in romanticized and background terms as a "colorful figure of the red light" and a "woman once widely known." Jazz historians often frame prostitution in that way: as a facet of the jazz scene separate from the music, liveliness, and "all that jazz." Prostitution is positioned, in the jazz canon, as a frequently mentioned but little discussed thread in the fabric of the "Jazz Age" backdrop. The common belief is that prostitution was important, but was not a direct influence on jazz scene life or the sounds later categorized as jazz music. The influential role of sex work and sex tourism in the jazz scenes of America, therefore, is not included in the official history of jazz. As this chapter will show, such representations of sex tourism and in Kansas City's jazz scene deny the important role that sex work played in the development, growth, and social formations of the jazz scene.

Kansas City existed in both urban and rural cultures, a western and eastern region, and such clashes of regional sensibilities are not prevalent in histories of prostitution. This is an extension of the problem created by traditional jazz historians, who insist that Kansas City was both an urban "wide-open" city on the road to New York and an isolated "southwestern" town where a jazz scene temporarily flourished. Kansas Citians did not see prostitution as simply a regional concern. For example Chief of Police Wentworth E. Griffin explained sex tourism to researcher Asa Martin with these words in 1913: "By reason of location and environment, Kansas City, Missouri, is confronted in its police work with conditions which have no parallel in any other inland city. Being the gateway for the entire West and Southwest, as evidenced by its size as a railway center, transient people in large numbers and for various causes are drawn here: a constant tide of emigration is passing through, and the criminal class comes with the throng."[4]

In the post-reform decades in Kansas City the popular belief was that prostitution had been eradicated, an opinion supported by historians of prostitution. Newspaper reports by historians in the 1940s and 1950s discussed the "former isolated zone" of the red-light district, in a false belief that the closing of downtown brothels was successful. It is clear, however, that jazz scene citizens in the city fully understood the relationship between the jazz scene and prostitution, and protected that relationship spatially. For instance Kansas City's Jazz District along Vine Street was traditionally a Republican stronghold. Henry McKissick was a ward boss for Casimir Welch in the Second Ward (bounded by Kansas City's Jazz District) who spoke at length about his "job" gathering votes and garnering support for Pendergast and his Democratic Party machine. Eventually the black vote in the Jazz District switched to Pendergast in order to protect both vice and Jazz District business.[5] There were fifty cabarets within the six blocks of Eighteenth and Vine, all of which catered to white middle-class "slummers" seeking a sexual encounter with the "other." It is clear, however, that city dwellers understood those areas as "deviant" due to their location. During his interview with Pearson and Litwak McKissick remembered: "[There was a red-light district] in my ward, [at] Fourteenth and Thirteenth, and Cherry and Holmes. I have always thought that [it was better to have prostitution concentrated in one area]."[6] McKissick's recollection clearly indicates that Pendergast and his leadership saw the enclosure of sex tourism as important. In Kansas City that meant that prostitution and jazz came to share the same spaces. Bennie Moten, leader of the Bennie Moten Orchestra and the first boss for such jazz greats as Count Basie and Eddie Barefield, started his career playing in Kansas City brothels where he "played mostly blues, because that's what people like. The gals, they always have a hang-up . . . feeling low."[7]

Like other jazz scene spaces sex tourism in Kansas City was inherently connected to contestations about race, gender, and economics. Prostitution was increasingly affiliated with racial mixing in the first half of the twentieth century.[8] Consequently a new racial taxonomy in this period likely affiliated African American and immigrant women with racial and ethnic inferiority. There were 128 brothels listed on Kansas City police fines lists in 1910 alone: 99 Caucasian "white houses," 22 African American "colored houses," and 7 with unlisted owners. It is unclear whether these houses were "white" and "colored" owned, or if that was simply an indicator of segregation among its workers and clientele. In addition there were 147 "assignation houses" in which rooms were available for rent for use by sex workers who found their clients on Kansas City streets.[9] The red-light district also revealed the city's continuing links to rural and western America. A 1910 survey of prostitutes found that one-third of Kansas City prostitutes were born in small towns, while only three percent were foreign born.[10] Since African American, immigrant, and poor white women inhabited the same city districts as the sex work district, the line between respectability and sex work was easily blurred by these changing discourses about race and sex work. Consequently sex workers likely depended on each other for social support denied to them in the larger hegemonic mainstream.

Though little information about Kansas City's red-light district survives, some details exist about the major brothels and madams of the city's pre–World War I period. As a railroad hub Kansas City inevitably developed a large and thriving red-light district controlled primarily by three women. Once the city's cribs and brothels became subject to municipal and state laws, the women of the "resorts" became targets for anti-vice Victorian reformers. The resulting clash with the Victorian elite did not destroy working-class women's labor or sexuality. In fact the events in Kansas City between 1880 and 1945 show that those Victorian upper-class moralists simply reasserted their control over sexuality by appropriating working-class city spaces and defining public sexual expression as "abnormal" according to regional values and laws. Kansas City's elite adopted the aspects of working-class sexuality they could reshape to their liking and successfully outlawed everything else.

Kansas City's urban elite was part of a national movement against the public display of working-class sexuality. With the advent of the Progressive Era, both evangelists and urban reformers considered mass amusements emblematic of declining morality and rising working-class anarchy.[11] Americans increasingly connected working-class leisure with immorality, especially with unregulated amusements. The biggest concern about leisure spaces was moral health, especially when it came to women and young people.[12] Urban reformers criticized mass amusements as a threat to public health, a danger that required both regulation and reform. Kansas Citians interested in amusement reform also discussed the danger of women seeking pleasure in the public sphere. According to one reformer working-class women in amusement spaces were a source of social danger. In his investigation of working-class girls the reformer wrote that he feared the cultural effect of "girls who were idling along, seeking some diversion, some amusement, girls who were loitering on the edge of that precipice over which so many fall to destruction."[13] Urban reformers often connected the immorality of theaters, movie houses, and amusement parks with prostitution and "fallen women." As Kevin Mumford explained, vice districts then became sites of commercial amusement, where working-class and African American women were commodities, not audiences.[14] Consequently, following the adoption of state laws and city ordinances governing most working-class leisure activities, all that remained for Kansas City's urban reformers to attack were the red-light districts.

This attack on sex work was particularly difficult to navigate for African Americans, both working-class women and men, who earned their incomes through the Kansas City's jazz scene spaces. African Americans were inherently criminal according to the city's white upper- and middle-class population, and when combined with the popular conception that African Americans were hypersexual, the policing and marginalization of African Americans in the city was likely the most stringent. Asa Martin, a Kansas City schoolteacher and graduate student, in 1913 undertook a study of Kansas City's African American population with the backing of the city's Board of Public Welfare. Martin was particularly focused on the study of African Americans as criminals. "Statistics show that the Negro is everywhere more criminal than the white man, and that his tendency towards crime increases," wrote Martin in 1913.[15] Using a 1911 report that the Kansas City Board of Police made to the Board of Public Welfare, Martin examined the role of prostitution in the increase of crime in Kansas City. According to Martin there were 957 arrests for running or owning a brothel in 1911; of those arrests 20 were African American men and 44 were African American women. In 1911 346 African American women were arrested for prostitution, compared to 471 white women, though Martin identified 834 white-owned and white-managed brothels in Kansas City.[16] How did Martin explain the "problem" of prostitution? Martin believed the root of the problem was race as a determinant of sex work among African American women. "The criminal tendency of Negro women, when compared with that either of white women or Negro men, is even more evident in city than State arrests," wrote Martin, "though there are less than one-tenth as many Negro women as white women."[17] Clearly the gendered aspects of Kansas City's jazz scene were inextricably linked to race.

Though Martin was obviously focused on the criminality of African American women, he was just as focused on the criminality of jazz scene spaces for African American men, specifically the saloon. Saloons were, as mentioned previously, a space for both leisure and survival in Kansas City's working-class districts. Different saloons catered to all racial and ethnic groups, giving men a homosocial atmosphere to socialize in and providing women with an outlet for income and assistance with anything from cooked meals to an assignation room for part-time crib girls. For Martin, however, the saloon represented the foundation of African American "race problems." As Martin wrote:

> The saloon is thus made the general loafing place for the idle Negro, where he spends his extra change, if he chances to possess any, endeavoring to satisfy his natural thirst for liquor or to display the appearance of wealth to his many friends gathered around him. If a canvass of all the Negro-pool halls, barber shops, and saloons were

made any evening between 7 and 10 o'clock, 1,800 or 2,000 Negro men would be found in them; and if the canvass were made on Saturday night, the number would probably exceed 3,000. . . . The hold the saloons now have upon the race as a whole, all go to make this [reform] a most difficult task—so much that any solution of the problem would require years of persistent labor with the proper application of the elevating agencies that might be thrown about him.[18]

Given all of these concerns about sex tourism, crime, class, and race, why did Kansas City reformers not try to simply eradicate prostitution? In addition to the moral zoning thought to defend "respectable" native-born white women, the enclosure of the red-light district led reformers to deal with other "problems" as a more immediate threat. First, defenders of Victorian American culture could see and criticize amusement parks and theaters because they were open to public view. Mass amusement advertisements appeared in newspapers and in public places, where upper-class reformers encountered them. Secondly, because prostitution was illegal the red-light districts of American cities supposedly did not exist. They were a part of an urban subculture that was out of sight to most people. Consequently mainstream Americans had little contact with the red-light culture, and those who did have knowledge of the red-light districts certainly never discussed their experiences in polite company. The blatant sexuality of red-light districts also slowed the bourgeois response. Open sexual expression was still suppressed in mainstream American culture.[19] Though mass amusements challenged the prevailing gender roles and moral codes at the turn of the century, sexuality remained a taboo subject. In urban red-light districts sexuality was recognized as a special context. In addition powerful women like Annie Chambers with political connections often controlled the establishments in red-light districts, and their connections to the economic success of the city and the city's Pendergast world gave them a certain level of protection from the incursion of reform.

Much of the force behind both life in the jazz scene and the written history that remains is the construction of sexuality. Kansas City's elite, and their counterparts in other American cities between 1880 and 1940, believed that sex as pleasure was inherently male-driven and acceptable only as a man's activity. Women were seen as reproductive, not sexual. During that period the diffusion of female sexual behavior from the wedding bed into mass amusements and social visibility resulted in a legal and moral "general policing of the gender order" in ways clearly differentiated by class and race.[20] The regulation and eradication of gender expressiveness in public amusements such as the red-light district affected both men and women, while keeping the dominant upper and middle classes in power. The class distinctions between urban white women and their working-class counterparts were a major factor in the marginalization of working-class women.[21] This marginalization included the control of working-class gender behavior in such public spaces as the red-light district.

For working-class white and African American women prostitution was much more complicated than reformers imagined. The transformation of American industry in the 1880s meant that working-class families could not survive on a single income. Single and widowed women could either marry or remarry, work in industry or domestic service, or become prostitutes.[22] These occupations were inherently sexualized as not "respectable" for women, and harassment, sexual objectification, and sexualization in the workplace was an everyday occurrence.[23] Just as the demand for prostitutes increased in the late nineteenth century, women were seeking some autonomy and economic security in the home by becoming part-time prostitutes known as "crib girls."[24] Upper-class women initially tolerated the rise of prostitution. According to Victorian moral codes prostitutes protected American wives from the male sex drive.[25] Though working-class women used prostitution as a source of income, moralistic reformers also explained prostitution as a product of inherently immoral working-class society.[26]

Of course upper-class women had little or no experience in red-light districts. Residents in red-light districts had their own commercial subculture with values and morals that outsiders hardly understood.[27]

KANSAS CITY'S WORLD OF SEX TOURISM

City Ordinance No. 291, which defined lewd behavior, was applied to everything from club entertainment to prostitution until the 1910s. Though this law existed it was seldom enforced. Numerous clubs, theaters, saloons, and brothels in Kansas City violated Ordinance No. 291. Kansas City civic leaders declined to close every saloon and brothel in town lest they offend workers and visiting businessmen. It seemed that Kansas City's economic success was largely supported by sex tourism in the city's red-light district and jazz spaces. An organized assault on the red-light districts developed in the 1900s. Increasingly reformers embraced movements to "purify" American life by ridding its cities of commercialized vice.[28] With accusations of the white enslavement of working-class girls, anti-prostitution movements appeared in tandem with park and movie house reform campaigns.[29] Along with their attacks on red-light districts reformers exhibited a sudden urge to "counterbalance the home" with various other establishments. Their efforts produced a series of seemingly disconnected reforms such as a 1914 regulation requiring Kansas City skating rinks to obtain official permits.[30] Civic reformers demanded public licensing of dancing and drinking establishments and the creation of censorship boards to control vice.[31] However these were all mass amusements, and urban reformers came to view the red-light districts as a "true form of evil." Located in the waterfront or tenement districts of a city, the bohemian red-light districts exemplified a more obvious threat to the purity of women and acceptable gender behavior.[32]

While Kansas City leaders certainly agreed with the avoidance of sexuality, they also depended on a public display of sexuality for good business. Kansas City was an important city in the 1880s, but it had not lost its "wild west" character. The city had a reputation for permissive behavior and was frequented by cattlemen and farmers who visited it on weekends in search of entertainment.[33] The city directory of 1878 listed eighty saloons—four times the number of city schools, libraries, and hospitals combined.[34] The key to Kansas City's success as a site of sex tourism was the railroad. Railroads were the cornerstone of the city's economic system, and as a railroad terminus Kansas City had national importance. The city's livestock and meatpacking industries attracted businessmen and investors as well as a large transient workforce.[35] Railroads brought seventy thousand people to Kansas City in 1869, the first year the Hannibal Bridge was open. Red-light districts were so named because of the red lights of railroad lanterns. During the development of Kansas City railroads train brakemen carried red signal lanterns to brothels during stops. By hanging the lantern on the brothel or crib door the brakemen were easily located in an emergency.[36] Prostitutes adopted the red railroad lanterns and hung them on their doorways when they were open for business.[37] Kansas City's red-light district was easy to find. "Crib girls," as part-time prostitutes were called in the 1880s, lived near the Levee in houses close to saloons or railroad tracks. Saloons were vital to life in red-light districts. Saloon owners frequently promoted or managed prostitution.[38] Owners built saloons near brothels to attract business and sometimes housed crib girls upstairs over their saloon. Boss Tom Pendergast had interests in prostitution and saloons in a manner similar to that of systems in other cities. For instance Pendergast owned at least two hotels where the availability of prostitution was an open secret. Pendergast simply paid a cut of the prostitution income payments to the city police.[39] Pendergast also protected other venues such as the all-nude Chesterfield Club in exchange for the club owner's agreement to purchase Pendergast liquor. In an effort to hide prostitution from Victorian sensibility city police allowed red-light districts to thrive without explicitly acknowledging the role of city leadership in keeping the districts alive. Saloon owners and madams paid police in return for such protection.[40] One Kansas City madam recalled her morning routine in the 1890s in an autobiography: "I always had plenty to do, getting the police and city hall cut of the night's take put in envelopes, inspecting the laundry with the housekeeper, the cleaning bills, replacing busted chairs, lamps, linens."[41] Kansas City's police essentially helped create the red-light district and punished saloon owners and madams only when they failed to make protection payments.[42] In this way Kansas City's elite derided and policed prostitution in certain districts and spaces but allowed it to flourish in order to protect the city's interests in sex tourism and its "wide-open" character. According to Fred Johnson, a Board of Public Welfare official who studied prostitution in 1911, the city's sex tourism was directly related to its geographical position as a railroad terminus and "wide-open" city.

> The houses of ill fame are the centers of infection that permeates all the territory which surrounds the city. Visitors from out of town are numerous. Some of them seek vice; to others when openly tolerated it is a source of morbid fascination. Not infrequently, as a result of his first visit, the country youth who has hitherto led a virtuous life will carry away with him a contagion which is poison not only to himself and family, but to the community in which he lives. Every convention or civic celebration which attracts visitors from outside the city brings an additional supply of men to swell the number of frequenters of these resorts. Nor can the evil influence which open toleration exerts on the youth of the city be overlooked. The high ideals which the teachings of home, church and school may have instilled in him receive a rude shock when he appreciates that his elders tolerate a system totally at variance with their teaching. Thrown into the abyss of temptation he is well worthy of commendation if possessed of sufficient moral stamina to remain pure.[43]

For Johnson and the reformers he represented, the indictment was clear. Kansas City's leaders were allowing sex tourism to continue while teaching their children that vice was criminal.

In order to maintain the facade of reforming prostitution while encouraging it as part of the city's tourist reputation, planners and leaders attempted to enclose sex tourism. Kansas City's red-light district was bounded by Second Street on the north, Main Street on the east, Sixth Street on the south, and May Street on the west. Those crib girls who were managed by a "madam" lived in female boarding houses called "resorts." By 1905 most resorts were located in the two-hundred block of West Fourth Street.[44] There were literally hundreds of resorts and cribs in the red-light district. Single women who simply put red lanterns on their doors ran some cribs. Other women worked in high-class resorts run by powerful and wealthy Kansas City women. The red-light district created $400,000 in Kansas City revenues each year.[45]

As Kansas City expanded south the red-light district expanded south along Main Street. Some of the better-known resorts and cribs on Main were Clara's Crib at 1801 Main and the Hotel Ester at 2035 Broadway. A crib at 1711 Walnut was called "The Irish Village" and catered mostly to Irish and German immigrants. Itinerant printer John Edward Hicks mentioned visiting several resorts or cribs in his memoirs. Hicks referred to the "high-priced beauties of Annie Chambers" and the "twenty-five cent crones at Lone Cottonwood."[46] Hicks's tour of the red-light district on one drunken evening took him to many cribs and resorts now forgotten. Hicks listed a series of what he termed "boarding houses": Mollie Paupaw's on West Fourth, Em Williams's on Third, Bessie Stevenson's on Broadway, Mollie O'Brien's at First and Main, "and the tent kept by the notorious Becky Ragan at the foot of Main Street."[47] Hicks also reported a sensational story he overheard about madam Jennie Armstrong "who kept a 'small place of sin' at Fifth and Bluff and got arrested for beating one of her three painted mermaids with the business end of a stovelifter."[48] These sensational stories added to the growing Victorian fear of the dangers of open female sexuality in Kansas City and to the city's titillating mystique as a site of sex tourism.

The most notorious and popular resorts in Kansas City were located in adjacent buildings in the two-hundred block of West Third and Fourth Streets. The madams of these three white resorts ran busy brothels that bore their names: Annie Chambers, Madame Lovejoy, and Eva Prince. One Kansas City reporter called these three resorts "the three most notorious houses of the kind in the 'red-light district.'"[49] A. B. McDonald also referred to the three resort owners as "the queens of the red-light" and mentioned that the "Salvation Army workers thereabout used to call them 'gilded palaces of sin.'"[50] Eva Prince's resort was located at 204 and 206 West Fourth Street. The Prince resort shared a wall with Madame Lovejoy's twenty-four rooms at 200 and 202 West Fourth Street.[51] The most famous of all these resorts was the house of Annie Chambers, a building at the southwest corner of Third and Wyandotte Streets just north of Lovejoy's.[52]

Reformers for social purity gained support in both public and government sectors after 1900. The growth of sexual reform was largely attributed to violence in the red-light districts. A lurid axe murder took place in 1880 when a rejected brothel customer murdered another customer in a crib at Nineteenth Street and Broadway.[53] In a report on New York's Tenderloin District a Kansas City reporter wrote of "girls who wearied of the monotony of rural life . . . and are frequently found by detective skill in the dens of infamy."[54] To combat crime associated with prostitution reformers and their government supporters classified prostitution as a crime. Special courts, police units, and correctional facilities were created especially for prostitutes.[55] The Kansas City Florence Crittenden Mission opened in the red-light district to rescue "fallen women." Social workers from Crittenden visited local saloons and dance halls to raise support for the mission.[56] Kansas City's Board of Public Welfare, the agency charged with managing correctional facilities, launched an investigation into the red-light district in

1910. Kansas City was one of forty-three cities that conducted formal vice investigations between 1900 and 1917.[57] Kansas City police were required to enforce new anti-vice laws. Consequently, and as discussed previously, 957 brothel owners and 471 prostitutes were arrested in 1911 alone.[58] The Board of Public Welfare appointed reformer Kate E. Pierson head of the Parole Department of Delinquent Women in 1910. Pierson managed women's jails, industrial work houses, and hospitals for prostitutes in Kansas City until 1912.[59] Board of Public Welfare investigators recommended new laws, increased arrests, and waged a "relentless warfare against the houses of prostitution."[60] As Board of Public Welfare investigator Fred Johnson stated in his 1910 study of Kansas City prostitutes: "The unprejudiced observer is convinced that no system of suppression can totally eliminate prostitution. First there must be a radical change in the amusements we tolerate, in public opinion, in our treatment of sex problems, in our economic system, in the attitude of the church, and in the teaching and influence of the home itself. As we have before noted, this evil is deep rooted."[61]

All of these brothels were the center of the city's "isolated zone," a red-light district centered in what is now Kansas City's downtown. As Mumford has explained, however, prostitution was not limited to the red-light district. Waitresses in jazz clubs and cabarets throughout the city were encouraged to turn tricks or work in underground sex shows.[62] It is likely that prostitution in the form of cribs and crib girls occurred all over the city, and certainly prostitution was a staple of life in the Jazz District. This was increased with the rise of the Pendergast machine in the Jazz District, a machine that ran prostitution and then funneled the proceeds into police protection and public works employment for blacks living in the district.[63] Little is written, however, about the effect that the sudden "reform" of prostitution had on the lived experience of working-class women engaged in sex work. As Kevin Mumford has proven, the *remapping of prostitution* shaped the lives of prostitutes and altered their lives in complex ways. Mumford explained that areas such as red-light districts "were in themselves complex social worlds, perhaps sites of cultural resistance, but certainly worthy of historical analysis."[64]

Of the few archival documents or records about prostitution in Kansas City only one seems to illuminate some aspects of prostitution according to the working women. As part of his 1911 study titled "The Social Evil in Kansas City" Board of Public Welfare official Fred Johnson published an informal survey of brothel madams and workers in Kansas City. Conducted by local pastors Rev. Frank Johnson and Dr. C. B. Miller, both members of the Board of Public Welfare board of directors, the survey data was collected from interviews of approximately 450 Kansas City sex workers.[65] Though the survey data is raw it provides an interesting window on the lives of Kansas City's workers in the sex tourism industry. For instance approximately half of the workers interviewed were married. One-third began working as prostitutes in their own homes, while only fifty-four worked in brothels.[66] The Johnson-led study also includes information that illuminates the race-differentiated aspects of prostitution in Kansas City during the early years of the jazz scene. While nearly one-third of the white women interviewed had worked in hotels or restaurants before working in prostitution, thirty-nine of the fifty-six African American women interviewed had worked as domestic labor. A large percentage of white women reported that they were introduced to prostitution through dancing or betrayal, while most African American women interviewed replied that they were "coaxed" into prostitution.[67] At the same time, however, much of the survey data belies shared concerns that crossed racial lines. For instance the women interviewed overwhelmingly stated that they *chose* prostitution in order to bring an income into their household after marriage, and regardless of race most of the women interviewed made four to six dollars per week.[68] In such a limited body of evidence the survey provides some insight into the backgrounds and concerns of women in Kansas City's sex tourism industry.

Unlike information from sex workers there is much in the written record by reformers about their reform movements against prostitution and how those reformers saw the "world" of prostitution. By the year 1900 reformers, who began to use the medical discourse of sexologists, classified prostitutes as sexual deviants.[69] The moral classification of prostitution led to "social purity" crusades intended to reform sexuality. Social purity reformers described prostitution as the result of working-class urban culture, often specifically African American and immigrant women.[70] In an effort to describe prostitution as a "social evil" reformers created a market for published memoirs of prostitutes as a form of education for urban women.[71] Interestingly enough, in this move to prove prostitution as a deviant practice in need of elimination the reformers created a record of the social worlds of prostitutes. At the same time, the reformers created a body of literature that described the sex tourism in American cities in voyeuristic and erotic terms. Such texts likely increased interest in red-light districts rather than proved the need for their elimination. Though little exists in written history about the lives of Kansas City's madams and crib girls, one first-hand account was published by social purity reformers in 1919. *Madeleine, an Autobiography* was the memoir of a prostitute who worked in the cribs of the Midwest. Though the publication of *Madeleine* was sponsored by reformers, according to historian Ruth Rosen *Madeleine* is one of the few memoirs whose details were later substantiated.[72] Madeleine worked in Kansas City in the late nineteenth century as a crib girl in Laura Lovejoy's brothel on West Fourth Street. Lovejoy's was known as the "Old Ladies Home" because the clientele was mostly local older men.[73] When she was seventeen Madeleine arrived at Lovejoy's after leaving Chicago because of illness. Though she had worked in brothels before, Madam Lovejoy insisted on interviewing Madeleine about her life and family. Madeleine was then given "'working clothes' and sent to the parlor to entertain a regular."[74] She worked at Lovejoy's for over a year before moving west. Madeleine described red-light life in Kansas City: "Red-light segregation was a name only, not a fact. . . . Vice flourished in all parts of the city; wine rooms were wide open for anyone having the price of a drink; private houses and assignation houses abounded—and the roadhouses ran full blast for twenty-four hours a day."[75]

Though most of Madeleine's memoir discussed Kansas City only briefly, it is clear from her memoir that the enclosure of the red-light district was not as successful as reformers imagined. Madeleine remembered the camaraderie among the women in the brothel, and explained late in the memoir that her life as a prostitute was not as damaging as reformers would lead the reader to believe.

ANNIE CHAMBERS, QUEEN OF THE RED LIGHT

Madeleine's short memoir about Kansas City reveals some information about the life of a working prostitute; there are limits on the information available about sex workers in Kansas City's jazz scene. Most of the information about prostitution in Kansas City lies in the story of a single brothel madam. Annie Chambers is probably the most famous madam in Kansas City history. She was born Leannah (last name unknown) in Kansas and was married as a young girl to a man named Loveall. In 1869 the Lovealls came to Kansas City, where they settled north of the Missouri River. However, when her husband died Leannah was forced to earn a living. She opened a resort in the Loveall home north of the river and welcomed visitors who came across the river by ferry.[76] Mrs. Loveall then changed her name to Annie Chambers and moved her resort to Kansas City in 1871. She met and married William Kearns, a bartender and gambler from the West Bottoms, but retained the name Chambers professionally. The resort house at Third and Wyandotte was built with Chambers's own money and completed according to her instructions. From the beginning the Chambers house was a brothel.[77] The Chambers brothel, with stained glass walls and a tiled entrance bearing Annie Chambers's name, operated daily until 1913. During a conversation with a missionary couple in 1924 Chambers defended her resorts as the only place where her girls could count on being safe and in control. As she told a newspaper reporter, Chambers told the young couple: "People think women of my sort are hard-hearted, but we have hearts, too, and sometimes they melt in sorrows. But we hide it from the world, for our business requires us to put on a gay front."[78]

How much of Chambers's interview was a performance of respectability, and how much was a performance of sex work? Her personal history indicates that she was a businesswoman first, and a strong factor in the Pendergast world and its dependence on sex tourism. For the wider public Chambers seemingly represented herself as a sad, tortured yet innocent woman, hardened by her years in "our business." Inside the Pendergast world it would seem more likely that she would worry about tourists first. These two worlds collided for Chambers in 1921, when her "hard-hearted" world clashed with the Victorian morality of the hegemonic mainstream. According to scholars Ryan and Hall sex tourism "presents an opportunity for people, male and female, to exploit their marginal status and their economic power to cross the line between the licit and illicit boundaries between the socially sanctioned and the 'socially suspect.'"[79] Chambers crossed the boundary of red-light district enclosure and used her marginal status to challenge the very nature of sex tourism and its reform.

The story of Annie Chambers represents a fascinating example of the complex social worlds of Kansas City's prostitutes and the ways in which red-lights served as sites of resistance and worldmaking. Chambers never shied away from attention in local newspapers and was anything but reticent about her work. She persisted in spite of the anti-prostitution campaign and successfully operated her resort again from 1913 through 1924, at times with the backing of Boss Pendergast. Progressive attacks against the resorts of the red-light district began in 1913. Chambers was called to appear before the newly formed all-male Society for the

Prevention of Commercialized Vice in November 1913.[80] The society was run by Kansas City's elite: the judges for both city courts, the pastor of the city's leading church, police chief Griffin, and Jackson County prosecutor Cameron Orr. When she appeared at the society's meeting in 1913 she spoke to the membership about the reform movement and the city's plan to eradicate the red-light district. The *Kansas City Journal* published Chambers's speech in full. Chambers expressed her view of the world of prostitution in the city: "When they come to us they have no place else to go. Their parents have turned against them, the church gives them no welcome, their friends spurn them and society kicks them further down. They are sick, heartbroken and weary and tell us if we do not admit them it will be either the river or poison. We do not send for them. It is the haven of the last resort when the whole world has cast them off."[81]

Chambers urged the society to stop its push to close the red-light district and suggested it would have an effect opposite to its intent. Chambers asked for the society to return to the system of fines for prostitutes that was stopped in 1912, and hoped that the society would them give some of the fines to build a women's reformatory rather than the "workhouse" that was in operation. When Chambers told the society that her girls were now dispersed around the city, the members asked her where they were. "You could not help them if you did [know where they were]. They would not accept a cent from this or any other organization. They'd die first."[82] Chambers then left the group with one parting sentence: "I am awfully sorry that this thing has gotten into politics."[83] According to the report about the meeting: "While admitting freely that the advice to 'begin at the beginning' was good and should be followed as far as possible, the committee did not take the rest of the talk seriously."[84]

One interesting aspect of Chambers's speech, and one that tells much about the actual mapping of prostitution, is her concern about plans for an injunction against brothels. According to the society meeting report,

Chambers said that injunctions "prevented the sale of it [property] if one chose. All insurance has been canceled, she said [Chambers] and thieves now run rife in the district. The casting aside carelessly of but one match, she said [Chambers], and all would be gone."[85] A month after Chambers's appearance the society pressured Kansas City's mayor to sign an injunction against "bawdy houses" under the explanation that prostitution was a public nuisance. The injunction briefly closed the Chambers resort in 1913, and Chambers herself was arrested and jailed.[86] The society secured injunctions against fifty brothels in 1913, closed their doors, and forced their residents onto the streets of the city.[87] Chambers refused to accept the ruling by city officials and reopened her house against city ordinance. In an act of overt resistance Chambers took the Jackson County prosecutor to the Supreme Court of Missouri seeking the return of her livelihood.

Kansas City's Society for the Prevention of Vice successfully pressured the state government for a nuisance law against brothels in 1921. The Act of 1921 prohibited the maintenance of "all buildings, erections, room and places, and the ground itself in or upon such bawdyhouse, assignation house, or place of prostitution is conducted."[88] According to the act, any county prosecuting attorney could "abate and perpetually enjoin" houses of prostitution and temporarily close the brothels for whatever period of time city officials deemed appropriate.[89] Jackson County prosecuting attorney Cameron Orr initiated a raid at the Chambers house in June 1921, only three months after the law passed. Orr was encouraged to raid the Chambers home by another city prosecuting attorney, William B. C. Brown. Brown was a Harvard-educated lawyer and one of the founders of the Society for the Prevention of Vice.[90] Kansas City police entered the Chambers house at 3:00 p.m. on June 29. According to police testimony there were ten women and two men in the brothel. Police found one girl hiding under a bed and another standing on the roof attempting to escape capture.[91] One police witness testified in 1921:

Q: When you got upstairs, what did you find up there?

A: Found several girls in the rooms with silk garments on and different colors.

Q: Bright?

A: Bright colors, yes, and in one room we found a man and a woman. This man was on the bed in his B.V.D.'s and this girl didn't have anything on but a teddybear.[92]

Following the raid Orr ordered the brothel closed for two months, and Annie Chambers was jailed until December. It was the first time in its history that Chambers's brothel had remained closed for more than a single day (Chambers's house closed for one day only upon her arrest in 1913). Orr successfully prosecuted Chambers in Jackson County Circuit Court and secured a permanent abatement for the infamous bawdyhouse. Throughout her incarceration and the abatement of her property Chambers insisted that she simply ran a boardinghouse and that she had not run a brothel in her home since the passage of Missouri's White Slave Act in 1913. Chambers was not prosecuted under her working name. Instead Kansas City's prosecutors filed against Leannah Kearns, a name she had not used since 1869.

Chambers, however, did not give up easily. She reopened her home as a "boardinghouse" for railroad workers and homeless women in late 1923. She appealed her case to the Missouri Supreme Court in 1924, where she successfully argued that "keeping a bawdy house is not a public nuisance in any sense of the term."[93] Before the state supreme court Chambers's lawyer J. Francis O'Sullivan argued that the 1921 act violated his client's Fifth and Fourteenth Amendment rights. In response Jackson County prosecutors Cameron Orr and Society for the Suppression of Commercialized Vice officer Leslie Lyons said the injunction was legal because the Chambers house caused immorality. As prosecutors Orr and Lyons stated: "Said defendant was, on said date, using said premises and property, furniture and equipment therein, for the purpose of keeping and harboring lewd, immoral, and lascivious women therein, and permitting and requiring said women so harbored therein, to receive and entertain men in rooms in said house and building for the purposes of unlawful sexual intercourse, assignation, and prostitution, and for immoral purposes and conduct. . . . [The brothels] are nuisances, and should be enjoined and abated, as prayed for in plaintiff's first amended petition."[94]

Along with the testimony of police officers and prosecutor Orr himself, the testimony of Annie Chambers was read for supreme court justices. Chambers stated for the record that she paid Kansas City police protection payments for forty years. Chambers testified that she paid weekly fines at the court clerk's office, and occasionally a uniform officer was sent to her home to collect the payments.[95] One witness was Kansas City police captain Frank H. Anderson, who patrolled Chambers's neighborhood for thirty-five years. When asked if anyone ever told him the Chambers house was a brothel, Anderson replied that "they didn't need to tell me."[96] The supreme court read Chambers's circuit court testimony into the record. Prosecutor Lyons questioned Chambers about her life as a madam during the Jackson County trial. When Annie Chambers was asked if she ran a bawdyhouse, she replied: "Not that I know of."[97] Chambers then told the court that her brothel closed at the date of her first arrest in 1913. According to Chambers she closed due to a "kind of wave or something . . . that drove them all out." When asked if that wave was the Society for Prevention of Commercialized Vice controlled by W. C. Brown, Chambers replied, "Yes."[98]

The Missouri Supreme Court found in favor of Chambers and remanded the decision of the Jackson County court. The decision of the court did not find Chambers innocent of running a brothel. However the justices did agree that the Act of 1921 was not entirely legal. "So much of the judgement as constitutes a perpetual injunction upon the defendant against using the premises, in the maintenance of a bawdyhouse, should be affirmed," wrote Justice Lindsay, "and so much of it as closes the premises against any use whatsoever should be reversed."[99] Chambers returned to Kansas City and opened her house to working-class boarders and former prostitutes.

With the closure of its high-profile brothels, Kansas City's underground urban culture was driven further from public view. What happened to the crib girls of Kansas City's red-light district is unknown. However the reporters and reformers of Kansas City carefully recorded the end of the three "queens of the red-light." These three paragons of Kansas City prostitution were watched, reported, and photographed as proof of the end of prostitution in the city. Shortly after the injunction law closed the resorts in 1921 Rev. David Bulkley moved to Kansas City to build a mission for the rehabilitation of drunkards and released criminals. Bulkley arranged for the purchase of the Madame Lovejoy house by coffee wholesaler Frank Ennis in the 1930s. "It had been vacant for years," wrote *Kansas City Star* reporter A. B. MacDonald, "ever since the moral revolution had wiped out the segregated district of this city."[100] Ennis then rented the Lovejoy house to Reverend Bulkley as the first building of the City Union Mission. Bulkley, along with his wife and young daughter, moved into the Lovejoy house and opened its doors to reform "fallen men."[101] As MacDonald wrote: "And in the room of Madame Lovejoy, on the first floor, with the trap door through which she used to draw up wine and other liquors from the iced troughs in the cellar, Dave [Bulkley] and his wife and daughter set up housekeeping."[102]

The resort next door to Madame Lovejoy's, the house of Eva Prince, was still in operation when Bulkley opened the City Union Mission. "Next door to the west was the old Eva Prince house," wrote MacDonald, "yet filled with women of the underworld, the very scum of it."[103] According to MacDonald the fall of the Prince house began there with the death of a "baby of the underworld," an illegitimate child of one of Prince's prostitutes. The mother appealed to Bulkley and his wife for help, so the baby's funeral was held in the old parlor of the Lovejoy house. The crib girls of Prince's sat on the steps and in the windows of the Lovejoy house to listen to the service. At the back of the Lovejoy house an elderly Annie Chambers opened her kitchen window to listen to the service. Shortly after the funeral Eva Prince agreed to lease the Prince resort to Bulkley as an addition to the City Union Mission.[104] Eventually Prince sold the house to the Bulkleys for $2,000 and a promise from Dave Bulkley that the house would be used as a home for wayward girls.

The funeral and the sale of the Prince house led Chambers to build a relationship with the Bulkley family. She became friends with Mrs. Bulkley and even lent Mrs. Bulkley her famous Alaskan seal coat for a trip to lectures at the Moody Bible Institute in Chicago.[105] Chambers did not, however, leave her work as a madam behind. Her home became a "halfway house" for young women in the city. Chambers ran the home with Murray Darling, an African American laborer and husband of Chambers's deceased longtime personal maid. Beginning in 1932, right after the court decision, Chambers began to give tours of her famous home. The house became a stop on "slumming tours" of the then dead red-light homes and other sites of prostitution, targeting upwardly mobile white couples as the tourists. As Kevin Mumford has explained, slumming was a part of sex tourism that provided access to "forbidden desires."[106] This was certainly the case for tourists at the Chambers home, who clearly came from upper- and middle-class Kansas City families. Reporter W. G. Secrest described the tour attendees as "well dressed men and women, husbands and wives" who knew Chambers as a "name familiar to people of these parts for more than a half a century, albeit a name mentioned only with extremest care in polite mixed company."[107] Chambers allowed tourists to freely examine every room of the home, telling stories of the girls who worked in the gilded bedrooms. As Secrest wrote of one tourist visit: "Paintings of nude women, which 'Miss Annie' classifies as art, hang from a moulding near the ceiling. . . . The rooms of 'her girls' are located on the second floor of the rambling, old brick structure. These also were visited by

her new class of patrons."[108] Eventually Chambers gave such tours of
the house every Tuesday and Thursday, since the house was rented as
a nightclub the rest of the time.[109]

Throughout her tours and her public appearances in the 1930s Chambers talked about her friendship with the Bulkley family. Shortly before
Chambers died in 1935 she willed her house to the Bulkley mission with
the stipulation that it be used to assist women in need.[110] In addition
Chambers required that Murray Darling be allowed to stay in the house
and supplied with a monthly stipend. The red-light district, which
once helped women in need earn a living, became a home for religious
reform and urban missionary work. While it might be expected that
the remapping and spatial identification of prostitution in the red-light
district would end with Chambers's death, it did not. Chambers home
was never used as a halfway house for women, as she requested in her
will. The Bulkleys used it intermittently as a flop house for railroad
workers, and Murray Darling continued to live there in a padlocked
room on the second floor. Upon Reverend Bulkley's death in 1940 his
widow and Chambers's friend Beulah Bulkley went before the circuit
court to have the Chambers home razed. While Mrs. Bulkley tried to
sell the house and land to a local truck company she was stopped by
an injunction placed by Murray Darling. According to Darling Chambers was coerced into giving the house and furnishing to the Bulkleys.
The court found, however, that Darling had no claim to the home or
its furnishings; he was forced onto the street and died in 1950. The
Chambers home was razed to the ground in 1943 and all remaining
rubble hauled off the old lot in 1946. As one reporter wrote in 1963:
"Today no hint of the 'scarlet' corner remains. Bare concrete covers
the corner where Kansas City's most notorious 'resorts' were located
and it serves as a truck terminal."[111]

Chambers, and with her the history of jazz scene prostitution in
Kansas City, was excavated once more in Kansas City's history of the
city's public spaces. The most famous painting in Chambers's brothel

CRIB GIRLS TO CRIMINALS

was a nearly seven-foot-tall oil painting of a nude woman. It hung in her entry parlor for forty years. Sometime in the 1920s, likely during her court cases against Jackson County, Chambers gave the painting to her pharmacist for storage at his store at 1408 Grand. Unable to hang the painting in his store, the pharmacist placed it in storage. It was rediscovered during an estate sale. The painting was cleaned and restored in the 1960s, where it found its way onto the walls of a bar and nightclub in Kansas City's Plaza shopping district. The painting was featured as the centerpiece of a wall "crowded with paintings, pastels, watercolors and drawings of nude women."[112] Decades after her crusade against anti-prostitution movements, Chambers was reduced to a nude on a nightclub wall.

That Chambers's image later became a symbol of female sexuality hanging on the wall is analogous to the representation of sex workers and sex tourism in traditional jazz history. Sex workers are reduced to wallpaper, interesting and colorful backgrounds for the master narrative. The world of sex tourism in Kansas City's jazz scene, however, was more than just a backdrop. It represented a zone of sexual commodification, a front line of economic power, and a clear example of the role of identification in Kansas City's jazz scene spaces. The experimentations with gender behavior and boundaries among sex tourists and sex workers created a new list of gendered identities: homosexual men, prostitutes, lesbians, strippers, New Women, and independent single men and women. The power of sexual division remained, but new gender divisions altered the popular understanding of sexuality and acceptability. These changing ideas about gender, sexuality, and respectability were not analogous or ancillary to the jazz scene. Sex tourism, and the challenges it represented to changing mainstream definitions, were an integral part of the jazz scene.

6

Queering Dante's Inferno

When the 1980 exhibition "Goin' to Kansas City" premiered it included in one section a black- and-white photograph of a performer known as "Mr. Half-and-Half." The photograph has since been reproduced in Pearson's *Goin' to Kansas City*, as well as the Kansas City Jazz website "Paris of the Plains," administered by Chuck Haddix. Both Pearson and Haddix point to this single photograph as evidence of gender, sexuality, and changing identities in Kansas City during its jazz heyday. It was this photograph that inspired me to study jazz spaces in Kansas City. I found the photograph in the Pearson book and followed it (like other scholars before me) as though it were a map to a history of queerness in Kansas City's jazz scene. While I was taking part in Christopher Nealon's search for myself in those moments, I also found a veritable goldmine of information about the jazz scene in Kansas City. I went on to transcribe the interview that Edna Mintirn and her daughter Ida Mintirn, the original owners of the photograph of "Mr. Half-and-Half," did with Pearson and Litwak in 1980. I was later informed about a collection of scrapbooks that included photographs of female impersonators from the 1920s and 1930s in Kansas City. I volunteered at the Spencer Library on the campus of the University of Kansas to complete a guide and finding aid for this collection. During my volunteer work cataloging the scrapbook collection I was surprised to turn a page and find the original photograph of "Mr. Half-and-Half." These were the scrapbooks and ephemera of Edna Mae Jacobs—mistakenly identified by Pearson and Litwak as Edna Mintirn.

While well-known jazz performers lived and worked in Kansas City during the jazz scene, little information exists about those performers who did not achieve even local fame. Thousands of house band musicians, territory players, vaudeville and burlesque dancers, and table singers worked throughout Kansas City, but they seldom appear in the official history of jazz as more than the background or opening act for the development of jazz as music. Edna Mae Jacobs, in many ways, is an exception to that dearth of information.[1] Jacobs appears in the city's collected archival records in two forms. The first is the interview completed in 1980 by Pearson and Litwak. The second source of Jacobs's narrative is a collection of her personal papers, donated to the Spencer Research Library at the University of Kansas in 1997. The Jacobs papers include Jacobs's own scrapbooks and mementos, clippings and matchbooks from the many clubs in which she performed across the United States, and photographs of the female impersonators at Kansas City clubs such as Dante's Inferno. These photographs and scrapbooks represent the collected memories of a cabaret singer and working-class white woman in Kansas City's jazz scene, and include a wealth of information on the previously ignored history of gender identity and expression in Kansas City. Given the seeming importance of these collections to an understanding of Kansas City's jazz scene, why is Edna Jacobs completely excluded from the written history of the jazz scene in Kansas City? How did a single photograph from her collection become representative of an entire category of jazz scene performance, while evidence of her world was subsumed?

The answer to that question lies in Jacobs's personal history. Jacobs worked as a table singer and waitress, and later as a club owner and manager, in Kansas City. She was not, according to the jazz canon, worthy of attention. The jazz canon, with its emphasis on the skill of famous male musicians and their ascension to New York's avant-garde, makes no attempt to include entertainers such as table singers. According to Nathan Pearson table singers were "usually working girls" (meaning prostitutes), and therefore not as important as the musicians and bands of Kansas City "Jazz."[2] In fact, of the 123 interviews completed by Pearson and Litwak, only two were done with performers who worked primarily as singers. Both were female: Edna Jacobs and Myra Taylor. Taylor, however, was a featured singer with the Harlan Leonard band and later gained national and international fame as a recording artist; according to Pearson she was a "vocalist."[3] Edna Jacobs is not listed as a vocalist at all, even though some of the Pearson biographical sketches of interview subjects list "vocals" as one of their skills. According to Pearson Jacobs was a "singer, dancer, and entertainer."[4] Driggs and Haddix discuss Taylor in more detail, listing her as" "a vocalist and entertainer."[5] According to Driggs and Haddix Taylor began her career as a singer and dancer in the Sunset and Reno clubs.[6] In their discussion of Taylor, however, this early work as a table singer and dancer was both temporary and important only for the training ground it provided Taylor for her later success. Given these examples it seems clear that in the jazz canon table singing and dancing were not "real jazz," and therefore did not deserve the attention of jazz historians. This also seems connected to the denial of gender and sexuality in the master narrative of jazz, if table singers could be explained into the unvisible simply by marking those singers as prostitutes.

The jazz canon practice of marginalizing table singers and dancers is what caused Edna Jacobs's story to be dominated by the master narrative. After the death of her friend and grandmother-in-law Edna Jacobs, Kansas Citian Donna Wilson contacted the American Jazz Museum and Hall of Fame about the possible donation of Jacobs's scrapbooks, costumes, and photographs. Representatives of the American Jazz Museum turned Wilson down on the grounds that Jacobs was "not famous enough."[7] Five years later, when I arrived at the Western

Historical Manuscripts Collections repository to listen to Jacobs's 1980 interview, the curator offered to find a tape of someone more famous. In the scrapbooks were the memories and mementos of a working-class woman, a jazz performer, a Kansas City native, and someone who seemingly represented a challenge to representations of gender and sexuality in Kansas City's jazz scene. How did all of those seemingly disparate events come together? After decades of storage and misidentification, how did the memories of Edna Jacobs, both in recorded interview and personal papers, come together over me? More importantly, how did Jacobs's photograph gain jazz canon fame, while Jacobs was herself subsumed by the canon?

The answers to those questions lie in the biography and memories of Edna Jacobs herself. Jacobs was a white working-class table singer, and on the surface does not represent any great challenge to the mainstream social order of the time. Clearly Jacobs considered her scrapbooks and memories important enough to keep and recollect for interviewers long after her career was over. Despite their vital personal connections, however, the sources still present a difficult test for researchers. While Jacobs's scrapbooks are interesting and important in terms of visual record, we have very little written information. Her 1980 interview was shaped as much by the preferences of her interviewers and her daughter Ida Mintirn as by Edna herself, who suffered from Alzheimer's disease at the time of the interview. It is clear from the interview tape that the collected group viewed the scrapbooks while Edna spoke in 1980, but no discussion of the photographs exists on the tape. The importance of these documents, and of Edna's life, lies not in the face value of the documents themselves. It lies in the unspoken *unvisible* aspects of gender and jazz in Kansas City included in the interstitial spaces of their pages and words.

According to Avery Gordon hypervisibility (where there is no distinction between presence and absence) leads to *unvisibility*: the presence of a true lack of the visible.[8] It is this unvisible space in the history of the Kansas City jazz scene that Edna Jacobs inhabits: always there in every reproduction of the "Mr. Half-and-Half" photograph, but always in its shadow. Edna Jacobs lurks in these shadows of the jazz scene, her experience neither explicit nor entirely lost, but subsumed in a process of jazz historicization and awaiting an encounter with recovery. Jacobs and her memories represent what Avery Gordon called *cultural blindness*, an aspect of cultural fear that leads to the ignorance of all but the most official knowledges.[9] This chapter is an attempt to write the story of this ghost and to deal with its desires. It is an attempt to answer Edna, to write her into the present, and to analyze the forces of historiography and discursive formation that rendered her unvisible. Avery Gordon, who also attempted to answer a ghost, wrote this on ghostly desires: "In order to manage this 'remembering which seems unsure,' it will be necessary to broach carefully and continuously the desires of the ghost itself. The ghost's desires? Yes, because the ghost is not just the return of the past of the dead. The ghostly matter is that always 'waiting for you,' and its motivations, desires, and interventions are remarkable only for being current."[10]

The "motivations, desires, and interventions" of the ghostly matters raised by researching Edna Jacobs in the present are directly connected to the spatialization of both her life and her memories. Jacobs lived in Kansas City's largest working-class district, the West Bottoms. Her recollections of growing up in the West Bottoms reveal that she identified strongly with the West Bottoms as a site of economic and class struggle. She later worked in Dante's Inferno, one of the city's most well-known female impersonator cabarets. The bits and pieces of Jacobs's biography and memories comprise the ghostly matters that help illuminate the ways that spaces such as Dante's were identified with specific groups in the city's jazz scene. These memories and connections are important, however, for what they haunt about the current. Within Jacobs's story is the discursive formation of spaces and the role that official knowledges played in silencing those not considered important to the "official" history of the jazz scene. By reducing Jacobs's work and life as a table singer to a single photograph the jazz canon essentially subjugated knowledges of table singers and dancers, Dante's Inferno, and the everyday life of a jazz scene performer in Kansas City's Pendergast world. By inviting Jacobs's work and life as a table singer to haunt that history, we can disturb the representations of "Jazz Age" gender, class, race, sexuality, and space seen so often in the jazz canon.

A BIOGRAPHY OF EDNA MAE JACOBS

Though her exact birthdate is unknown Edna Mae Whithouse was likely born in 1905 or 1906. She told Pearson and Litwak in 1980 that she was born "in the Indian Territory of Oklahoma" and came to Kansas City with her mother and younger brother upon the death of her father.[11] Edna's father was a religious singer who evidently recorded songs on wax cylinders before his death.[12] Young Edna and her family moved to the city to be near their maternal grandmother, a widow who lived at 2911 Gillham Street, a house in Kansas City's West Bottoms District. Home to meat packing houses, railroad yards, and factories, the West Bottoms was the center of Kansas City's overcrowded tenements for the working-class population, whether white, black, or immigrant.[13] Because the West Bottoms was the city's industrial center its tenements primarily housed newly arrived native and European immigrant packinghouse workers, along with most of the city's African American population.[14] Edna Jacobs moved to Kansas City with her family in the early 1900s and lived in a five-room canvas tent home in the Bottoms as a child.[15] The West Bottoms, because of its concentration of working-class and racially marginalized people, was often the site of labor disputes. Kansas City reformers, in fact, struggled with residents in the West Bottoms throughout the early 1900s and into the jazz scene. While it was not the only clash, one labor strike in the First Ward was particularly violent. Kansas City's upper- and middle-class residents often sent their cleaning to steam laundries, where women and girls worked in 120-degree temperatures for $4.50 a week.[16] By comparison, as previously noted, women working in prostitution could expect to make up to eight dollars a week. In late 1917, demanding an eight-hour workday and better pay, the laundry workers at Minger Laundry on Twelfth Street (in the heart of the Jazz District) tossed laundry bundles into the street and burned them.[17] As the strike gained support women strikers began to vandalize city laundry trucks. A Walker Laundry truck was pushed over Cliff Drive, the city's most famous and elite block of homes. An attack on a Silver Laundry truck at Seventeenth and Cherry resulted in the death of a non-striking laundry guard.[18] Eventually twenty-six thousand union members in Kansas City went on strike in support of laundry workers. Working class–owned movie houses, breweries, and saloons in the First Ward closed in support as well.[19] The strike lasted nearly six months, causing shutdowns and economic hardship across the city. Edna Jacobs, who was an eleven-year-old girl when the strike occurred, recalled the ways in which it affected her West Bottoms family. "When we lived at 2911 Gillham and the strike was on it was really, really hard times. . . . They wanted you to pick all up any kind of metal. Screws, nuts, and bolts, anything. We got ten cents a pound for it, little brother and I with that wagon [a childhood wagon]."[20]

Edna Jacobs lived and worked in Kansas City during the preeminence of the Pendergast-controlled machine. The spatial control of race, gender, sexuality, and popular amusement in Kansas City was integral to the Pendergast machine. Edna Jacobs's life reveals that contested spatial territory that the residents of the First and Second Wards navigated as part of the Pendergast world, especially Pendergast's reliance on segregation. For instance, when interviewers Pearson and Litwak asked Jacobs if Dante's Inferno allowed African Americans at the tables, Jacobs replied that club owners "didn't like colored people in there." She also remembered spending after-hours time in the Sunset Club and the Subway Club, two African American clubs that often appear in the jazz canon as sites of performances by Kansas City's jazz greats.

"Oh yeah!" Jacobs told interviewers. "We'd always have to go some-place and wind down. We'd go down to Niggertown and watch them jam. Oh boy."[21] Jacobs saw herself as a West Bottoms native but also as a white person. Though she worked in jazz spaces all over the city, Jacobs evidently also went "slumming" in the Jazz District. Was Jacobs "slumming" though, or was she following the popular identification of that area of the Jazz District? After all, Jacobs does mention "winding down." What pressures caused Jacobs to need to "wind down"?

Due largely to Pendergast's segregation rules, this alignment of vice in working-class and racial minority neighborhoods followed the mainstream codes of morality in the Kansas City. First Ward constituents like Edna Jacobs were perceived as deviant, although most patrons of vice districts in the city came from outside the wards. At the same time, Jacobs saw herself as superior to African Americans in the First Ward. The result was a double-edged life for people in the Pendergast world. While vice brought money and employment to the Pendergast wards, it also brought violence, sexual objectification, and an aura of exoticism to African American and working-class city dwellers. The income and control that First and Second Ward city dwellers and their Pendergast patrons gained from the jazz scene came at the cost of racial segregation and the objectification of working-class women across racial lines.

Another example of the role of segregation in the Pendergast world, and Edna Jacobs's place in that world, is in her memories of African American jazz clubs. While clubs such as the Chesterfield served white patrons, another group of clubs operated for African American patrons. Most African American music lovers listened to jazz at cabarets such as the Sunset and Subway clubs along Highland Avenue in Little Tammany.[22] The African American Cherry Blossom Club was the home of Count Basie, and included a "no whites" policy to protect its female customers from slumming whites.[23] While Edna Jacobs remembered these clubs, her perspective was clearly that of a white woman. Jacobs recalled feeling welcome in African American clubs she visited after a night's work, and she told interviewers that she never felt endangered. Jacobs, however, also stated that while she knew musicians and cooks she was not friends with any of the African Americans in the clubs. In fact Jacobs remembered the Subway as "rowdy" and the Reno as a "dump." Her greatest recollection of the African American clubs was the availability of marijuana. "I never smoked a stick in my life," Jacobs told Pearson and Litwak, "but you'd breathe it. You'd see smoke coming up off the ashtrays."[24] For Jacobs, a working-class white woman perform- ing as a table singer, the African American clubs were not respectable.

PERFORMING IN DANTE'S INFERNO

Beginning around 1920 Jacobs began working in Kansas City's jazz scene districts. Though she eventually built a singing career, she spent her early adulthood working as a waitress. Jacobs recalled her experi- ences working as a young waitress in Nicholl's Lunch, a popular diner in Kansas City near the Jazz District. "You didn't want to sing there, you wanted to go squat, sit down a while. Oh, it was a work house, but I loved it. I loved the whole family. They had the cutest bunch of kids . . . little monsters, they'd come in there. . . . They had floors [garbled tape]. I'd have the room all nice and clean, and they'd get in there and start skating."[25]

Her career as a diner waitress, however, was short-lived. Sometime in the mid-1920s Jacobs became a table singer and waitress at Dante's Inferno. Another landmark in Kansas City's Pendergast world, Dan- te's featured drag performers, including "Mr. Half-and-Half," along with a house band and floor show featuring special effects created by stage designer Frank Villareal. "He made monsters in there, and made them move," recalled Jacobs about the special effects floor show, "It's come crawl out of the cave. Bring over somebody's drinks, and they'd jump!"[26] In 1933, when Dante's Inferno gained enough popularity to outgrow its original location near Cherry Avenue, it was relocated to 1104 Independence Avenue at the corner of Independence and Troost.

Near the heart of the Jazz District, the new Dante's attracted not only customers but newspaper attention. The December 1933 reopening of Dante's was recorded in the *Kansas City Journal-Post* "Night Club Notes" section as the "hottest of the hot spots." "Old M. Satan himself holds sway with all his little devils in a setting that surely must make him feel at home," wrote the reporter. "Many novelty numbers keep the temperature at a high degree."[27] That veiled reference to "hot" shows no doubt enticed and titillated city dwellers aroused by the thought of sexuality on display. Jacobs began work as a waitress in Dante's in 1929 when the club was still located near Cherry Avenue; she eventually became a table singer and then a headlining act. As a waitress Jacobs was required to wear revealing red satin uniforms to entice patrons of Dante's. "A little devil's suit and the horns," recalled Jacobs in 1980. "We had a tail but that caused a little business. You'd go by with a tray of drinks and some sucker'd get a hold of your tail and stop ya."[28] Jacobs performed under a variety of names, including Lorelei Lynn and Eddie Lynn. Newspaper clippings in Jacobs's scrapbooks include reviews from Kansas City newspapers about her performances, along with copies of Dante's menu and flyers that list her among the performers. Jacobs's scrapbooks also include photographs of Jacobs and her peers at Dante's dressed in their mandatory uniforms.

Cabarets like Dante's, unlike other more mainstream jazz clubs, were spaces for experimentation with gender roles. Patrons of Dante's Inferno came not only for the music and the entertainment, but for the desire-driven chance to blur boundaries as well. Perhaps it was that same desire that brought Jacobs to Dante's Inferno looking for work and kept her there until the club closed permanently. That Jacobs saw Dante's as a transgressive space that represented a particular period of her life is a plausible reading of her scrapbooks. Of the two scrapbooks in the Jacobs papers at the University of Kansas only one is complete. That scrapbook contains Jacobs's mementos and memories of her career as a singer and club owner. Over half of the scrapbook is dominated by clippings, photographs, and ephemera from Dante's Inferno. Each page was carefully arranged by Jacobs herself, and each page focuses on a specific aspect of her time at Dante's. For example one page early in the scrapbook shows a young Edna at the beginning of her career: in her Nicholl's Lunch uniform in the bottom left corner, Jacobs and an unidentified Dante's employee wearing their devil costumes in the upper right corner, with remaining space showing club manager Eli Madloff, clippings about Dante's from the newspaper, a portrait of Jacobs and the same unidentified employee in evening gowns, and a pair of small portraits. Who is this unidentified person? For some reason Jacobs did not put captions, details, or descriptions on any of her scrapbook pages. No people are identified nor are dates placed on the pages. Through the photographs and clippings it is clear that the scrapbooks are in chronological order. On another page of the scrapbook Jacobs arranged a series of clippings and photographs from Dante's after it reopened on Independence Avenue. The photographs show Jacobs with the same unidentified employee as seen in previous pages. A photograph in the top left corner show Jacobs, other Dante's employees, and the house band posing in an empty Dante's. Surrounding clippings are predominantly announcements of the schedule of performances at Dante's and a clipping about club owner Joe Lusco, along with one photograph of a female impersonator. Again, however, there are no notes, details, or identifications, not even on the backs of the photographs. According to Donna Wilson Edna Jacobs did not allow anyone else in the family to touch her scrapbooks or to look in them without her knowledge. In fact Wilson explained that Jacobs kept the scrapbooks hidden and allowed no one else to work on them at any time. Wilson also said that "Grandmother was a woman ahead of her time."[29] It seems clear that Jacobs considered her time as a jazz performer, and specifically her time at Dante's, to be time spent in a transgressive space where silence was important. What were Jacobs and her family not saying?

The secret in the scrapbooks lies not in the visible but in the unvisible and tacit details it includes. Beginning with the opening of the second Dante's Inferno on Independence Avenue, Jacobs moved from table singer to floor show performer as half of the Lynn Sisters—Eddie (Edna) and Billie. According to existing records Edna Jacobs had no sisters, and Billie was actually Billy Richards, a well-known female impersonator. Richards made several appearances at Dante's as a "toe tap dancer and blues singer extraordinary."[30] While it was a frequent occurrence in cabarets to have fictional "sister acts," the Lynn Sisters were special— they were supposed to be a pair of female impersonators. While Richards was locally well-known as a female impersonator, Jacobs entered the performance representing a much-contested identity: biologically female, Jacobs represented a man performing as a female impersonator. Through the early 1930s "the Lynn Sisters—the Sisters of Harmony" performed nightly at Dante's. Jacobs's papers include several loose photographs of Richards, dressed both in drag and in more masculine street clothing. Inscriptions on the photographs from Richards read: "For Eddie, A girl I shall always remember as a real and true friend" and "For Eddie, one gay girl I know shall go far."[31]

Female impersonators were far from unknown in Kansas City's jazz scene. Homosexual performers, drag performers, and sex shows were understood components of the "sin palaces" of the city, even if historians did not make it seem so. As noted in chapter 1 Kansas City Ordinance No. 291 was in existence and should have applied to such performances. While this law was available such laws were ignored in the Pendergast world where money and patronage were law. Since these clubs were marginal even within the jazz scene, however, their history has since been silenced. Though historians such as Pearson, Driggs, and Haddix did not associate such performances with the jazz scene, they were part of the professional world of performers in America's jazz scenes. Gender impersonators traveled a circuit from Chicago to Kansas City, and then from Kansas City to San Francisco. In fact the now infamous

"Mr. Half-and-Half" was Arthur West-Brussard, a well-known circuit performer based in Chicago who performed under names including A. Brussard and Art West. In an announcement in the *Kansas City Call* in 1935, Brussard's performance impersonating Mae West was publicized. "Known all over the east and in Chicago as 'Mae West,'" wrote the columnist, "in private life he is A. Brussard."[32] Kansas City, as a railroad terminus, was far from unknown in the world of gender impersonation. In fact, as discussed in chapter 3, such performances likely served as a signpost of Kansas City's jazz scene for its queer audiences. In a 1978 interview band leader Woodie Walder remembered the "sexual attractions" this way: "In the black clubs they had female impersonators' night. . . . And everybody's come to see 'em dance. It's like a big ball they have in New Orleans, for the Mardi Gras. They have a big drag act where all the gays in town came out and do their show. Hell, man, we judge people by what they want to be themselves, you dig what I mean? These people were good, they're always good to you. They'd fill up the kitty if they make some money."[33]

According to Walder drag performances were clearly gathering places for queer city dwellers, as well as popular spaces in the Kansas City jazz scene. Their popularity, however, did not reflect the opinion of the city's genteel reformers, who found the atmosphere at Dante's Inferno an increasingly dangerous threat to the city. Reformers, in fact, were especially troubled by the display of gender variance and sexuality in Dante's. Some of Kansas City's reformers published a newsweekly titled *The Future*, aimed at reformers interested in preparing the city for middle-class modernity. In a 1935 article titled "Night Life of the Mortals," anonymous *Future* writers spent the night touring some of the city's well-known nightclubs, including the Chesterfield and Dante's Inferno. At the Chesterfield the investigators recalled seeing a "tiny child, certainly not yet five" singing a song titled "Oh! You Nasty Man!"[34] Their description of a visit to Dante's illustrates the mainstream attitude about the club and the dangers of sexuality it represented.

The interior is decorated with a lurid red substance which must be inflammable as the flames of hell it symbolizes. We were there for the first show, an extremely unpleasant ordeal, for the female impersonators who gave it were an inept and pitiful lot. One of them came to our table, sat down in all his finery and ordered a sherry flip. Kansas City, he lisped, was the crudest place he had ever worked in. "The folks here are sure dumb. They don't get nothing subtle." He went on to explain that he worked on a circuit which extended from New York to New Orleans; made pretty good money but had to spend a lot of it on snappy costumes. He was wearing, at the time, a little tulle model decorated grotesquely with a bunch of bananas. One look at the croupiers behind the gambling table decided against trying our luck there. We left just as the soft-spoken Mr. Lusco was arguing with two young men patrons in an attempt to prevent them from dancing together.[35]

The attitude displayed in this "expose" of Dante's Inferno seems indicative of the mainstream attitude toward gender impersonators. The investigators willingly identify the impersonator, club owner, and patrons as suspect and feminine, while proposing that the painted flames of hell are more than just illusion. While this attitude was likely prevalent outside the Pendergast world, it did not stop the flow of customers to Dante's and other "sexual attractions" in the city.

There is no way to know how much Jacobs said during her 1980 interview about her work with and as a gender impersonator at Dante's. Regardless of the numerous photographs in her scrapbooks, there are no captions in the Jacobs papers that identify Richards as her partner in the "sister act." Other than matching signatures there is no method Jacobs used in her papers to identify the costumed and street-clothed photographs of Richards as the same person. The fact that Richards gave Jacobs both types of photographs clearly demonstrates that Jacobs was more than just a fan. In addition the ownership of both types of photographs demonstrates the interstitial space that gender impersonators occupied in the city: both genders, and perhaps both as performances, only came together in the dressing rooms at Dante's Inferno. From the lack of captions it is also apparent that Jacobs distinctly identified her career among gender impersonators as a spatially identified period in her life. In the chronological scrapbooks, later pages on Jacobs's career as a female singer at World War II military bases include many photographs of Jacobs with clippings and captions. Meanwhile, when the scrapbooks were donated to the University of Kansas the donation arrived with all the photographs of female impersonators at Dante's in an unmarked envelope tucked inside the back cover of the Dante's scrapbook. In that envelope each photograph is signed and inscribed to "Eddie." They are not contextualized, captioned, or further mentioned by Jacobs. According to Donna Wilson these scrapbooks were never touched by family members after Jacobs died and were donated to the Spencer Library as Jacobs left them.[36] In this way Jacobs continues to haunt the jazz scene and the photographs of performers such as "Mr. Half-and-Half." Like other forgotten members of the jazz scene Jacobs felt the need to hide desires represented by interstitial spaces such as Dante's Inferno, even though she was an insider in that contested space.

Given all the silence and performance inherent in Jacobs's career as an impersonator at Dante's, can researchers identify her with a particular gender? Pearson, in his 1980 book, clearly represented Jacobs as a patron of female impersonation—there is no indication that Jacobs told Pearson she worked in Dante's as part of the impersonator floor show. In a section of interview appearing in the Pearson book but now lost, Jacobs seemed to empathize with the impersonators while separating herself from them. "A lot of people didn't like impersonators, but I learned a lot from them all," Jacobs told interviewers, "They're wonderful people, very talented, and our crowd loved them."[37] What did she learn from "them," and who was included in "our crowd?" Does this tell us anything about Jacobs's identity? Jacobs, perhaps, felt included in the community at Dante's, the world she "learned a lot from," and did not want to endanger that world by revealing her own sexual desires, whatever they were. Another aspect of this question of identity is pivotal to understanding the subjectification of gender impersonators: we cannot forget that they were performers. According to Drorbaugh performers of gender impersonation resisted being read as one gender or another, preferring ambiguity to identification.[38] Did Jacobs hide her scrapbooks and exclude captions in an effort to resist identification? Jacobs did, after all, allow Pearson and Litwak to identify her as "Mintirn" though that was not her name. In addition Jacobs did not tell them about either her work in Dante's or her three marriages to men. Perhaps Jacobs most identified with, and felt comfortable in, ambiguity. Taken together the gender impersonation work of Jacobs illustrates the fact that gender and sexuality are inherently performative and defy attempts to determine their position in historical individuals. Such ambiguity, however, likely contributed to the subsumation of Jacobs in the historical record. After all, if it was the threat of discovery and the comfort of ambiguity that kept Jacobs from contextualizing her scrapbooks, or that prevented Jacobs and her daughter from being more detailed in the 1980 interview, then it is that same combination of factors that leaves Jacobs lurking in the shadows of the jazz scene.

LIFE AFTER DANTE'S

Club owner and Pendergast crony Joe Lusco was shot by Pendergast rivals in 1938, and as a result he closed Dante's and opened the independent New York–style Stork Club downtown on Baltimore Street.[39] Jacobs, now without a job, signed with a touring group. Beginning in 1938 and continuing through 1943 Jacobs worked as the singer in a vocal-piano duo known as Lorelei and Lillian. Jacobs, who took the name Lorelei, worked with pianist Lillian May along a circuit that ran from Kansas City to Los Angeles.[40] Jacobs also joined the circuit performers by signing with the McConkey Orchestra Company, a talent agency headquartered in Kansas City. McConkey had strict rules about the behavior and attire of booked performers, and, as Jacobs recalled in 1980, cross-dressing was not one of the options. "He [Mr. McConkey] interviewed me. He said, uh, how's your wardrobe. He said, I insist you have . . . one black skirt, and a outfit for Sundays. We worked Sundays all the time. And you didn't wear naked clothes on Sunday you know, we wore sleeves. Look like a lady."[41]

While Jacobs was appearing as part of the performers in the McConkey books, she was also a young mother of three. While she was on tour Jacobs's children lived for a short time with her mother on Gillham Road. During her first three years of touring her first husband Riggs died, her son enlisted during World War II, and her two daughters separated. Her eldest daughter, Ida, stayed in Kansas City and worked on the Plaza while living with her grandmother.[42] Though Jacobs's daughter mentions her mother's separation from the family in the 1980 interview, the scrapbooks are filled instead with matchbooks, photographs, and newspaper reviews of her performances on the McConkey circuit. It seems that the scrapbooks were a remembrance of her professional career, not her home life. One such clipping, from the November 13, 1943, issue of *Billboard*, included an announcement about Lorelei and Lillian's recent performance in Chicago: "Take feminine beauty, add musical talent and lovable personality, and you really have something—-in this popular duo," wrote the reviewer. "Lorelei, 'Duchess of Memory Songs,' with Lillian, 'Princess of Piano Capers.'"[43] In one trip to San Francisco in the 1940s Jacobs visited Finocchio's, a famous impersonator club. According to historian Nan Alamilla Boyd Finocchio's was a queer nightclub and enclave gathering space where impersonators included both genders and cross-racial representation.[44] A program, matchbook, and menu from Finocchio's were tucked in the back of Jacobs's scrapbook, left unassociated with the ticket stubs, clippings, and matchbooks from her other stops in San Francisco.

Finished with touring as part of the McConkey circuit in 1943, Jacobs did not return home to Kansas City. Telling interviewers that her children "were all growed up," Jacobs chose instead to spend two years singing with Lillian May for boot-camp soldiers in Alexandria, Louisiana.[45] Jacobs's granddaughter recalled that Jacobs used a special songbook to take requests in Louisiana. Jacobs's "hook" was her claimed ability to sing any song requested. Evidently she kept a scrapbook of clipped sections from the lyrics of songs. Whenever someone requested a song she would look up the lyric in her scrapbook and use the clipped lyric as a mnemonic tool to recall the melody for both herself and Lillian May. She also kept a scrapbook of military insignia in Louisiana so that she could address her male fans by rank correctly.[46] The Jacobs papers include dozens of photographs and request cards from Alexandria, frequently signed with such words as "To Lorelei, who lures men on."[47] One photograph shows two soldiers posed before a jeep with the word "Lorelei" painted on the wheel well.[48]

Jacobs's performance time in Louisiana was her last. She returned to Kansas City around 1945, quit singing, and returned to her world as a table waitress in the city's cabarets. When interviewers asked Jacobs in 1980 why she stopped singing, she revealed that her time in Louisiana was not pleasant. "That was, that was rough," Jacobs told Pearson and Litwak. "And, I think I just kind of burned out."[49] Upon her return to Kansas City Jacobs worked as a hostess at the Tropics, a club downtown that included a nightly "tropical storm" and waitresses dressed in sarongs.[50] Sometime shortly after her return to Kansas City, however, Edna married Joe Jacobs. It seems likely that Joe and Edna had known each other before World War II, when Edna was performing at Dante's. Joe Jacobs was an enforcer for the Pendergast machine who purchased the Kentucky Bar-B-Q from its original owners sometime in the late 1930s. The Kentucky was a well-known eatery and jazz space made famous by its early-morning jam sessions attended by musicians leaving their nightly gigs in nearby Jazz District establishments. Edna

Jacobs frequented the Kentucky for both food and entertainment.[51] In her scrapbooks there are photographs and clippings about Joe Jacobs mixed with news about other Pendergast employees such as Dante's owner Joe Lusco and emcee Eli Madloff.

While it is not clear exactly when Joe and Edna Jacobs met, what they did after their marriage is part of the Jacobs papers. By the time the Jacobses married in 1945 the power of the Pendergast machine was broken. With Pendergast's arrest and subsequent death the Pendergast machine was dismantled by reformist city officials and attorneys general. Jacobs remembered the post-Pendergast era as a more peaceful one in the city. "It seems like people . . . got along better," she told interviewers. "Between the factions there used to be so much unrest."[52] Together Edna and Joe Jacobs purchased the abandoned Riverside Jockey Club on Highway 40. The Riverside Track and Club had originally been opened and managed by Tom Pendergast in 1928, but it reopened under the ownership of the Jacobses as the Paradise Club and Riverside Supper Club. Newspaper announcements from 1945 mentioned the fact that the Paradise was owned by Joe Jacobs, with "Eddy Lynn" "in charge of floor and hostess."[53] Joe ran the Paradise and Riverside, while Edna worked as hostess and booked the nightly entertainment. Large sections of Jacobs's scrapbooks are devoted to the opening and operation of the Paradise, including photographs of Joe and Edna seated in the center of their jointly owned dance floor. The nightly house band was led by Sam "Baby" Lovett and his "Gentlemen of Jive." With Lovett as the headlining act the Paradise became a popular jazz club in the 1940s and remained open until Joe Jacobs died in the 1950s.

Edna Jacobs's granddaughter Donna Wilson recalled playing as a child at the Paradise, where Edna introduced her daughter Ida to future son-in-law Charles Minturn. Once the Paradise Club closed in the 1950s Jacobs opened the small Eastwood Hills Tavern nearby, where patrons could hear jazz music and eat fried chicken dinners. The last entries in Jacobs's scrapbooks concern the Paradise Club. While Jacobs's granddaughter recalls spending afternoons playing with her siblings in the Eastwood Hills Tavern, Jacobs did not put anything about the tavern in her scrapbooks.[54] Edna Jacobs retired from work in the 1960s.[55] Her grandchildren lived with her for a number of years, and Jacobs married a man named Mears. Only one clipping in the Jacobs scrapbooks mentioned any activity after 1950—a short letter from the director of Kansas City's Veteran's Home thanking Edna and her daughter Ida for singing for the veterans.[56] Late in life Edna Jacobs developed Alzheimer's disease and moved in with her daughter Ida Minturn. The 1980 interview with Pearson and Litwak was recorded in the Minturn home. The Jacobs papers were donated to the University of Kansas in 1997 by Donna Wilson, after Edna's death and Ida's deterioration due to Alzheimer's disease made the security of the papers somewhat precarious.

JACOBS AND KANSAS CITY'S JAZZ SCENE HISTORY

Jacobs's story is representative of the problematic work of researching marginalized groups, such as working-class women and table singers, in Kansas City's jazz scene history. The lack of working-class women such as Jacobs is a direct result of the inherent gendering of the written history of the city's jazz scene. The concept of Kansas City's "cock-sure," Pendergast era "Jazz Age" past in essence silences any other subjects in the jazz canon. This subsumation of individuals such as Jacobs is evident in everything from the texts of the jazz canon to the treatment of collections in archival repositories. For example the Jacobs papers at the University of Kansas are listed as the Edna Mae (Whithouse Riggs) Jacobs Papers. Jacobs, however, never performed under any of those names. Her various stage names are described in the collection's accession records as: "Lorelei Lynn (changed her name later to Eddy Lynn) was a singer, 18th and Vine, Kansas City."[57] Jacobs did not perform in the Eighteenth and Vine Jazz District, nor did she perform in Kansas City as Lorelei Lynn. Given that description, patrons could easily assume that Jacobs collected the papers of Lorelei Lynn—not that Jacobs performed under a variety of stage names. In fact the description of Jacobs's collection presents Jacobs as a patron, not a performer. Perhaps the greatest reflection of the role of gender and sexuality in avoidance of subjects such as Jacobs, especially in the jazz canon writings about Kansas City, pertains to the 1980 interview by Pearson and Litwak. Pearson always referred to this interview as the Mintirn interview, using the last name of Jacob's married daughter.[58] In *Goin' to Kansas City* Pearson discussed the "Mintirn interview" as one with primary evidence of homosexuality in Kansas City's jazz scene. Despite that proclamation Jacobs never said the word "homosexual," and Pearson did not identify passages he thought specifically discussed homosexuality. It seems, instead, that Pearson took Jacobs's stories about female impersonation as evidence of homosexuality. In addition, and despite Pearson's statements about the interview's importance, only a small section of the interview was transcribed for the Pearson book. Though the original Jacobs interview was nearly two hours long, only thirty-five minutes of the interview now exist on tape. The tapes from Pearson's project were originally deposited at the Smithsonian Institution, Rutgers University, and the University of Missouri–Kansas City, along with Pearson's personal copies. Today only the thirty-five-minute fragment in Kansas City remains. The full interview was never transcribed and is no longer available for transcription.[59] The fact that the original interview is lost possibly explains some of the power dynamics related to gender and sexuality, class, and professional historians' concepts of propriety that subsumed not only Jacobs's narrative but the contested territory of Kansas City's jazz scene altogether. The exact cause of the loss of Jacobs's narrative will likely never be known. It is, however, interesting to note that the interviews Pearson and Litwak conducted with famous male performers, such as Count Basie and Jay McShann, were fully transcribed in 1987 and are available to researchers in all three archival repositories.

Another problematic area associated with Jacobs's biography lies in her relationship to the events narrated in the 1980 interview. Jacobs is listed in the Pearson book as an important source on the history of sexuality in the city, but her interview reveals some reticence about talking openly. Pearson later remembered the Jacobs interview: "We [Pearson and Litwak] both recall her being interested in the interview, and interesting, but somewhat coy about some aspects of her professional life in that era."[60] It was not Edna Jacobs, however, but her daughter Ida who had the most contentious relationship with her mother's past. The 1980 interview was conducted in the home of Ida Minturn, and it is obvious from the recording that the interview was practiced. Ida Minturn shaped the interview through interruptions, clarifications, and the use of archival material in the scrapbooks to supplement her mother's memories. This power dynamic was as much personal as cultural, and reflected her daughter's understanding of Edna Jacobs's personal history. In a sense Ida Minturn interpreted Jacobs's narrative before it reached the tape recorder. During the course of the interview Jacobs lost control of her own narrative as her daughter guided both questions and answers for the interviewers. This level of performance in the Jacobs interview poses a methodological challenge, because an interpretation of the interview depends on untangling the memories of mother and daughter.

According to Donna Wilson Edna Jacobs suffered from Alzheimer's disease, which doubtless affected Jacobs's ability to recall the past, and likely facilitated Ida Minturn's guidance during the interview.[61] There are sections of the interview, however, where it seems that Minturn's concern is not her mother's memory but the stories her mother might tell. These sections are concerned primarily with race and specifically with "Baby" Lovett. An example is this fragment from the 1980 interview:

INTERVIEWER: Would, um, would you have any friends who were black? That band members, like Lovett, maybe Lovett knows folks. But just members of the audience, would you socialize much?

EDNA JACOBS: Oh, I was always close to Baby because, uh . . .

IDA MINTURN: No, black people. Besides in the band, were there black people that you were friendly with?[62]

It is clear from Jacobs's scrapbooks who "Baby" was: drummer and bandleader Sam "Baby" Lovett. The word "Lovett" appears only once in the existing interview tape, in the passage above when mentioned by the interviewers. The passage is also indicative of another feature of the interview. Whenever Jacobs uttered the word "Baby" her daughter redirected the question or changed the subject. Jacobs's scrapbooks, however, are filled with matchbooks, flyers, and photographs of Lovett in clubs and cabarets around Kansas City. In addition there are many photographs of Lovett at dinner tables, on dance floors, and even in the stands at a Kansas City Monarchs baseball game. Who is the photographer for this collection of snapshots? Who haunts these images? As mentioned previously the scrapbooks were tightly controlled by Jacobs alone.

Samuel Lovett was born in Louisiana in 1894. He arrived in Kansas City in 1922 and played with George and Julia Lee, the Kansas City Rockets, and occasionally filled in for Jo Jones, the drummer for the Count Basie Orchestra.[63] Known today in the jazz canon as an originator of Kansas City bebop style drumming, Lovett was inducted into the Kansas City Jazz Hall of Fame in 1972—an honor he followed with a week of shows at the Hotel President.[64] In a 1957 interview with jazz stakeholder Frank Driggs (in preparation for his 1959 essay), Lovett recalled the foundations of his musical style: "When I was just a young kid I used to go to the holy roller churches and get as close to the window as I could, and I heard the rhythm and it kind of grew in me. With just a drum, tambourine and a guitar, they'd get one solid beat and it would last about an hour. The longer they'd play the happier the congregation would get. It's something that grows in you and I'm still playing the same way today, nothing's changed."[65]

Though it is impossible to know exactly when Lovett and Edna Jacobs met, they likely were introduced when Lovett played drums at Kentucky Bar-B-Q. Jacobs frequented the Kentucky; the club/restaurant located at Nineteenth and Vine eventually became home of the first Gates BBQ restaurant. Lovett played at the Kentucky as part of Woodie Walder's Kentucky Club Swing Unit, the Kentucky house band from 1934 until approximately 1939.[66] Lovett played various shows at the Sunset, Subway, and Spinning Wheel clubs, among other clubs in Kansas City. Each of these clubs was mentioned in the Jacobs interview, along with occasional mentions of "hearing Baby." Though Jacobs left Kansas City and performed across the country, when she returned to Kansas City and opened the Paradise Club Lovett and his band became the nightly headlining act.

An example of the ways in which the combination of desire and space worked in Kansas City's jazz scene lies in the unvisible story of Edna Jacobs and Baby Lovett. Throughout her interview Jacobs made frequent mention of "Baby," including his skill as a musician and his friendship with Jacobs. Each mention of his name, however, resulted in Ida Minturn changing the subject or interrupting her mother to speak to the interviewers directly. Was the act of interrupting the narrative event simply racism on Ida's part, an attempt to avoid racism from Edna, or a deeper reaction by Ida to her mother's life experiences? While the interviewers seemed to sidestep the question of "Baby" through choice or suggestion, the presence of Baby Lovett in Edna Jacobs's life is unmistakable in her scrapbooks. The scrapbooks span nearly forty years, and each section contains clippings, flyers, and/or photographs of Baby Lovett. While some of these mementos show Lovett in performance, the rest show much more personal and private moments. What exactly was Jacobs's relationship to Baby Lovett?

It seems clear that Lovett and Jacobs were at least friends, even though Jacobs told interviewers that she had no African American friends. The frequent inclusion of Lovett in the scrapbooks, however, might indicate a more serious relationship. Jacobs, for instance, wrote details and captions on photographs of her performances on the road in the 1940s and about her co-ownership of the Paradise Club. While the photographs of Lovett in performance are sometimes captioned, the photographs and mementos associated with more private representations of Lovett have no context or captions at all. Like the photographs of female impersonators, images of Lovett in anything but a professional context are kept unvisible. Coupled with Ida Minturn's avoidance of the subject of Lovett, Jacobs's mentions and remembrances of Lovett suggest that, even if a relationship did exist, Jacobs considered it a taboo subject on a number of levels. Did Jacobs have a deeper relationship with Baby Lovett in the segregated Pendergast world? If so, what pressures caused her to continue to segregate their relationship in her scrapbooks?

Whether an intimate relationship between Lovett and Jacobs existed or not, why was Ida Minturn constantly avoiding the subject? The answer lies in the links between desire and space. The desiring body defies boundaries, whether those boundaries are between races, genders, sexualities, or classes. Hegemony, however, seeks to reterritorialize those bodies by suppressing desire and replacing it with the representation of acceptability. Given the geography of desires and its jazz scene spaces within which Jacobs and Lovett existed, it is obvious that whatever personal or cultural desires they may have had were suppressed by the hegemonic representation of interracial relationships as criminal and deviant. This same reason governs the lack of cross-identification for separate photographs of Billy Richards and the disappearance of the complete Jacobs interview from the historical records. These images, these memories, were deviant and belonged in limited times and spaces. Once those spaces were ignored by the jazz canon, excavating their history was deemed unacceptable. As a scholar of Deleuze and Guattari wrote: "The ethical question is not one of inside/outside, but rather of how one or a collective inhabits an unavoidably corrupted context for which there is no outside."[67] Trapped inside this corrupted context are Jacobs, Richards, and Lovett.

Another important part of the corrupted context of Jacobs's memories is its intersections. Though there are multiple levels of information and evidence of overlapping discursive formations in Jacobs's story, the main thread is her portrayal of spatial segregation. This spatialization includes female impersonators and table singers, working-class Kansas Citians, and segregated racial and ethnic minority people. Edna Jacobs engaged her interviewers in several short discussions about spatialization in Kansas City's jazz scene, as well as her experiences as a "slummer" in black clubs. Her memories of race in Kansas City reflect her position as a white woman, but they also reveal her understanding and empathy with other performers in a context driven by music. Her scrapbooks further demonstrate this duality in Jacobs's position. Her scrapbooks are filled with signed photographs of African American jazz performers and bands. In addition Jacobs frequently discussed band leader Baby Lovett in her interview and signed Lovett as her headlining act at the Paradise Club. Another major strain of discourse and analysis in the Jacobs materials are her memories of living as a woman in the Kansas City jazz scene. As a woman performer in a gendered and sexualized jazz scene, Jacobs's recollections of clubs, performers, and environments in the jazz scene reveal her position as a performer and an insider in a spatialized and contested territory. Finally Jacobs's interview serves as evidence of working-class life in Kansas City before World War II. Throughout the 1980 interview Jacobs discussed her childhood and adulthood in Kansas City's working-class neighborhoods. Her recollections of collecting scrap metal as a child, waiting tables while her mother worked as a maid, and living in a tent in the West Bottoms excavate a largely forgotten aspect of Kansas City's jazz scene. The evidence of working-class life in Jacobs's experience creates a concept of the past that greatly diverges from the common popular and historical representation of "pink and pretty" girls in a "wide-open" town.

According to Avery Gordon, haunting transforms the shadow of a life into an undiminished life history.[68] Edna Mae Jacobs has lurked in Kansas City's jazz canon shadow for decades, her life a footnote and her memories reduced to a fetishized photograph. She was never famous, and the single photograph of "Mr. Half-and-Half" has been continually marginalized by traditional jazz historians. Jacobs's story is representative of the problematic work of researching marginalized jazz scene lives in Kansas City's history. Her story, however, also illustrates the importance of examining identity and subjectivity as a discursive production of both space and knowledge. Jacobs's haunting of the jazz scene reveals and produces an encounter with many subjects whose voices were not preserved on tape but whose images survived despite their liminal position in the jazz canon. Through Edna Jacobs the spaces of the jazz scene, and the contested lives of those who lived and worked in the Pendergast world, are excavated. According to Muñoz worldmaking is inherently a collection of practices that critique the oppression of difference.[69] In the scrapbooks and interviews, the photographs and recollections, lies Edna Jacobs's worldmaking practice: the maintenance of memories and ephemera of a world so marginalized it was rendered unvisible. Jacobs could have burned her photographs, refused an interview request, thrown her Finocchio's program in the trash. She did not, because her critique of oppression was not an act of open defiance or an overt performance of the subjugated. Her critique was (and is) in her refusal to be quiet and in her remembrance of difference otherwise silenced by family, disease, and the historians who used one of her photographs as proof of some kind of illusory and modern acceptance. Edna haunts jazz history and represents an oppositional practice that still results in a worldmaking of the present.

7

Remembering KC

Two events that were based on Kansas City's representation in the jazz canon took place in September 2006. First, the corner of Twelfth and Vine was officially dedicated as "Goin' To Kansas City Plaza" on September 11. The blocks known for their "neon riot of bars, gambling dens and taxi dance halls" were turned into a monument of commemoration. "Kansas City, and the world, has a physical symbol to help us all remember, and relive, the wonderfully vibrant early days of Kansas City jazz," wrote Juanita Moore, executive director of the American Jazz Museum, at the plaza's dedication. "I urge you all to go see the 'Goin' to Kansas City Plaza' at 12th Street and Vine and reminisce."[1] During the weekend celebration of the plaza, the Kansas City, Missouri, City Council adopted the song "Kansas City" as the official city song. The classic song was written by Mike Stoller and Jerry Leiber; the two composers had never been to Kansas City.[2] First recorded under the title "K.C. Lovin'," the song was based on the mythos of Kansas City as a "wide-open" town. Given the sexualized and the spatially identified lyrics, the song reveals much about the pervasiveness of the myth of Kansas City's jazz scene.

> . . . Kansas City, here I come
> They got a crazy way a-lovin' an I wanna get me some![3]

Much has changed in Kansas City since the days of the jazz scene suggested in the Leiber and Stoller song. Through a reminiscent nod to the "genteel lady" of Kansas City, however, traditional jazz historians have failed to understand how jazz scene history and its spatialization were linked through reterritorialization. The changing identification and use of jazz scene spaces in Kansas City were not simply effects of development—it was a reterritorializing subsumation of the city's jazz scene history through the destruction of space and the production of a written history that denied the historical meanings of such spaces. Through this reterritorialization and the master narrative of jazz history, Kansas City's jazz scene spaces became melancholy plazas where the contested meanings of music, sex, race, and space were reduced to lyrics.

This reterritorialization of spaces is visible when examining the current state of some of the spaces associated with the city's jazz scene in this study. Many of these spaces are now gone. The site of 2911 Gillham, once home to a tent city where Edna Jacobs and her family stayed in the early 1900s, now contains a warehouse. Dante's Inferno, the famous home of female impersonation, was torn down to make way for an interchange between Independence Avenue and Interstate 35. Used by a trucking company for many years as an extra parking lot, the lot that was home to Annie Chambers's brothel was left vacant and abandoned until 2000. In that year the City of Kansas City and the Missouri Department of Natural Resources approved the lot for development. In the development report officials for the Missouri Department of Natural Resources identify the lot this way: "This 1.8-acre Kansas City site saw many uses throughout its history, including a saloon, a warehouse, a theatre, and a couple of trucking companies. At the time of cleanup, it was a parking lot." After four years of work Hok Sports Venue opened their international corporate headquarters on the site in 2004.[4] Hok is an internationally known architectural firm specializing in sports arenas and stadiums. Hok is the architectural firm that produced the City of Kansas City's plans for redesign of Kauffman Stadium and Arrowhead Stadium, as well as the downtown Sprint Arena.[5]

While those spaces were reterritorialized by their destruction, others remained on the city's map as historical sites of the "Jazz Age." The most famous of these is the Eighteenth and Vine Jazz District, which Driggs and Haddix explained this way:

> Eighteenth and Vine miraculously escaped the urban renewal wrecking ball that leveled surrounding neighborhoods during the 1960s. A multi-million-dollar redevelopment effort, launched in 1997, featuring the American Jazz and Negro Leagues Baseball Museums, has sparked a minor renaissance in the historic district. New housing units have been erected, and two new restaurants anchor the stretch of 18th Street between Paseo and Highland. The renovated Gem Theater has reopened as a performing arts venue. The jazz museum, situated on the corner of 18th and Vine, showcases the legacies of Ella Fitzgerald, Louis Armstrong, Duke Ellington, and Charlie Parker.[6]

False storefronts erected at Eighteenth and Vine for production of the film *Kansas City* (1997) remain attached to the buildings, and, as Krin Gabbard explained in a review of the film, the only musician with dialogue in the film is Charlie Parker.[7] As Driggs and Haddix explained in their book, however, the Gem Theater was not a club where "jazz" musicians played. It was a small theater that "offered second-run photoplays and modest theatrical productions."[8] While Parker was a Kansas City native, as traditional jazz historians have continually emphasized, Fitzgerald, Ellington, and Armstrong were musicians who only appeared in Kansas City occasionally as a tour stop. In these examples the spaces that "miraculously escaped the wrecking ball" were not jazz scene spaces at all, but recreations of a jazz scene discursively produced by traditional jazz historians. The spaces of the "wide-open" and contested jazz scene were reterritorialized under the guise of "development," while spaces built to represent Kansas City's "Jazz Age" were produced as multipurpose monuments of a master narrative.

In this reterritorialization of jazz scene spaces, the master narrative of Kansas City's "Jazz Age" also enclosed the worldmaking aspects of those spaces. Critical geographer Gill Valentine wrote that performance and its manipulation of an audience can inscribe a geography of desires on that audience.[9] According to James Duncan it is this very inscription of desire that makes a space representational. In what Duncan called the "spatialities of representation," desires become inscribed not just on the body, but on the space where such desires are performed.[10] These desiring-performances become spectacles, but not spectacles of the hegemonic mainstream. Instead, as Jose Esteban Muñoz wrote, such spectacles give minoritarian subjects a representational space in which to position themselves, and thus an avenue to create community and obtain agency.[11] According to Muñoz identity is produced in a space between self and society.[12] These spaces, in the case of Kansas City's jazz scene, were not psychological or theoretical. They were the actual cabarets, brothels, and clubs of the jazz scene where a counterpublic spectacle could be performed, watched, and desired.

With the denial of such desires in Kansas City's jazz canon, and the reterritorialization of their spaces, traditional jazz history in Kansas City created a disciplinary monotony. According to Foucault the enclosure of a heterogeneous body requires first a disciplinary monotony. Kansas City's jazz scene history put this monotony into practice.[13] Second, Foucauldian discipline requires the breaking up of collectives by giving each subject a discursively formed "place," a move Foucault called the "principle of partitioning." The third step in Foucault's theory of discipline is functional sites, or the creation of a multipurpose space that is coded by hegemonic discourse.[14] The American Jazz Museum, the "Goin' to Kansas City Plaza," and the Hok Sports company are all sites of multipurpose spaces that reify and support the version of Kansas City history memorialized in the jazz canon. Finally, according to Foucault the last step in disciplining bodies is to rank units. For Foucault this meant that individual subjects had to be classified, and meanings about those subjects disciplined according to their discursive formations. By relegating subjects such as madams, gender impersonators, and table singers to the backdrop of the jazz scene, traditional jazz successfully ranked those subjects: musicians who played the music later classified as "jazz," jazz men who displayed the masculinity and skill inherent in such a classification, were given a place in the canon, while those who contested disciplinary monotony were represented as an anomaly. Charlie Parker became the subject of "Kansas City Jazz," and Edna Jacobs became the table singer who was not famous enough. As Avery Gordon demonstrated, Parker remained visible in the history of the jazz scene, while Jacobs was rendered unvisible through the cultural blindness of traditional jazz historians, scholars, and Kansas City jazz history stakeholders.

Historians, scholars, stakeholders, and fans—none will ever know exactly how the patrons of Dante's Inferno felt about that space and their place in it, if that question ever entered their minds. None will ever know if the women employed by Annie Chambers felt a sense of kinship, or if the gender impersonators of Kansas City lived and worked in an enclave of queer community. What is important is that they were part of the jazz scene, and that they signaled a challenge to the discursive formations of gender, sexuality, race, class, and space that traditional jazz historians have represented as truth. In their performances these Kansas City jazz scene dwellers worked on, with, and against formations of difference in the city. Their world, the intersectional and contested Pendergast world, was more than just a backdrop for "Kansas City Jazz." It was a geography of desires, of desire-producing spaces, that traversed the city. The concept that such spaces gave minoritarian subjects a space of agency is, in itself, a challenge to those historians and the "Jazz Age" they claim to represent.

Notes

1. RETHINKING KANSAS CITY'S JAZZ STORY

1. Nealon, *Foundlings*, 96.
2. Muñoz, *Disidentifications*, 195–96.
3. Brooks, *Bodies in Dissent*, 8.
4. Montgomery and Kasper, *Kansas City*, 85.
5. Russell, *Jazz Style*, 4.
6. DeVeaux, "Constructing the Jazz Tradition," 545.
7. Nathan Pearson Jr. and Howard Litwak, "Final Narrative Report: Kansas City—The Oral History of a Jazz Scene, 1924–1942," 2, Folder #KC0012, Kansas City Jazz Oral History Collection, Western Historical Manuscripts Collection, University of Missouri–Kansas City.
8. Sears, *Arresting Dress*, 76.
9. Russell, *Jazz Style*, 8.
10. Schirmer, *A City Divided*, 126.
11. Brown, *Closet Space*, 4.
12. Adams, Hoelscher, and Till, "Place in Context," xvii, xiv.
13. Board of Public Welfare, *Fifth Annual Report*, 53.
14. Montgomery and Kasper, *Kansas City*, 87.
15. Schirmer, *A City Divided*, 126.
16. Donna Wilson, telephone interview with the author, April 30, 2004.

2. KANSAS CITY'S JAZZ SCENE

1. Richard Rodgers and Oscar Hammerstein, "Kansas City," http://www .lyricsondemand.com/soundtracks/o/oklahomalyrics/kansascitylyrics .html, accessed July 3, 2007.

2. Goldberg, *Disoriented America*, 40.

3. Pearson, *Goin' to Kansas City*, xvii.

4. Mumford, *Interzones*, xv.

5. Thelen, *Paths of Resistance*, 270.

6. Ogren, *The Jazz Revolution*, 62–63.

7. Dahl, *Morning Glory*, 71.

8. Williams, "Jazz," 171.

9. Stowe, "Jazz in the West," 56.

10. Becker, "Jazz Places," 17.

11. Gabbard, "Review: *Kansas City*," 1275.

12. Comer, *Landscapes*, 27.

13. Lewis and Smith, *Oscar Wilde*, 327.

14. Mobley and Harris, *A City Within a Park*, 3.

15. Mobley and Harris, *A City Within a Park*, 3.

16. Crabb, "Music in Kansas City," 51.

17. Lewis and Smith, *Oscar Wilde*, 327.

18. Lewis and Smith, *Oscar Wilde*, 328.

19. Dorsett, *The Pendergast Machine*, 4.

20. Comer, *Landscapes*, 157.

21. Pearson, *Goin' to Kansas City*, 78.

22. Montgomery and Kasper, *Kansas City*, 85.

23. Dorsett, *The Pendergast Machine*, 4.

24. Dorsett, *The Pendergast Machine*, 5.

25. Montgomery and Kasper, *Kansas City*, 102.

26. Montgomery and Kasper, *Kansas City*, 130.

27. Dorsett, *The Pendergast Machine*, 5.

28. Brown and Dorsett, *K.C.*, 45.

29. Montgomery and Kasper, *Kansas City*, 88.

30. Miller, *From Prairie to Prison*, 12.

31. Montgomery and Kasper, *Kansas City*, 118.

32. Wilson, *The City Beautiful*, 15.

33. Wilson, *The City Beautiful*, 15.

34. *Kansas City Evening Star*, January 5, 1893, 1(A).

35. *Kansas City Evening Star*, January 5, 1893, 1(A).

36. Miller, *From Prairie to Prison*, 14.

37. Montgomery and Kasper, *Kansas City*, 80.

38. Brown and Dorsett, *K.C.*, 50–51.

39. Montgomery and Kasper, *Kansas City*, 107.

40. Montgomery and Kasper, *Kansas City*, 111.

41. Montgomery and Kasper, *Kansas City*, 127.

42. Dorsett, *The Pendergast Machine*, 4.

43. Dorsett, *The Pendergast Machine*, 13.

44. Dorsett, *The Pendergast Machine*, 7.

45. Dorsett, *The Pendergast Machine*, 7.

46. Dorsett, *The Pendergast Machine*, 12.

47. Dorsett, *The Pendergast Machine*, 26.

48. Butsch, "Introduction," 12.

49. Peiss, "Commercial Leisure," 109.

50. McBee, *Dance Hall Days*, 45.

51. Wilson, *The City Beautiful*, 32.

52. Montgomery and Kasper, *Kansas City*, 174.

53. Dorsett, *The Pendergast Machine*, 68.

54. Dorsett, *The Pendergast Machine*, 58.

55. Dorsett, *The Pendergast Machine*, 88–89.

56. Pearson, *Goin' to Kansas City*, 85.

57. Morris, *Wait Until Dark*, 1–2.

58. Pearson, *Goin' to Kansas City*, 93.

59. Russell, *Jazz Style*, 8.

60. Larsen and Hulston, *Pendergast!*, 92.

61. Larsen and Hulston, *Pendergast!*, 104–5.

62. Larsen and Hulston, *Pendergast!*, 93.

63. Larsen and Hulston, *Pendergast!*, 105.

64. Schirmer, *A City Divided*, 97.

65. Schirmer, *A City Divided*, 100.

66. Schirmer, *A City Divided*, 125.

67. Schirmer, *A City Divided*, 166.

68. Schirmer, *A City Divided*, 131.

69. Schirmer, *A City Divided*, 169.

70. Morris, *Wait Until Dark*, 12.

71. Morris, *Wait Until Dark*, 12.

72. Morris, *Wait Until Dark*, 105.

73. Pearson, *Goin' to Kansas City*, 94.

74. Morris, *Wait Until Dark*, 186.

75. Mumford, "Homosex Changes," 389.

76. Larsen and Hulston, *Pendergast!*, 104.

77. Long, *The Great Southern Babylon*, 156.

78. Schirmer, *A City Divided*, 172.

79. Perry, *Women Artists*, 11.

80. History Project, *Improper Bostonians*, 98.

81. Sandra Wayne, interview with the author, Warrensburg, Missouri, March 2007.

82. de Graaf, "Race, Sex, and Region," 84.

83. Alexander, *The "Girl Problem,"* 20.

84. de Graaf, "Race, Sex, and Region," 93.

85. Larsen and Hulston, *Pendergast!*, 96–97.

86. Larsen and Hulston, *Pendergast!*, 107.

87. Larsen and Hulston, *Pendergast!*, 101.

88. Larsen and Hulston, *Pendergast!*, 102.

89. Morris, *Wait Until Dark*, 1.

90. Pearson, *Goin' to Kansas City*, 95.

91. Morris, *Wait Until Dark*, 5.

92. Morris, *Wait Until Dark*, 15.

93. Larsen and Hulston, *Pendergast!*, 101.

94. Larsen and Hulston, *Pendergast!*, 103.

95. Pearson, *Goin' to Kansas City*, 103.

96. Larsen and Hulston, *Pendergast!*, 103.

97. Russell, *Jazz Style*, 16.

98. Russell, *Jazz Style*, 17.

99. Pearson, *Goin' to Kansas City*, 94.

100. Russell, *Jazz Style*, 22–23.

101. Russell, *Jazz Style*, 19.

102. Russell, *Jazz Style*, 24; Driggs and Haddix, *Kansas City Jazz*, 203–4.

103. Pearson, *Goin' to Kansas City*, 121.

104. Pearson, *Goin' to Kansas City*, 133; Driggs and Haddix, *Kansas City Jazz*, 124–25.

105. Pearson, *Goin' to Kansas City*, 121.

106. Martin, *Our Negro Population*, 3.

107. Pearson, *Goin' to Kansas City*, 133.

108. Morris, *Wait Until Dark*, 140.

109. Pearson, *Goin' to Kansas City*, 227.

110. Personal Papers of Mary Lou Williams, Series 5, Box 1, Folder 1, Autobiographical Book #1 131, Mary Lou Williams Collection, Institute of Jazz Studies, Rutgers University, Newark, New Jersey.

111. Dahl, *Morning Glory*, 71.

112. Personal Papers of Mary Lou Williams, Series 5, Box 1, Folder 2, Autobiographical Notes 155, Mary Lou Williams Collection, Institute of Jazz Studies, Rutgers University, Newark, New Jersey.

113. Personal Papers of Mary Lou Williams, Series 5, Box 1, Folder 2, Autobiographical Notes 180–82.

114. Personal Papers of Mary Lou Williams, Series 5, Box 1, Folder 2, Autobiographical Notes 203–5.

115. Havig, "Mass Commercial Amusements," 319.

116. Havig, "Mass Commercial Amusements," 319.

117. Havig, "Mass Commercial Amusements," 319–20.

118. Kenney, "Historical Context," 107.

119. Pearson, *Goin' to Kansas City*, 185.

3. THE MYTH OF THE WIDE-OPEN TOWN

1. Clark, "'Nothin' Over There,'" 57. See also Hentoff and McCarthy, *Jazz*; Williams, *The Jazz Tradition*.

2. DeVeaux, "Constructing the Jazz Tradition," 552.

3. Gabbard, "Writing the Other History," 7.

4. Ogren, *The Jazz Revolution*, 139.
5. DeVeaux, "Constructing the Jazz Tradition," 540.
6. O'Meally, Edwards, and Griffin, *Uptown Conversations*, 2.
7. Ake, *Jazz Cultures*, 10.
8. Ake, *Jazz Cultures*, 10.
9. Ake, *Jazz Cultures*, 41.
10. Washington, "'All the Things,'" 29.
11. Vincent, *Keep Cool*, 14.
12. Tucker, *Swing Shift*, 12.
13. Gendron, *Between Montmartre*, 12.
14. Crouch, *Kansas City Lightning*, 68.
15. Peretti, "Oral Histories," 128.
16. Peretti, "Oral Histories," 122.
17. Ogren, "'Jazz Isn't Just Me,'" 112.
18. Peretti, "Oral Histories," 127.
19. Harlos, "Jazz Autobiography," 132.
20. Harlos, "Jazz Autobiography," 132.
21. Driggs, "Kansas City and the Southwest," 196.
22. Driggs, "Kansas City and the Southwest," 190.
23. Driggs, "Kansas City and the Southwest," 228.
24. Driggs, "Kansas City and the Southwest," 228.
25. Driggs, "Kansas City and the Southwest," 198.
26. Driggs, "Kansas City and the Southwest," 229–30.
27. Driggs, "Kansas City and the Southwest," 207–8.
28. Driggs, "Kansas City and the Southwest," 191.
29. Driggs, "Kansas City and the Southwest," 195.
30. Becker, "Jazz Places," 17.
31. Gillis, "Review: *Jazz Style*," 316.
32. DeVeaux, "Constructing the Jazz Tradition," 539.
33. DeVeaux, "Constructing the Jazz Tradition," 540.
34. Russell, *Jazz Style*.
35. Gillis, "Review: *Jazz Style*," 316.
36. Russell, *Jazz Style*, 15–16.

37. Russell, *Jazz Style*, 17–22.

38. Russell, *Jazz Style*, 23.

39. Russell, *Jazz Style*, 11.

40. Russell, *Jazz Style*, 24.

41. Russell, *Jazz Style*, 9.

42. Russell, *Jazz Style*, 3.

43. Russell, *Jazz Style*, 9.

44. Dyson, "Review: *Pops Foster*," 222.

45. Gillis, "Review: *Jazz Style*," 316.

46. Nathan W. Pearson Jr., interview with the author, Greenwich, Connecticut, September 12, 2006.

47. Peretti, "Oral Histories," 119.

48. Pearson, interview with the author.

49. Pearson and Litwak, "Final Narrative Report," 2.

50. Peretti, "Oral Histories," 120.

51. Peretti, "Oral Histories," 120.

52. Pearson and Litwak, "Final Narrative Report," 2.

53. Pearson and Litwak, "Final Narrative Report," 2.

54. Pearson, interview with the author.

55. Pearson and Litwak, "Final Narrative Report," 3.

56. Pearson and Litwak, "Final Narrative Report," question outline.

57. Pearson and Litwak, "Final Narrative Report," question outline.

58. Peretti, "Oral Histories, 121.

59. Ernest Williams, interview with Nathan W. Pearson Jr. and Howard Litwak, May 18, 1977, transcript, Goin' to Kansas City Collection, Western Historical Manuscripts Collection, University of Missouri–Kansas City. Any typographical errors are original to the transcript.

60. Pearson, *Goin' to Kansas City*, xv.

61. Pearson, *Goin' to Kansas City*, 127.

62. Pearson, *Goin' to Kansas City*, 134n3.

63. Pearson, *Goin' to Kansas City*, 112n2.

64. Pearson, *Goin' to Kansas City*, xiii.

65. Terry Teachout, "Goin' to Kansas City: In Search of Heroes," *Kansas City Star*, May 4, 1980, 8(A) and 18(A).

66. Pearson and Litwak, "Goin' to Kansas City."

67. Teachout, "Goin' to Kansas City," 18(A).

68. Brofsky, "Review: *Goin' to Kansas City*," 334.

69. Driggs and Haddix, *Kansas City Jazz*, ix.

70. Driggs and Haddix, *Kansas City Jazz*, x.

71. Driggs and Haddix, *Kansas City Jazz*, x.

72. Chuck Haddix, Frank Driggs Jazz Oral History Collection, Special Collections, Miller-Nichols Library, University of Missouri–Kansas City, https://library2.umkc.edu/marr-collections/archival/driggs.

73. Haddix, Frank Driggs Jazz Oral History Collection.

74. Driggs and Haddix, *Kansas City Jazz*, xi.

75. Driggs and Haddix, *Kansas City Jazz*, 39.

76. Driggs and Haddix, *Kansas City Jazz*, 101.

77. Driggs and Haddix, *Kansas City Jazz*, 1.

78. Driggs and Haddix, *Kansas City Jazz*, 57.

79. Driggs and Haddix, *Kansas City Jazz*, 25.

80. Driggs and Haddix, *Kansas City Jazz*, 26.

81. Driggs and Haddix, *Kansas City Jazz*, 225.

82. Driggs and Haddix, *Kansas City Jazz*, 69.

83. Dahl, *Morning Glory*, 66–67.

84. Driggs and Haddix, *Kansas City Jazz*, 101.

85. Driggs and Haddix, *Kansas City Jazz*, 132.

86. Driggs and Haddix, *Kansas City Jazz*, 101.

87. Driggs and Haddix, *Kansas City Jazz*, 12.

88. Driggs and Haddix, *Kansas City Jazz*, 7.

89. Driggs and Haddix, *Kansas City Jazz*, 5.

90. Driggs and Haddix, *Kansas City Jazz*, 233.

91. Driggs and Haddix, *Kansas City Jazz*, 234–35.

92. Rawlins, "Review: *Kansas City Jazz*," 695.

93. Rawlins, "Review: *Kansas City Jazz*," 695.

94. Priestley, "Review: *Kansas City Jazz*," 91.

95. Priestley, "Review: *Kansas City Jazz*," 97.

4. SISSY NIGHTS AT THE SPINNING WHEEL

1. Mumford, "Homosex Changes," 398.
2. Levine, "Jazz and American Culture," 13.
3. Smith-Rosenberg, "The Female World," 60.
4. Sinfield, *Out on Stage*, 39.
5. Smith-Rosenberg, "The New Woman," 266.
6. Recreation Department, *Annual Report*, 242–43.
7. Peiss, "Commercial Leisure," 106.
8. Chauncey, "Female Deviance," 93.
9. Drorbaugh, "Sliding Scales," 120.
10. Boyd, *Wide-Open Town*, 11.
11. Boyd, *Wide-Open Town*, 13.
12. Boyd, *Wide-Open Town*, 26.
13. Mumford, "Homosex Changes," 394.
14. History Project, *Improper Bostonians*, 104.
15. Luce, "A History of the Standard Theatre," 4.
16. Havig, "Mass Commercial Amusements," 327.
17. Crabb, "A History of Music," 49.
18. Allen, *Horrible Prettiness*, 221.
19. Allen, *Horrible Prettiness*, 221.
20. Peiss, "Commercial Leisure," 109.
21. Peiss, "Commercial Leisure," 110.
22. Board of Public Welfare, *The Kansas City Child: A Handbook of the Child Welfare Exhibit*, 48, handbook from 1911 Convention Hall exhibition, Special Collections, Kansas City (MO) Public Library.
23. Havig, "Mass Commercial Amusements," 327.
24. Recreation Department, *Annual Report*, 205.
25. Recreation Department, *Annual Report*, 205.
26. DeAngelo, *What About Kansas City*, 115.
27. Ken Weyand, "Electric Park: Kansas City's Glowing Attraction of 1899–1925," 11, Vertical File—Electric Park, Special Collections, Kansas City (MO) Public Library.
28. Pearson, *Goin' to Kansas City*, 12.

29. Ernest Williams, interview with Nathan W. Pearson Jr. and Howard Litwak, May 18, 1977, transcript, 40, private collection of Nathan Pearson.
30. Sexton, "Blackface Minstrelsy," 5–8.
31. Gaines, "Sexuality and Race," 319.
32. History Project, *Improper Bostonians*, 111.
33. Crabb, "A History of Music," 55.
34. Crabb, "A History of Music," 55.
35. Crabb, "A History of Music," 55.
36. History Project, *Improper Bostonians*, 11.
37. Erenberg, *Steppin' Out*, 81.
38. Erenberg, *Steppin' Out*, 113.
39. Erenberg, *Steppin' Out*, 83.
40. Kenney, "Historical Context," 107–8.
41. Peiss, "'Charity Girls,'" 59.
42. Morris, *Wait Until Dark*, 187.
43. Friedman, *Prurient Interests*, 8.
44. Recreation Department, *Annual Report*, 205.
45. DeAngelo, *What About Kansas City*, 114.
46. Montgomery and Kasper, *Kansas City*, 86.
47. Luce, "A History of the Standard Theatre," 51.
48. Recreation Department, *Annual Report*, 271.
49. Allen, *Horrible Prettiness*, 201.
50. Allen, *Horrible Prettiness*, 219.
51. Allen, *Horrible Prettiness*, 214.
52. Williams, interview with Pearson and Litwak, 41.
53. Williams, interview with Pearson and Litwak, 41.
54. Bean, "Transgressing the Gender Divide," 255.
55. Lewis, *When Harlem Was in Vogue*, xxvii.
56. McBreen, "Biblical Gender Bending," 23.
57. Pearson, *Goin' to Kansas City*, 100.
58. Chuck Haddix, discussion with the author, April 2004. The author would like to thank Chuck Haddix for copies of newspaper clippings about gender impersonators in Kansas City.

59. The word "queer" has multiple meanings, both historical and political, that make it a highly problematic term. Its use here is not meant as an ahistorical referent but rather as a way of discussing nonheteronormative behavior and performance in the jazz scene period. The term "queer" was not unknown in the jazz scenes of America. Biographer David Hadju suggested that "queer" meant "unusual" or "eccentric" in the 1920s but that its use to describe same-sex sexuality was not unheard of. According to David Hurewitz, historian Sharon Ullman found archival records indicating that "queer" was a common subcultural, insider term for homosexual men in Los Angeles in the 1920s and 1930s. In this study the definition of "queer" follows historian Nan Alamilla Boyd in positioning "queer" as a signifier of any behavior marked by sexual and gender transgression of the dominant norms, and therefore anyone resisting heteronormativity in the jazz scene. See also Hadju, *Lush Life*; Hurewitz, *Bohemian Los Angeles*.
60. Ullman, "'The Twentieth-Century Way,'" 547.
61. Hurewitz, *Bohemian Los Angeles*, 37. Hurewitz's use of the term "fairy" is from George Chauncey's *Gay New York*, in which Chauncey wrote that the identification as a "fairy" was for early twentieth-century men in New York City who performed feminine gender characteristics as a way to signal their sexual desire for men. See also Chauncey, *Gay New York*.
62. Kukla, *Swing City*, 1.
63. Boyd, *Wide-Open Town*, 14.
64. Boyd, *Wide-Open Town*, 26.
65. McBreen, "Biblical Gender Bending," 24.
66. Mumford, *Interzones*, 143.
67. Kennedy and Davis, *Boots of Leather*.
68. Ullman, "'The Twentieth-Century Way,'" 591–96. Ullman also explains that this spatialization of queerness caused problems for police, who were troubled when the "deviants" they were sent to arrest (specifically performance patrons) were not dressed in drag.
69. Boyd, *Wide-Open Town*, 33.
70. Moore, "Remapping Resistance," 93.

71. Hamilton, "'I'm the Queen,'" 115.
72. Drorbaugh, "Sliding Scales," 124.
73. Drorbaugh, "Sliding Scales," 126.
74. Senelick, "Introduction," ix.
75. Senelick, "Lady and the Tramp," 29.
76. Senelick, "Lady and the Tramp, 37.
77. Hamilton, "'I'm the Queen,'" 108.
78. Hamilton, "'I'm the Queen,'" 111.
79. Straub, *Sexual Suspects*, 20.
80. Hall, *Representation*, 268.
81. Straub, *Sexual Suspects*, 20.
82. Straub, *Sexual Suspects*, 129.
83. Straub. *Sexual Suspects*, 143.
84. Muñoz, *Disidentifications*, 99–100.
85. Muñoz, *Disidentifications*, 114.
86. Hatheway, *The Gilded Age Construction*, 59.
87. Phelan, *Unmarked*, 21.
88. Foucault, *The History of Sexuality*, 1:116.
89. Boyd, *Wide-Open Town*, 26.
90. Newton, *Mother Camp*, 7.
91. Chauncey, *Gay New York*, 331–54.
92. Hamilton, *When I'm Bad*, 149.
93. Senelick, "Lady and the Tramp," 33.
94. Senelick, "Boys and Girls Together," 89.
95. Board of Public Welfare, *Fifth Annual Report*, 53.
96. Montgomery and Kasper, *Kansas City*, 87.
97. Straub, *Sexual Suspects*, 134.
98. *Kansas City Star*, January 21, 1927.
99. Booker Washington, interview with Nathan Pearson Jr. and Howard Litwak, July 8, 1977, transcript, 141–42, Goin' to Kansas City Collection, Western Historical Manuscripts Collection, University of Missouri–Kansas City.
100. Herman L. Walder, interview with Nathan W. Pearson Jr. and Howard Litwak, June 8, 1977, transcript, 81–82, Goin' to Kansas City

Collection, Western Historical Manuscripts Collection, University of Missouri–Kansas City.

101. Walder, interview with Pearson and Litwak, 199.
102. Walder, interview with Pearson and Litwak, 201.
103. Walder, interview with Pearson and Litwak, 202–3.
104. Butler, *Gender Trouble*, 179.
105. Pearson, *Goin' to Kansas City*, 92.
106. Pearson, *Goin' to Kansas City*, 92.
107. Gabbard, "Introduction," 2.

5. CRIB GIRLS TO CRIMINALS

1. Driggs and Haddix, *Kansas City Jazz*, 8.
2. Long, *The Great Southern Babylon*, 1.
3. Long, *The Great Southern Babylon*, 7.
4. Martin, *Our Negro Population*, 129.
5. Schirmer, *A City Divided*, 166.
6. Pearson, *Goin' to Kansas City*, 101.
7. Pearson, *Goin' to Kansas City*, 100.
8. Mumford, *Interzones*, 21.
9. Johnson, "Social Evil," 127.
10. Johnson, "Social Evil," 138.
11. Erenberg, *Steppin' Out*, 63.
12. Havig, "Mass Commercial Amusements," 341.
13. Recreation Department, *Annual Report*, 242–43.
14. Mumford, *Interzones*, 29.
15. Martin, *Our Negro Population*, 129.
16. Martin, *Our Negro Population*, 132.
17. Martin, *Our Negro Population*, 133.
18. Martin, *Our Negro Population*, 160–61.
19. Sinfield, *Out on Stage*, 72.
20. Chauncey, *Gay New York*, 28.
21. See Stansell, *City of Women*.
22. Rosen, *Lost Sisterhood*, 3.
23. Peiss, "'Charity Girls' and City Pleasures," 61.

24. Rosen, *Lost Sisterhood*, 4.

25. Rosen, *Lost Sisterhood*, 5.

26. Rosen, *Lost Sisterhood*, 6.

27. Rosen, *Lost Sisterhood*, xiv.

28. Burnham, "Progressive Era Revolution," 887.

29. Burnham, "Progressive Era Revolution," 887.

30. Havig, "Mass Commercial Amusements," 338.

31. McGovern, "American Women's Pre–World War I Freedom," 331.

32. Sinfield, *Out on Stage*, 50.

33. Pearson, *Goin' to Kansas City*, 78.

34. Montgomery and Kasper, *Kansas City*, 85.

35. Miller, *From Prairie to Prison*, 14.

36. Rosen, *Lost Sisterhood*, 105.

37. Lee, "High Toned Brothel," 83.

38. Rosen, *Lost Sisterhood*, 44.

39. Dorsett, *The Pendergast Machine*, 68.

40. Dorsett, *The Pendergast Machine*, 4.

41. Kimball, *Nell Kimball*, 9.

42. Rosen, *Lost Sisterhood*, 5.

43. Johnson, "Social Evil," 10.

44. Lee, "High Toned Brothel," 83.

45. Rosen, *Lost Sisterhood*, 71.

46. Hicks, *Tramp Printer*, 29.

47. Hicks, *Tramp Printer*, 29.

48. Hicks, *Tramp Printer*, 29–30.

49. A. B. McDonald, "Gift to Union Mission of Old North Side Resort," *Kansas City Star*, February 18, 1934, A5.

50. McDonald, "Gift to Union Mission."

51. Lee, "High Toned Brothel," 84.

52. Lee, "High Toned Brothel," 84.

53. "A Bloody Tragedy," *Kansas City Times*, February 3, 1880, 5.

54. "Gotham Dance Houses," *Kansas City Times*, January 30, 1880, 2.

55. Rosen, *Lost Sisterhood*, 19.

56. Miller, *From Prairie to Prison*, 16.

57. Rosen, *Lost Sisterhood*, 14.
58. Martin *Our Negro Population*, 132.
59. Board of Public Welfare, *Third Annual Report*, 295.
60. Johnson, "Social Evil," 137.
61. Johnson, "Social Evil," 135.
62. Schirmer, *A City Divided*, 169.
63. Schirmer, *A City Divided*, 169.
64. Mumford, *Interzones*, 49.
65. Johnson, "Social Evil," 1.
66. Johnson, "Social Evil," 13.
67. Johnson, "Social Evil," 16.
68. Johnson, "Social Evil," 14.
69. Rosen, *Lost Sisterhood*, 13.
70. Rosen, *Lost Sisterhood*, xiii.
71. Rosen, *Lost Sisterhood*, 11.
72. Rosen, *Lost Sisterhood*, 78.
73. Madeleine, *Madeleine*, 65.
74. Madeleine, *Madeleine*, 63.
75. Madeleine, *Madeleine*, 70.
76. Lee, "High Toned Brothel," 83.
77. Lee, "Gone but Not Forgotten," 88.
78. McDonald, "Gift to Union Mission."
79. Ryan and Hall, *Sex Tourism*, 47.
80. Flynn, *Kansas City Women*, 26.
81. "Says Scattering of Vice Is Wrong," *Kansas City Journal*, September 12, 1913, 10.
82. "Says Scattering of Vice Is Wrong."
83. "Says Scattering of Vice Is Wrong."
84. "Says Scattering of Vice Is Wrong."
85. "Says Scattering of Vice Is Wrong."
86. Social Improvement News, "Case of Annie Chambers," 12.
87. Social Improvement News, "Condensed Information," 28.
88. State v. Kearns.
89. State v. Kearns.

90. Marshall and Morrison, *Political History*, 85.
91. Marshall and Morrison, *Political History*, 85.
92. State v. Kearns.
93. Social Improvement News, "Case of Annie Chambers," 12.
94. State v. Kearns.
95. State v. Kearns, Appellant's Abstract of the Record and Bill of Exceptions, 137.
96. State v. Kearns, Appellant's Abstract, 93.
97. State v. Kearns.
98. State v. Kearns, Appellant's Abstract, 139.
99. State v. Kearns, Appellant's Abstract, 139.
100. McDonald, "Gift to Union Mission."
101. McDonald, "Gift to Union Mission."
102. McDonald, "Gift to Union Mission."
103. McDonald, "Gift to Union Mission."
104. McDonald, "Gift to Union Mission."
105. McDonald, "Gift to Union Mission."
106. Mumford, *Interzones*, 115.
107. W. G. Secrest, "South Siders Getting Thrill from Sights: Colorful Figure in Red Light District for Half Century Relates Her Story Nightly," *Kansas City Journal Post*, May 15, 1932, 1(B).
108. Secrest, "South Siders Getting Thrill," 2(B).
109. Secrest, "South Siders Getting Thrill," 1(B).
110. Social Improvement News, "Case of Annie Chambers," 12.
111. "Mysterious 'Lady' Won't Reveal Her Past," *Kansas City Star*, December 6, 1963.
112. Umland, "Gambling Halls," 41.

6. QUEERING DANTE'S INFERNO

1. Edna Mae Whithouse was married three times (Riggs, Jacobs, and Mears). Pearson and Litwak mistakenly listed her as Edna Minturn, the last name of her daughter Ida. Though her last name was Mears at the time of her death, when her papers were donated to the University

of Kansas they were listed as the Edna Mae Jacobs Papers. For the sake of clarity, she will be referred to as Edna Jacobs throughout this work.

2. Pearson, interview with the author.

3. Pearson, *Goin' to Kansas City*, 227.

4. Pearson, *Goin' to Kansas City*, 226.

5. Driggs and Haddix, *Kansas City Jazz*, 188.

6. Driggs and Haddix, *Kansas City Jazz*, 188.

7. Wilson, interview with the author.

8. Gordon, *Ghostly Matters*, 16–17.

9. Gordon, *Ghostly Matters*, 207.

10. Gordon, *Ghostly Matters*, 169.

11. Edna (nee Jacobs) and Ida Mintirn, interview with Nathan Pearson Jr. and Howard Litwak, January 24, 1980, transcript by the author, October 18, 2002, Folder #KC0012, Tape #T.123 (12), Kansas City Jazz Oral History Collection, Western Historical Manuscripts Collection, University of Missouri–Kansas City.

12. Jacobs, interview with Pearson and Litwak, 5.

13. Dorsett, *The Pendergast Machine*, 4–5.

14. Montgomery and Kasper, *Kansas City*, 102.

15. Jacobs, interview with Pearson and Litwak, 3.

16. Montgomery and Kasper, *Kansas City*, 169.

17. Montgomery and Kasper, *Kansas City*, 180.

18. Montgomery and Kasper, *Kansas City*, 180.

19. Montgomery and Kasper, *Kansas City*, 182.

20. Jacobs, interview with Pearson and Litwak, 5.

21. Jacobs, interview with Pearson and Litwak, 16.

22. White, "Kansas City," 238.

23. Schirmer, *A City Divided*, 172.

24. Jacobs, interview with Pearson and Litwak, 13–14.

25. Jacobs, interview with Pearson and Litwak, 1.

26. Jacobs, interview with Pearson and Litwak, 11.

27. "Night Club Notes," *Kansas City Journal-Post*, December 3, 1933, 4(A).

28. Jacobs, interview with Pearson and Litwak, 10.

29. Wilson, interview with the author.
30. Scrapbooks, #97-05-04, Edna Mae Jacobs Collection, Spencer Research Library, University of Kansas–Lawrence.
31. Folder 1, Edna Mae Jacobs Collection.
32. "'Mae West' Well Known Female Impersonator Here," *Kansas City Call*, June 14, 1935, 11(A).
33. Pearson, *Goin' to Kansas City*, 102.
34. "Night Life of the Mortals," *Future*, March 29, 1935, 1 and 8.
35. "Night Life of the Mortals," 1 and 8.
36. Wilson, interview with the author.
37. Pearson, *Goin' to Kansas City*, 102.
38. Drorbaugh, "Sliding Scales," 139.
39. Scrapbooks, Edna Mae Jacobs Collection.
40. Jacobs, interview with Pearson and Litwak, 8–9.
41. Jacobs, interview with Pearson and Litwak, 10.
42. Jacobs, interview with Pearson and Litwak, 9.
43. Scrapbooks, Edna Mae Jacobs Collection.
44. Boyd, *Wide-Open Town*, 52.
45. Jacobs, interview with Pearson and Litwak, 9.
46. Wilson, interview with the author.
47. Scrapbook 1, Edna Mae Jacobs Collection.
48. Folder 4, Edna Mae Jacobs Collection.
49. Jacobs, interview with Pearson and Litwak, 8.
50. Wilson, interview with the author.
51. Scrapbooks 1 and 2, Edna Mae Jacobs Collection.
52. Jacobs, interview with Pearson and Litwak, 8.
53. Folder 3, Edna Mae Jacobs Collection.
54. Wilson, interview with the author.
55. Edna Mae Jacobs Collection.
56. Edna Mae Jacobs Collection.
57. Accession records, Edna Mae Jacobs Collection.
58. Pearson and Litwak not only mistakenly used Jacobs's daughter's last name, they also misspelled the name. Ida married Charles MINTURN, not MINTIRN as listed in the Pearson collections.

59. Despite extensive searching, Nathan Pearson cannot locate the (Jacobs) Mintirn tape in his private collection.
60. Nathan Pearson, email to the author, June 14, 2006.
61. Wilson, interview with the author.
62. Jacobs, interview with Pearson and Litwak, 15.
63. Rye, "Lovett, Baby," 629.
64. "Music in Mid-America," *Kansas City Times*, September 20, 1972, 8(A).
65. Interview with Samuel Lovett, transcript, Frank Driggs Jazz Oral History Collection, Special Collections, Miller-Nichols Library, University of Missouri–Kansas City, photocopy located in File Baby Lovett, Special Collections, Kansas City (MO) Public Library.
66. Martin, *Kansas City*, 27.
67. Sexton, "No Interracial Sexual Relationship," 145.
68. Gordon, *Ghostly Matters*, 208.
69. Muñoz, *Disidentifications*, 195–96.

7. REMEMBERING KC

1. Fenner, "Goin' to Kansas City Revisited," 25.
2. Fenner, "Goin' to Kansas City Revisited," 24.
3. Jerry Lieber and Mike Stoller, "K.C. Lovin'," http://www.bluesforpeace.com/lyrics/kansas-city.htm, accessed June 30, 2007. The lyric "an' I wanna get me some" is the original Lieber and Stoller lyric. When the song was recorded by Wilbert Harrison in 1959, he altered the lyric to the more familiar version in which Harrison speaks of "crazy little women" and plans to "get me one." While Harrison altered the lyric, the credit stayed with Lieber and Stoller.
4. Missouri Department of Natural Resources, "Wyandotte 300 Project," http://www.dnr.mo.gov/env/hwp/bvcp/docs/Wyandotte%20300%20Project.pdf, accessed June 30, 2007.
5. Hok.Sports+Venue+Event, corporate website, http://www.hoksve.com/, accessed June 30, 2007.
6. Driggs and Haddix, *Kansas City Jazz*, 234–35.
7. Gabbard, "Review: *Kansas City*," 1274.
8. Driggs and Haddix, *Kansas City Jazz*, 29.

9. Valentine, "Creating Transgressive Space," 478.

10. Duncan, Johnson, and Schein, *Companion to Cultural Geography*, 90.

11. Muñoz, *Disidentifications*, 1.

12. Muñoz, *Disidentifications*, 6.

13. Foucault, *Discipline and Punish*, 141.

14. Foucault, *Discipline and Punish*, 143.

Bibliography

ARCHIVAL SOURCES

Institute of Jazz Studies, Rutgers University, Newark, New Jersey
   Institute of Jazz Studies Administrative Records Collection
   Mary Lou Williams Collection
Kansas City (MO) Public Library
   Historic Photographs Collection
   Missouri Valley Special Collections
   Newspaper Collection
Lesbian Herstory Archives, Brooklyn, New York
   Books and Monographs Collection
   Jewel Box Revue Subject File
   Musicians Subject File
   Music Subject File
   Stormé DeLarverie Subject File
   T-Shirt Collection
Missouri State Archives
   Records of the Missouri Supreme Court
Private Collection of Nathan Pearson
Special Collections, Miller-Nichols Library, University of Missouri–Kansas City
   Frank Driggs Jazz Oral History Collection
Spencer Research Library, University of Kansas–Lawrence
   Edna Mae Jacobs Collection

Western Historical Manuscripts Collection, University of Missouri–
Kansas City
Goin' to Kansas City Collection
Kansas City Jazz Oral History Collection

PUBLISHED SOURCES

Adams, Paul C., Steven Hoelscher, and Karen E. Till. "Place in Context:
Rethinking Humanist Geographies." In *Textures of Place: Exploring Human-
ist Geographies*, edited by Paul C. Adams, Steven Hoelscher, and Karen
E. Till, xiii–xxxiii. Minneapolis: University of Minnesota Press, 2001.

Ake, David. *Jazz Cultures*. Berkeley: University of California Press, 2002.

Aldama, Frederick Lewis. "Review: *Disidentifications* by Jose Esteban
Muñoz." *Modern Drama* 43, no. 4 (Winter 2000): 641–42.

Alexander, Ruth. *The "Girl Problem": Female Sexual Delinquency in New York,
1900–1930*. New York: Cornell University Press, 1995.

Allen, Robert C. *Horrible Prettiness: Burlesque and American Culture*. Chapel
Hill: University of North Carolina Press, 1991.

Anderson, Karen. "Western Women: The Twentieth-Century Experience."
In *The Twentieth-Century West: Historical Interpretations*, edited by Gerald
P. Nash and Richard Etulain, 99–122. Albuquerque: University of New
Mexico Press, 1989.

Armitage, Susan. "Women and Men in Western History: A Stereotypical
Vision." In *The Gendered West*, edited by Gordon Morris Bakken and
Brenda Farrington, 1–17. The American West: Interactions, Intersections,
and Injunctions. New York: Garland, 2000.

Bean, Annemarie. "Transgressing the Gender Divide: The Female Impersonator in Nineteenth-Century Blackface Minstrelsy." In *Inside the Minstrel Mask: Readings in Nineteenth-Century Blackface Minstrelsy*, edited
by Annemarie Bean, James V. Hatch, and Brooks McNamara, 245–56.
Hanover and London: Wesleyan University Press, 1996.

Becker, Howard S. "Jazz Places." In *Music Scenes: Local, Translocal, and Virtual*, edited by Richard A. Peterson and Andy Bennett, 17–27. Nashville:
Vanderbilt University Press, 2004.

Bederman, Gail. *Manliness and Civilization: A Cultural History of Gender and Race in the United States, 1880–1917*. Women in Culture and Society, edited by Catharine R. Stimpson. Chicago: University of Chicago Press, 1995.

Best, Joel. *Controlling Vice: Regulating Brothel Prostitution in St. Paul, 1865–1883*. Columbus: Ohio State University Press, 1998.

Best, Steven, and Douglas Kellner. *Postmodern Theory: Critical Interrogations*. New York: Guilford Press, 1991.

Blanchard, Mary W. "The Soldier and the Aesthete: Homosexuality and Popular Culture in Gilded Age America." *Journal of American Studies* 30 (1996): 25–46.

Board of Public Welfare. *Fifth Annual Report of the Board of Public Welfare of Kansas City, Missouri, April 21, 1913–April 20, 1914*. Kansas City MO: Cline Printing, 1914.

———. *Second Annual Report of the Board of Public Welfare of Kansas City, Missouri, April 19, 1910–April 18, 1911*. Kansas City MO: Fratcher Printing, 1911.

———. *Third Annual Report of the Board of Public Welfare of Kansas City, Missouri, April 18, 1911–April 15, 1912*. Kansas City MO: Cline Printing, 1912.

Borland, Katharine. "That's Not What I Said: Interpretive Conflict in Oral Narrative Research." In *The Oral History Reader*, edited by Robert Perks and Alistair Thomson, 320–32. London and New York: Routledge, 1998.

Boyd, Nan Alamilla. *Wide-Open Town: A History of Queer San Francisco to 1965*. Berkeley: University of California Press, 2003.

Brofsky, Howard. "Review: *Goin' to Kansas City* by Nathan Pearson Jr." *Ethnomusicology* 33, no. 2 (Spring/Summer 1989): 334.

Brooks, Daphne A. *Bodies in Dissent: Spectacular Performances of Race and Freedom, 1850–1910*. Durham NC: Duke University Press, 2006.

Brown, A. Theodore, and Lyle W. Dorsett. *K.C.: A History of Kansas City, Missouri*. Western Urban History. Boulder CO: Pruett, 1978.

Brown, Michael P. *Closet Space: Geographies of Metaphor from the Body to the Globe*. Critical Geographies, edited by Tracy Shelton and Gill Valentine. London: Routledge, 2000.

Brown, Stuart, Diane Collinson, and Robert Wilkinson, eds. *One Hundred Twentieth-Century Philosophers*. London: Routledge, 1998.

Burnham, John C. "The Progressive Revolution in American Attitudes Toward Sex." *Journal of American History* 59, no. 4 (March 1973): 885–908.

Butler, Anne M. *Daughters of Joy, Sisters of Misery: Prostitutes in the American West, 1865–1890*. Urbana and Chicago: University of Illinois Press, 1985.

Butler, Judith. *Bodies That Matter: On the Discursive Limits of "Sex."* New York: Routledge, 1993.

———. *Gender Trouble: Feminism and the Subversion of Identity*. New York: Routledge, 2000.

Butsch, Richard. "Introduction: Leisure and Hegemony in America." In *For Fun and Profit: The Transformation of Leisure into Consumption*, edited by Richard Butsch, 3–27. Philadelphia: Temple University Press, 1990.

Castiglia, Christopher. "Review: *Foundlings: Lesbian and Gay Historical Emotion Before Stonewall*." *Journal of American History* 89, no. 4 (March 2003): 1590–91.

Chauncey, George. "Christian Brotherhood or Sexual Perversion? Homosexual Identities and the Construction of Sexual Boundaries in the World War One Era." *Journal of Social History* 19 (Winter 1985): 189–211.

———. "From Sexual Inversion to Homosexuality: The Changing Medical Conceptualization of Female 'Deviance.'" In *Passion and Power: Sexuality in History*, edited by Kathy Peiss and Christina Simmons, 87–117. Philadelphia: Temple University Press, 1989.

———. *Gay New York: Gender, Urban Culture, and the Making of Gay Male World, 1890–1940*. New York: Basic Books, 1994.

Clark, Andrew. "'Nothin' Over There but Critics': Jazz and History (criticism, canon, historiography)." In *Riffs and Choruses: A New Jazz Anthology*, edited by Andrew Clark, 57–61. London and New York: Continuum, 2001.

Comer, Krista. *Landscapes of the New West: Gender and Geography in Contemporary Women's Writing*. Chapel Hill: University of North Carolina Press, 1999.

Cook, Susan C. "Passionless Dancing and Passionate Reform: Respectability, Modernism, and the Social Dancing of Irene and Vernon Castle." In

The Passion of Music and Dance, edited by William Washabaugh, 133–50. Oxford: Berg Press, 1998.

Crabb, James Milford. "A History of Music in Kansas City." PhD diss., University of Missouri–Kansas City Conservatory of Music, 1967.

Crouch, Stanley. *Kansas City Lightning: The Rise and Times of Charles Parker*. New York: Harper, 2013.

Crunden, Robert M. *Body and Soul: The Making of American Modernism, Art, Music, and Letters in the Jazz Age, 1919–1926*. New York: Basic Books, 2000.

Dahl, Linda. *Morning Glory: A Biography of Mary Lou Williams*. New York: Pantheon, 1999.

Davies, Charlotte Aull. *Reflexive Ethnography: A Guide to Researching Selves and Others*. London and New York: Routledge, 1999.

Dean, Carolyn. "The Productive Hypothesis: Foucault, Gender and the History of Sexuality." *History and Theory* 33 (1994): 271–96.

DeAngelo, Dory. *What About Kansas City! A Historical Handbook*. Kansas City MO: Two Lane Press, 1995.

de Graaf, Lawrence B. "Race, Sex, and Region: Black Women in the American West, 1850–1920." In *The Gendered West*, edited by Gordon Morris Bakken and Brenda Farrington, 73–101. The American West: Interactions, Intersections, and Injunctions. New York: Garland, 2000.

DeLeon, Charles Ponce. "Spectacular Women: A Review of *Female Spectacle*." *Reviews in American History* 30 (2002): 295–301.

Deleuze, Giles, and Felix Guattari. *Anti-Oedipus: Capitalism and Schizophrenia*. Minneapolis: University of Minnesota Press, 1983; 10th edition, 2000.

Deutsch, Sarah. *Women and the City: Gender, Space and Power in Boston, 1870–1940*. New York: Oxford University Press, 2000.

DeVeaux, Scott. "Constructing the Jazz Tradition: Jazz Historiography." *Black American Literature Forum* 25, no. 3 (Autumn 1991): 525–60.

Donovan, Brian. *White Slave Crusades: Race, Gender, and Anti-Vice Reform, 1887–1917*. Chicago: University of Illinois Press, 2006.

Dorsett, Lyle W. *The Pendergast Machine*. New York: Oxford University Press, 1968.

Douglas, Ann. *Terrible Honesty: Mongrel Manhattan in the 1920s.* New York: Farrar, Straus and Giroux, 1995.

Dreyfus, Hubert L., and Paul Rabinow. *Michel Foucault: Beyond Structuralism and Hermeneutics.* 2nd ed. Chicago: University of Chicago Press, 1983.

Driggs, Frank, and Chuck Haddix. *Kansas City Jazz: From Ragtime to Bebop—A History.* New York: Oxford University Press, 2005.

Driggs, Franklin A. "Kansas City and the Southwest." In *Jazz: New Perspectives on the History of Jazz by Twelve of the World's Foremost Jazz Critics and Scholars,* edited by Nat Hentoff and Albert J. McCarthy, 190–230. New York: Holt, Rinehart and Winston, 1959. Reprint, New York: DaCapo Press, 1974. Page references are to the 1974 edition.

———. "Women in Jazz: A Survey." New York: Stash Records, 1977. Lesbian Herstory Archives, File Number 09220: Music—Blues and Jazz, Brooklyn, New York.

Drorbaugh, Elizabeth. "Sliding Scales: Notes on Stormé DeLarverie and the Jewel Box Review, the Cross-Dressed Woman on the Contemporary Stage, and the Invert." In *Crossing the Stage: Controversies on Cross-Dressing,* edited by Lesley Ferris, 120–43. New York: Routledge, 1993.

DuCille, Anne. "'Othered' Matters: Reconceptualizing Dominance and Difference in the History of Sexuality in America." *Journal of the History of Sexuality* 1 (1990): 102–30.

Duggan, Lisa. *Sapphic Slashers: Sex, Violence, and American Modernity.* Durham NC: Duke University Press, 2000.

Dumenil, Lynn, and Eric Foner. *The Modern Temper: American Culture and Society in the 1920s.* New York: Hill and Wang, 1995.

Duncan, James S., Nuala C. Johnson, and Richard H. Schein, eds. *A Companion to Cultural Geography.* Blackwell Companions to Geography. Oxford: Blackwell, 2004.

Dyson, Ernest F. "Review: *Pops Foster: The Autobiography of a New Orleans Jazzman* by Tom Stoddard and Brian Rust and *Jazz Style in Kansas City and the Southwest* by Ross Russell." *Journal of Negro History* 58, no. 2 (April 1973): 221–22.

Erenberg, Lewis A. *Steppin' Out: Nightlife and the Transformation of American Culture, 1890–1930.* Westport CT: Greenwood Press, 1981.

Faderman, Lillian. *Odd Girls and Twilight Lovers: A History of Lesbian Life in Twentieth-Century America*. New York: Columbia University Press, 1991.

Fass, Paula. *Damned and the Beautiful: American Youth in the 1920s*. Baltimore: Johns Hopkins Press, 1979.

Fenner, Ed. "Goin' to Kansas City Revisited." *JAM: Jazz Ambassador Magazine* 19, no. 6 (December 2005/January 2006): 24–25.

Finkel, Alicia. "A Tale of Lilies, Sunflowers, and Knee Breeches: Oscar Wilde's Wardrobe for His American Tour." *Dress* 15 (1989): 4–15.

Fischer, Gayle V. *Pantaloons and Power: A Nineteenth-Century Dress Reform in the United States*. Kent OH: Kent State University Press, 2001.

Flanagan-Saint-Aubin, Arthur. "'BlackGayMale' Discourse: Reading Race and Sexuality Between the Lines." In *American Sexual Politics: Sex, Gender and Race Since the Civil War*, edited by John C. Fout and Maura Tantillo, 381–403. Chicago: University of Chicago Press, 1993.

Flynn, Jane Fifield. *Kansas City Women of Independent Minds*. Kansas City MO: Fifield Publishing, 1992.

Foucault, Michel. *The Archaeology of Knowledge and the Discourse on Language*. Translated by A. M. Sheridan Smith. New York: Pantheon Books, 1972.

———. *Discipline and Punish: The Birth of the Prison*. Translated by Alan Sheridan. New York: Vintage, 1977. Reprint, 1995.

———. *The History of Sexuality*. Vol. 1, *Introduction*. Translated by Robert Hurley. New York: Random House, 1978. Reprint, 1990.

———. "Of Other Spaces." Translated by Jay Miskoweic. *Diacritics* 16, no. 1 (Spring 1986): 22–27.

———. *The Order of Things: An Archaeology of the Human Sciences*. Translated by A. M. Sheridan Smith. New York: Random House, 1970. Reprint, New York: Vintage Books, 1994.

———. *Politics, Philosophy, Culture: Interviews and Other Writings, 1977–1984*. Translated by Alan Sheridan. New York: Routledge, 1988.

———. "The Subject and the Power." In *Michel Foucault: Beyond Structuralism and Hermeneutics*, by Hubert L. Dreyfus and Paul Rabinow, 208–26. 2nd ed. Chicago: University of Chicago Press, 1983.

Friedlander, Peter. "Theory, Method, and Oral History." In *The Oral History Reader*, edited by Robert Perks and Alistair Thomson, 311–19. London and New York: Routledge, 1998.

Friedman, Andrea. *Prurient Interests: Gender, Democracy, and Obscenity in New York City, 1909–1945*. Columbia Studies in Contemporary American History, edited by William E. Leuchtenberg and Alan Brinkley. New York: Columbia University Press, 2000.

Gabbard, Krin. "Introduction: The Jazz Canon and Its Consequences." In *Jazz Among the Discourses*, edited by Krin Gabbard, 1–28. Durham NC: Duke University Press, 1995.

———. "Introduction: Writing the Other History." In *Representing Jazz*, edited by Krin Gabbard, 1–8. Durham NC: Duke University Press, 1995.

———, ed. *Representing Jazz*. Durham NC: Duke University Press, 1995.

———. "Review: *Kansas City* produced by Robert Altman and Frank Barhydt." *American Historical Review* 102, no. 4 (October 1997): 1274–75.

Gaines, Stanley O., Jr. "Sexuality and Race." In *The African American Experience: An Historical and Bibliographical Guide*, edited by Arvarh E. Strickland and Robert E. Weems Jr., 315–25. Westport CT: Greenwood Press, 2001.

Gendron, Bernard. *Between Montmartre and the Mudd Club: Popular Music and the Avant Garde*. Chicago: University of Chicago Press, 2002.

Gillis, Frank J. "Review: *Jazz Style in Kansas City and the Southwest* by Ross Russell and *Bird Lives! The High Life and Hard Times of Charlie (Yardbird) Parker* by Ross Russell." *Ethnomusicology* 19, no. 2 (May 1975): 315–16.

Glenn, Susan. *Female Spectacle: The Theatrical Roots of Modern Feminism*. Cambridge: Harvard University Press, 2000.

Goldberg, David. *Discontented America: The United States in the 1920s*. Baltimore: Johns Hopkins University Press, 1999.

Gordon, Avery. *Ghostly Matters: Haunting and the Sociological Imagination*. Minneapolis: University of Minnesota Press, 1997.

Gregory, Derek. *Geographical Imaginations*. Cambridge: Blackwell, 1994.

Gutting, Gary. "Michel Foucault: A User's Manual." In *The Cambridge Companion to Foucault*, edited by Gary Gutting, 1–27. London: Cambridge University Press, 1994.

Hadju, David. *Lush Life: A Biography of Billy Strayhorn*. New York: Farrar, Straus and Giroux, 1996.

Hall, Stuart. *Representation: Cultural Representations and Signifying Practices*. London: Sage, in association with The Open University, 1997.

Halperin, David. *Saint Foucault: Toward a Gay Hagiography*. New York: Oxford University Press, 1995.

Hamilton, Marybeth. "'I'm the Queen of the Bitches': Female Impersonation and Mae West's *Pleasure Man*." In *Crossing the Stage: Controversies in Cross-Dressing*, edited by Lesley Ferris, 107–19. New York: Routledge, 1993.

———. *When I'm Bad I'm Better: Mae West, Sex, and American Entertainment*. New York: Harper Collins, 1995.

Harlos, Christopher. "Jazz Autobiography: Theory, Practice, Politics." In *Representing Jazz*, edited by Krin Gabbard, 131–66. Durham NC: Duke University Press, 1995.

Haskell, Henry C., and Richard B. Fowler. *City of the Future: A Narrative History of Kansas City, 1850–1950*. Kansas City MO: Frank Glenn Publishing, 1950.

Hatheway, Jay. *The Gilded Age Construction of Modern American Homophobia*. New York: Palgrave Macmillan, 2003.

Havig, Alan. "Mass Commercial Amusements in Kansas City before World War I." *Missouri Historical Review* 75 (April 1981): 316–45.

Hennessey, Thomas J. *From Jazz to Swing: African-American Jazz Musicians and Their Music, 1890–1935*. Jazz History, Culture and Criticism, edited by William J. Kennedy III. Detroit: Wayne State University Press, 1994.

Hentoff, Nat, and Albert J. McCarthy. *Jazz: New Perspectives on the History of Jazz by Twelve of the World's Foremost Jazz Critics and Scholars*. New York: Holt, Rinehart and Winston, 1959. Reprint, New York: DaCapo Press, 1974.

Hicks, John Edward. *Adventures of a Tramp Printer, 1880–1890*. Kansas City MO: MidAmerica Press, 1950.

Higham, John. "The Reorientation of American Culture in the 1890s." In *The Origins of Modern Consciousness*, edited by John Weiss, 25–48. Detroit: Wayne State University Press, 1965.

History Project. *Improper Bostonians: Lesbian and Gay History from the Patriots to Playland*. Boston: Beacon Press, 1998.

Hurewitz, Daniel. *Bohemian Los Angeles and the Making of Modern Politics*. Berkeley: University of California Press, 2007.

Johnson, Fred. "The Social Evil in Kansas City." In *Second Annual Report of the Board of Public Welfare of Kansas City, Missouri, April 19, 1910–April 18, 1911*, by Board of Public Welfare, 126–41. Kansas City MO: Fratcher Printing, 1911.

Julien, Kyle. *Sounding the City: Jazz, African American Nightlife and the Articulation of Race in 1940s Los Angeles*. PhD diss., University of California, 2002.

Kelley, Robin D. G. *Race Rebels: Culture, Politics, and the Black Working Class*. New York: The Free Press, 1994.

Kennedy, Elizabeth, and Madeline Davis. *Boots of Leather, Slippers of Gold: The History of a Lesbian Community*. New York: Penguin, 1994.

Kenney, William Howland. "Historical Context and the Definition of Jazz: Putting More History in 'Jazz History.'" In *Jazz Among the Discourses*, edited by Krin Gabbard, 100–116. Durham NC: Duke University Press, 1995.

Kimball, Nell. *Nell Kimball: Her Life as an American Madam by Herself*. New York: Macmillan, 1970.

Kukla, Barbara J. *Swing City: Newark Nightlife, 1925–1950*. Philadelphia: Temple University Press, 1991.

Kurzweil, Edith. *The Age of Structuralism*. New York: Columbia University Press, 1980.

———. "Michel Foucault's History of Sexuality as Interpreted by Feminists and Marxists." *Social Research* 53 (Winter 1986): 647–63.

Larsen, Lawrence, and Nancy J. Hulston. *Pendergast!* Columbia: University of Missouri Press, 1997.

Lee, Fred L. "Annie Chambers' High Toned Brothel." *Kansas City Genealogist* 39, no. 1 (Spring 1998): 83–85.

———. "Gone but Not Forgotten: Annie Chambers, Kansas City Madam, Dead at Age Ninety-Two." *Kansas City Genealogist* 38, no. 2 (Fall 1998): 88–89.

Levine, Lawrence W. "Jazz and American Culture." *Journal of American Folklore* 102, no. 403 (January–March 1989): 6–22.

Lewis, David Levering. *When Harlem Was in Vogue*. 3rd ed. New York: Penguin, 1997.

Lewis, Lloyd, and Henry Justin Smith. *Oscar Wilde Discovers America, 1882*. New York: Harcourt, Brace, 1936.

Long, Alecia P. *The Great Southern Babylon: Sex, Race, and Respectability in New Orleans, 1865–1920*. Baton Rouge: Louisiana State University Press, 2004.

Luce, Michael G. "A History of the Standard Theatre, Kansas City, Missouri, 1900–1920." Master's thesis, Central Missouri State University, 1981.

Macey, David. *The Lives of Michel Foucault: A Biography*. New York: Pantheon, 1993.

Mackey, Thomas C. *Red Lights Out: A Legal History of Prostitution, Disorderly Houses, and Vice Districts, 1870–1917*. American Legal and Constitutional History: Garland Series of Outstanding Dissertations, edited by Harold Hyman. New York: Garland, 1987.

Madeleine. *Madeleine: An Autobiography*. New York: Harper and Brothers, 1919.

Marquis, Eva M. *A Survey of the Extent, Financial and Social Cost of Desertion and Artificially Broken Homes in Kansas City, Missouri, During the Year 1915*. Kansas City MO: Board of Public Welfare and Cline Printing, 1915.

Marshall and Morrison Publishers. *Political History of Jackson County: Biographical Sketches of Men Who Have Helped to Make It*. Kansas City MO: Marshall and Morrison, 1902. Reprint, Berwyn Heights MD: Heritage Books, 1997.

Martin, Asa E. *Our Negro Population: A Sociological Study of the Negroes of Kansas City, Missouri*. Kansas City MO: Franklin Hudson, 1913.

Martin, Donna, ed. *Kansas City . . . and All That's Jazz: The Kansas City Jazz Museum*. Kansas City MO: Andrews McMeel, 1999.

May, Larry. *Screening Out the Past: The Birth of Mass Culture and the Motion Picture Industry*. New York: Oxford University Press, 1980.

McBee, Randy D. *Dance Hall Days: Intimacy and Leisure among Working-Class Immigrants in the United States*. New York: New York University Press, 2000.

McBreen, Ellen. "Biblical Gender Bending in Harlem: The Queer Performance of Nugent's Salome." *Art Journal* 57, no. 3 (Autumn 1998): 22–28.

McClintock, Anne. *Imperial Leather: Race, Gender and Sexuality in the Colonial Context*. New York: Routledge, 1995.

McGovern, James R. "The American Women's Pre–World War I Freedom in Manners and Morals." *Journal of American History* 55, no. 2 (September 1968): 315–33.

McRuer, Robert. *Crip Theory: Cultural Signs of Queerness and Disability*. Cultural Front Theory, edited by Michael Berube. New York: New York University Press, 2006.

Megill, Allan. "Foucault, Structuralism, and the Ends of History." *Journal of Modern History* 51 (September 1979): 451–503.

Miller, James. *The Passion of Michel Foucault*. New York: Simon and Schuster, 1993.

Miller, Sally M. *From Prairie to Prison: The Life of Social Activist Kate Richards O'Hare*. Missouri Biography Series, edited by William E. Foley. Columbia: University of Missouri Press, 1993.

Mobley, Jane, and Nancy Whitehall Harris. *A City Within a Park: One Hundred Years of Parks and Boulevards in Kansas City, Missouri*. Kansas City MO: American Society of Landscape Architects and Kansas City, Missouri, Board of Parks and Recreation Commissioners, 1991.

Montgomery, Rick, and Shirl Kasper. *Kansas City: An American Story*. Edited by Monroe Dodd. Kansas City MO: Kansas City Star Books, 1999.

Moore, Donald S. "Remapping Resistance: 'Ground for Struggle' and the Politics of Place." In *Geographies of Resistance*, edited by Steve Pile and Michael Keith, 87–106. New York: Routledge, 1997.

Morris, Ronald L. *Wait Until Dark: Jazz and the Underworld, 1880–1940*. Bowling Green OH: Bowling Green University Popular Press, 1980.

Mumford, Kevin J. "Homosex Changes: Race, Cultural Geography, and the Emergence of the Gay." In *Locating American Studies: The Evolution of a Discipline*, edited by Lucy Maddox, 385–404. Baltimore: Johns Hopkins Press, 2002.

———. *Interzones: Black/White Sex Districts in Chicago and New York in the Early Twentieth Century*. New York: Columbia University Press, 1997.

Muñoz, Jose Esteban. *Disidentifications: Queers of Color and the Performance of Politics*. Minneapolis: University of Minnesota Press, 1999.

Nasaw, David. *Going Out: The Rise and Fall of Public Amusements*. New York: Basic Books, 1993.

Nealon, Christopher. *Foundlings: Lesbian and Gay Historical Emotion Before Stonewall*. Durham NC: Duke University Press, 2001.

Newton, Esther. *Mother Camp: Female Impersonators in America*. Chicago: University of Chicago Press, 1979.

Ogren, Kathy J. "'Jazz Isn't Just Me': Jazz Autobiographies as Performance Personas." In *Jazz in Mind: Essays on the History and Meaning of Jazz*, edited by Reginald Buckner and Steven Weiland. Detroit: Wayne State University Press, 1991.

———. *The Jazz Revolution: Twenties America and the Meaning of Jazz*. New York: Oxford University Press, 1992.

O'Meally, Robert G., Brent Hayes Edwards, and Farah Jasmine Griffin, eds. *Uptown Conversations: The New Jazz Studies*. New York: Columbia University Press, 2004.

O'Neill, William L. "Reflections on Feminism: Implications for Today." In *Women, the Arts, and the 1920s in Paris and New York*, edited by Kenneth Wheeler and Virginia Lee Lussier. New Brunswick NJ: Transcation Books, 1982.

Padgug, Robert. "'Sexual Matters': On Conceptualizing Sexuality in History." *Radical History Review* 20 (Spring/Summer 1979): 3–23.

Pannuck, Francine, and Shannon Dowling. "The Gendered and Racialized Space Within Australian Prisons." In *Gender Nonconformity, Race, and Sexuality: Charting the Connections*, edited by Toni Lester, 44–61. Madison: University of Wisconsin Press, 2003.

Pearson, Nathan, Jr. *Goin' to Kansas City*. Music in American Life Series. Urbana: University of Illinois Press, 1987.

Pearson, Nathan, Jr., and Howard Litwak. "Goin' to Kansas City: A Catalogue for the *Goin' to Kansas City* Exhibit." Kansas City MO: Mid-America Arts Alliance, 1980.

Peiss, Kathy. "'Charity Girls' and City Pleasures: Historical Notes on Working-Class Sexuality, 1880–1920." In *Passion and Power: Sexuality in*

History, edited by Kathy Peiss and Christina Simmons, 57–69. Philadelphia: Temple University Press, 1989.

———. *Cheap Amusements: Working Women and Leisure in Turn-of-the-Century New York*. Philadelphia: Temple University Press, 1986.

———. "Commercial Leisure and the 'Woman Question.'" In *For Fun and Profit: The Transformation of Leisure into Consumption*, edited by Richard Butsch, 105–17. Philadelphia: Temple University Press, 1990.

Peretti, Burton W. "Oral Histories of Jazz Musicians: The NEA Transcripts as Texts in Context." In *Jazz Among the Discourses*, edited by Krin Gabbard, 117–33. Durham NC: Duke University Press, 1995.

Perry, Gill. *Women Artists and the Parisian Avant-Garde: Modernism and "Femme" Art 1900 to the Late 1920s*. Manchester: Manchester University Press, 1995.

Peterson, Richard A. *Creating Country Music: Fabricating Authenticity*. Chicago: University of Chicago Press, 1997.

Peterson, Richard A., and Andy Bennett. "Introducing Music Scenes." In *Music Scenes: Local, Translocal, and Virtual*, edited by Richard A. Peterson and Andy Bennett, 1–15. Nashville: Vanderbilt University Press, 2004.

Phelan, Peggy. *Unmarked: The Politics of Performance*. London and New York: Routledge, 1993.

Porter, Eric. *What Is This Thing Called Jazz? African American Musicians as Artists, Critics, and Activists*. Berkeley: University of California Press, 2002.

Priestley, Brian. "Review: *Kansas City Jazz: From Ragtime to Bebop—A History* by Frank Driggs and Chuck Haddix and *One O'Clock Jump: The Unforgettable History of the Oklahoma City Blue Devils* by Douglas Henry Daniels." *Jazz Perspectives* 1, no. 1 (April 2007): 89–97.

Rawlins, Robert. "Review: *Kansas City Jazz: From Ragtime to Bebop—A History* by Frank Driggs and Chuck Haddix." *Journal of Popular Culture* 39, no. 4 (August 2006): 694–95.

Recreation Department. *Annual Report of the Recreation Department of the Board of Public Welfare, April 18, 1911–April 15, 1912*. Kansas City MO: Cline Printing, 1912.

Rhodes, Chip. *Structures of the Jazz Age: Mass Culture, Progressive Education, and Radical Discourse in American Modernism*. The Haymarket Series. New York: Verso, 1998.

Rosen, Ruth. *The Lost Sisterhood: Prostitution in America, 1900–1918*. Baltimore: Johns Hopkins University Press, 1982.

Russell, Ross. *Jazz Style in Kansas City and the Southwest*. Berkeley: University of California Press, 1971.

Ryan, Chris, and C. Michael Hall. *Sex Tourism: Marginal People and Liminalities*. New York: Routledge, 2001.

Rye, Howard. "Lovett, Baby." In *The New Grove Dictionary of Jazz*, 629. New York: Grove Dictionaries Limited, 2000.

Sangster, Joan. "Telling Our Stories: Feminist Debates and the Use of Oral History." In *The Oral History Reader*, edited by Robert Perks and Alistair Thomson, 87–106. London and New York: Routledge, 1998.

Sargeant, Winthrop. *Jazz: Hot and Hybrid*. New York: Dutton, 1946.

Schirmer, Sherry. *A City Divided: The Racial Landscape of Kansas City, 1900–1960*. Columbia: University of Missouri Press, 2002.

Schrager, Samuel. "What Is Social in Oral History?" In *The Oral History Reader*, edited by Robert Perks and Alistair Thomson, 284–99. London and New York: Routledge, 1998.

Scott, Joan Wallach. "Experience." In *Feminists Theorize the Political*, edited by Joan Scott and Judith Butler, 22–40. New York: Routledge, 1992.

———. "Gender as a Useful Category of Analysis." In *Gender and the Politics of History*, 28–50. New York: Columbia University Press, 1988.

Sears, Clare. *Arresting Dress: Cross-Dressing, Law, and Fascination in Nineteenth-Century San Francisco*. Durham NC: Duke University Press, 2015.

Senelick, Laurence. "Boys and Girls Together: Subcultural Origins of Glamour Drag and Male Impersonation on the Nineteenth-Century Stage." In *Crossing the Stage: Controversies on Cross-Dressing*, edited by Lesley Ferris, 80–95. New York: Routledge, 1993.

———, ed. *Gender in Performance: The Presentation of Difference in the Performing Arts*. Hanover NH: University Press of New England, 1992.

———. "Introduction." In *Gender in Performance: The Presentation of Difference in the Performing Arts*, edited by Laurence Senelick, 1–3. Hanover NH: University Press of New England, 1992.

———. "Lady and the Tramp: Drag Differentials in the Progressive Era." In *Gender in Performance: The Presentation of Difference in the Performing Arts*, edited by Laurence Senelick, 26–45. Hanover NH: University Press of New England, 1992.

Sexton, Alexander. "Blackface Minstrelsy and Jacksonian Ideology." *American Quarterly* 27, no. 1 (March 1975): 3–28.

Sexton, Jared. "There Is No Interracial Sexual Relationship: Race, Love, and Sexuality in the Multiracial Movement." In *The Problems of Resistance: Studies in Alternate Political Cultures*, edited by Steve Martinot and Jory James, 135–54. Radical Philosophy Today Series, edited by Bat-Ami Bar On and Andrew Light. New York: Humanity Books, 2001.

Sigerman, Harriet. "An Unfinished Battle: 1848–1865." In *No Small Courage: A History of Women in the United States*, edited by Nancy F. Cott, 237–88. New York: Oxford University Press, 2000.

Sinfield, Alan. *Out on Stage: Lesbian and Gay Theatre in the Twentieth Century*. New Haven: Yale University Press, 2000.

Smith-Rosenberg, Carroll. "The Female World of Love and Ritual: Relations Between Women in Nineteenth-Century America." In *Disorderly Conduct: Visions of Gender in Victorian America*, 53–76. New York: Alfred A. Knopf, 1985.

———. "Hearing Women's Words: A Feminist Reconstruction of History." In *Disorderly Conduct: Visions of Gender in Victorian America*, 11–52. New York: Alfred A. Knopf, 1985.

———. "The New Woman as Androgyne: Social Disorder and Gender Crisis, 1870–1936." In *Disorderly Conduct: Visions of Gender in Victorian America*, 245–96. New York: Alfred A. Knopf, 1985.

Social Improvement News. "From Dark to Dawn: Condensed Information on a Great Moral Victory." *Social Improvement News* 2, no. 7 (January 1944): 28.

———. "From Dark to Dawn: No. 3—The Case of Annie Chambers; Sinner, Saint." *Social Improvement News* 1, no. 3 (September 1943): 121.

Soja, Edward W. "Postmodern Geographies: Taking Los Angeles Apart." In *NowHere: Space, Time and Modernity*, edited by Roger Friedland and Deirdre Boden, 127–62. Berkeley: University of California Press, 1994.

Somerville, Siobhan. *Queering the Color Line: Race and the Invention of Homosexuality in America*. Durham NC: Duke University Press, 2000.

Stansell, Christine. *City of Women: Sex and Class in New York, 1789–1860*. Urbana: University of Illinois Press, 1987.

The State ex rel. Cameron L. Orr v. Leannah Kearns, alias Annie Chambers. Supreme Court of Missouri Case No. 24023 (264 S.W. 775), July 31, 1924.

Stearns, Carol Z., and Peter N. Stearns. "A Traditional View of Victorian Sexuality." In *Major Problems in American Women's History*, edited by Mary Beth Norton, 248–54. Major Problems in American History, edited by Thomas G. Paterson. Lexington MA: D. C. Heath, 1989.

Stoler, Laura Ann. *Race and the Education of Desire: Foucault's History of Sexuality and the Colonial Order of Things*. Durham NC: Duke University Press, 1995.

Stowe, David W. "Jazz in the West: Cultural Frontier and Region During the Swing Era." *Western Historical Quarterly* 23, no. 1 (February 1992): 53–73.

Straub, Kristina. *Sexual Suspects: Eighteenth-Century Players and Sexual Ideology*. Princeton: Princeton University Press, 1992.

Thelen, David. *Paths of Resistance: Tradition and Democracy in Industrializing Missouri*. Columbia: University of Missouri Press, 1986.

Thompson, E. P. *The Making of the English Working Class*. New York: Pantheon, 1964.

Tucker, Sherrie. *Swing Shift: "All-Girl" Bands of the 1940s*. Durham NC: Duke University Press, 2000.

Turner, Victor. *From Ritual to Theater: The Human Seriousness of Play*. New York: PAJ Publications, 1982.

Ullman, Sharon. "'The Twentieth-Century Way': Female Impersonation and Sexual Politics in Turn-of-the-Century America." *Journal of the History of Sexuality* 5, no. 4 (April 1995): 573–600.

Umland, Rudolph. "Gambling Halls, Saloons and Bawdy Houses." *The Attic Window: The Monthly Magazine for the Audience of Tiffany's Attic* (July 1972): 6–10, 17.

Valentine, Gill. "Creating Transgressive Space: The Music of kd lang." *Transactions of the Institute of British Geographers, New Series* 20, no. 4 (1995): 474–85.

Vincent, Ted. *Keep Cool: The Black Activists Who Built the Jazz Age*. New York: Pluto Press, 1993.

Washington, Salim. "'All the Things You Could Be Now': *Charles Mingus Presents Charles Mingus* and the Limits of Avant-Garde Jazz." In *Uptown Conversations: The New Jazz Studies*, edited by Robert O'Meally, Brent Haynes Edwards, and Farah Jasmine Griffin, 27–49. New York: Columbia University Press, 2004.

Weiss, Andrea, and Greta Schiller. *Before Stonewall: The Making of a Gay and Lesbian Community*. New York: Naiad Press, 1988.

White, Hayden. "Michel Foucault." In *Structuralism and Since: From Levi-Strauss to Derrida*, edited by John Sturrock, 81–115. London: Oxford University Press, 1979.

White, John. "Kansas City, Pendergast, and All That Jazz." In *American Studies: Essays in Honour of Marcus Cunliffe*, edited by Brian Holder and John White, 231–48. New York: St. Martin's Press, 1990.

White, William Allen. *The Autobiography of William Allen White*. New York: MacMillan, 1946. Reprint, 1966.

Williams, Martin. *The Jazz Tradition*. New York: Oxford University Press, 1970. Reprint, 1973.

———. "Jazz: What Happened in Kansas City?" *American Music* 3, no. 2 (Summer 1985): 171–79.

Wilson, William H. *The City Beautiful Movement in Kansas City*. University of Missouri Studies 40. Columbia: University of Missouri Press, 1964.

Index

To order or obtain more information on these or other University of Nebraska Press titles, visit nebraskapress.unl.edu.

www.ingramcontent.com/pod-product-compliance
Lightning Source LLC
Chambersburg PA
CBHW020337100426
42812CB00029B/3166/J